Critical Perspectives on International Political Economy

Also by Jason P. Abbott

OFFSHORE FINANCE CENTRES AND THE RISE OF GLOBAL CAPITAL
(*with Mark P. Hampton*)

STATE STRATEGIES IN THE GLOBAL POLITICAL ECONOMY
(*with Ronen Palan*)

Critical Perspectives on International Political Economy

Edited by

Jason P. Abbott
Senior Lecturer in International Political Economy
Nottingham Trent University

and

Owen Worth
Department of International Studies
Nottingham Trent University

palgrave
macmillan

Editorial matter and selection © Jason P. Abbott and Owen Worth 2002
Foreword © Barry K. Gills 2002
Individual chapters (in order) © Christopher Farrands; Chris White;
Louise Amoore and Paul Langley; Gary Burn; Iain Watson; Owen Worth;
Jason P. Abbott; Craig N. Murphy and Douglas R. Nelson 2002

First published 2002 by
PALGRAVE MACMILLAN
Houndmills, Basingstoke, Hampshire RG21 6XS and
175 Fifth Avenue, New York, N.Y. 10010
Companies and representative throughout the world

PALGRAVE MACMILLAN is the global academic imprint of
the Palgrave Macmillan division of St. Martin's Press, LLC and of
Palgrave Macmillan Ltd. Macmillan® is a registered trademark in
the United States, United Kingdom and other countries. Palgrave is a
registered trademark in the European Union and other countries.

ISBN 0–333–96427–6

This book is printed on paper suitable for recycling and made from fully
managed and sustained forest sources.

A catalogue record for this book is available from the British Library.

Library of Congress Cataloging-in-Publication Data
Critical Perspectives on International Political Economy
Edited by Jason P. Abbott and Owen Worth; foreword by Barry K. Gills
    p. cm.
  Includes bibliographical references and index.
  ISBN 0–333–96427–6
    1. International economic relations. 2. Globalization. I.
Abbott, Jason, 1971–II. Worth, Owen, 1974–
HF1359. C75 2002
337–dc21   2002025103

10   9   8   7   6   5   4   3   2   1
11   10   09   08   07   06   05   04   03   02

Printed and bound in Great Britain by
Antony Rowe Ltd, Chippenham and Eastbourne

*To the memory of **Joan Abbott**, who encouraged me to read*

Contents

Being Critical: A Foreword

It is a privilege to be asked to write a foreword to a collection of essays such as this, personally, professionally and practically. First, it is a personal privilege because I have known most of the contributors in this volume either as a teacher or in collaborative research projects here at Newcastle, where I have taught International Political Economy (IPE) for the past twelve years. I have been privileged to watch them develop as scholars and I am very proud of their accomplishments. They represent the next generation of critical IPE scholarship, and judging by the work presented in this volume, they are well able to take the field forward in new, useful, and above all 'critical' directions. I also speak in this regard, I have no doubt, for my former colleagues here at Newcastle, including Randall Germain and Ronen Palan, to whom I and many of the contributors to this volume owe thanks and recognition for their contributions to critical IPE, here and in their subsequent careers. We are all travelling together, on a long journey, and our conversations and relations are the substance of much of our practice, as we struggle to enlighten ourselves, one another, and those who may read what we produce.

It is a professional pleasure and a privilege to write a foreword for this volume not only because of the life connections mentioned above, but also because this is truly a fine collection of essays on a most centrally important subject. We should not make the facile assumption that all IPE is 'critical' for indeed it is certainly not. Much that passes for 'IPE' is still remarkably mainstream in both theory and praxis, and focuses on the understanding of the status quo, whether of trade, finance or economic diplomacy. What unites this little band of 'critical' IPE theorists is precisely their desire for 'being critical' and therefore challenging the status quo, whether this be 'received theory' or the perceived power structure dominating the world or even our local workplace or home. The editors are to be commended for having brought this collection together and having done so under the explicit heading of new attempts to grapple with defining and understanding what 'being critical' is in IPE. They rightly identify this unresolved problem as a strategic one for the discipline and set the terms of reference in an open, negotiated and dialogic frame of reference. This is precisely what the field requires and

I sincerely hope that this volume will stimulate new debate and research on these most pivotal problems of both theory and of practice.

It is a privilege in the 'practical' sense, which I regard as indistinguishable from the 'political' to be associated with this new volume of critical IPE essays because it is through such mutual understandings and dialogue that we as scholars make our most central contribution to practice in the world about us. If we make no false separation between the realm of ideas and the realm of action, as surely we must not if we are to practise a critical knowledge construction, then surely we realise the import of our own work and the potential of intellectual action. This is the 'reflexive' aspect of critical theorising, i.e. being both aware of our social, moral and intellectual responsibilities as scholars in this field, while at the same time exercising a self-critical reflection on the act of knowledge construction. This vital epistemological and ontological theme is openly addressed in this book. This volume stands not only for conscious moral and intellectual purpose, the first principle of critical IPE theory, but likewise for critical engagement with the real world of political action, undertaken at whatever 'level' or terrain of politics, and we should address as many as possible. Therefore, the reader of this volume will find a very useful discussion of the many contributions to the formation of critical IPE over the past fifteen years or so, and in previous intellectual history. She will also find a wide range of 'practical' frameworks of action addressed as well. This is precisely as it should be, and the editors wisely and correctly chose not to prefigure the readers' imagination or perception by separating the contributions too strictly into 'theory' and 'practice' sections. The ideal is to combine both, not only in one volume, but also in one piece of work, as many of the contributors to this volume do admirably.

As for the timeliness and practical importance of this volume, we certainly all recognise that all politics, as well as life itself, is 'contested' and that there is everything to play for and no excuse for default or inaction. In the present era of 'globalisation', which is fast becoming one of 'the politics of resistance', in my view at least, there is so much social motion about us that it would be remarkable if we were to be indifferent to it. We are always in the process of re-interpreting the nature of social power and the ways by which we might pursue emancipatory strategies of action. In the past, rightly or wrongly, there often seemed to be a conventional or recognisable 'subject' of action for the 'critical or progressive' scholar, whether this was the labour movement, anti-colonial and revolutionary movements, peasants' movements, or women's, peace and environmentalist movements. Today we realise that the scope for 'critical' reflection and action has actually expanded, rather than contracted. This expanded scope for action is the paradox of globalisation and also its greatest opportunity. Far from being on the margins of the real world of social action, the new critical IPE theory is central to it. Action and idea cannot be separated. What matters is the nature of the critique of reality and how we translate this understanding into meaningful action. I can say without doubt that this volume and these contributors are dedicated to these propositions and to the possibility of imagining real alternatives to the present world order and power structures, to emancipatory theory and its concretisation, and to the transformation of our world. What could be more important than that?

In closing I commend these authors once again for taking another step on the long journey we have embarked upon together, to develop new understandings of IPE and to practise a self awareness of what it means to us to be critical. I look forward to the contributions that these and many other new critical theorists in IPE will make in the future. They remind us that even 'critical' theorists must never be complacent nor succumb to a defence of (new) orthodoxy. By critical dialogic understanding we can all move forward together. They also remind us that to practise a narrowing of our intellectual horizons would be a tragedy for critical theory in IPE. Above all, we must listen to the admonition of this volume to remain as open as possible to new perspectives and to undertake a sincere dialogue with each other. The fruitful discussion waiting to happen between the many varieties of the new critical IPE theory, whether post-structuralist, post-modern, neo-Gramscian, world system, neo-structuralist, or some other perspective, is perhaps the single most important message of this volume, and the harbinger of many volumes to follow in the future I hope. Through this process, which this volume fruitfully seeks to initiate, we can surely enhance our mutual understandings of IPE and of what 'being critical' within it will continue or come to mean.

BARRY K. GILLS

Acknowledgements

First and most obviously we would like to thank all of our contributors for their hard work in producing their chapters, and for their patience in revising their work in response to our queries. We hope that they are as pleased as we are with the final output. A special thanks here must go to both Barry Gills and Craig Murphy for their support and contributions and Chris Farrands for, well … being 'Chris' (he knows what we mean).

The genesis of this collection emerged from several post-session 'bar-room debates' at the British International Studies Association and the International Studies Association. To thank all of those who listened to our respective rants would take far too long. However among those colleagues who had a particular input to the project at various stages special thanks must go Randall Germain. Thanks also to the anonymous referees whose comments and advice were particularly helpful, and to Nicola Viinikka for her faith in the project.

Any shortcomings in this collection are, of course, our responsibility.

JASON P. ABBOTT
OWEN WORTH

Notes on the Contributors

Jason P. Abbott is Senior Lecturer in the Department of International Studies, Nottingham Trent University. He is co-author (with Ronen Palan) of *State Strategies in the Global Political Economy* (1999) and co-editor of *Offshore Finance Centres and Tax Havens: The Rise of Global Capital* (Palgrave Macmillan, 1999). His work has appeared in *Asian Studies Review, Development Policy Review, Pacifica Review, Roundtable: The Commonwealth Journal of International Affairs, Security Dialogue* and *Third World Quarterly*. He is currently working on the Internet and democratisation in developing countries.

Louise Amoore is Lecturer in International Politics at the University of Newcastle upon Tyne, having formerly taught at the University of Northumbria. Her most recent work has been published in *Global Society, New Political Economy*, and the *Review of International Political Economy*. She is currently researching the relationships between social experiences of production and work and processes of globalisation.

Gary Burn is Visiting Research Fellow in the Centre for Global Political Economy, University of Sussex. He received an MA in International Political Economy from the University of Newcastle and a doctorate from the University of Sussex. He won the Robert Cox Award in 2000 for his article 'The State the City and the Euromarkets'. His work has been published in the *Review of International Political Economy* and the French journal *Alternatives Economiques*. He is currently working on a book on the political economic history of sterling entitled *Sterling and the British People*.

Chris Farrands is Principal Lecturer in International Relations at Nottingham Trent University. He has recently been Scholar in Residence at American University in Washington, DC, and was formerly visiting professor in the University of Grenoble. He has published widely in international theory and international political economy, including several single and co-authored books on technology and IPE. His most recent publications include articles in *Alternatives, Global Society* and *Swords and Ploughshares* and the co-edited collection, *Technology, Culture and Competitiveness* (1997).

Barry K. Gills is Reader in International Politics at the University of Newcastle upon Tyne. Founding editor of the *Review of International Political Economy*, he has also been a frequent guest editor for *Third World Quarterly* and editorial contributor to *New Political Economy*. He is also the founder of the World Historical Systems theory group of the ISA, and Secretary of the British Association of Korean Studies. Among his most recent works are *Globalization and the Politics of Resistance* (Palgrave Macmillan, 2000), *World System History* (2000) and 'Re-orienting the New (International) Political Economy' (in *New Political Economy*, vol. 6, no. 2, 2001). Past works include *The World System* (with Andre Gunder Frank, 1996), *Korea versus Korea* (1996) and *Low Intensity Democracy* (with J. Rocamora and R. Wilson, 1993).

Paul Langley is Lecturer in International Politics at the School of Social, Political and Economic Sciences, University of Northumbria at Newcastle (UNN). His work has been published in *New Political Economy*, *Review of International Political Economy*, *Millennium*, *Global Society* and *International Studies Perspectives*. He is also author of *World Financial Orders and World Financial Centres: An Historical International Political Economy* (Routledge/RIPE Series, forthcoming).

Craig N. Murphy is Professor and Chair of Political Science at Wellesley College in Wellesley, Massachusetts, and served as President of the International Studies Association in 2000–1. He has published widely on international relations theory and international political economy, international organisations and north-south relations, including several single and co-authored books. His articles have appeared in many professional and scholarly journals including *International Interactions*, *International Organization*, the *International Political Science Review*, *International Studies Quarterly* and the *Review of International Political Economy*. His current research examines the global political economy of inequality across lines of race, gender, region and class.

Douglas R. Nelson is Professor of Economics at the Murphy Institute of Political Economy at Tulane University, New Orleans, Louisiana, and Recurring Visiting Professor of Economics at the University of Nottingham. He has contributed to several edited collections on international political economy and published numerous articles in scholarly journals including *American Journal of Political Science*, *Economics and Politics*, *Journal of Economic Studies* and *World Economy*. His current research focuses on questions of international trade and migration especially in developing manufacturing countries.

Iain Watson was awarded his doctorate from the University of Newcastle upon Tyne and is currently a teaching associate at the University of Durham. His work has been published in *Global Society, New Political Economy* and the *Review of International Political Economy* and more recently in B. K. Gills (ed), *Globalization and the Politics of Resistance* (Palgrave Macmillan, 2000), M. Ebata and B. Neufeld eds, *Confronting the Political in International Relations* (Palgrave Macmillan, 2000) and R. Higgott and A. Payne eds, *The New Political Economy of Globalisation* (2000). He has a forthcoming book *Rethinking the Politics of Globalisation: Theory, Concepts and Strategy* (2002).

Chris White is a doctoral candidate and Graduate Teaching Assistant in the Department of International Studies, Nottingham Trent University. He is currently researching intra Institutional issues connected with the political economy of the World Bank.

Owen Worth is a doctoral candidate and part-time teaching assistant in the Department of International Studies, Nottingham Trent University. He also teaches government and politics at the University of Lincolnshire. He is currently researching forms of contestation to the dominant norms of the global political economy.

Introduction: The 'Many Worlds' of *Critical* International Political Economy[1]

Jason P. Abbott and Owen Worth

How much easier it is to be critical than to be correct.[2]

The study of International Political Economy (IPE) or of its lesser known but comprehensive twin Global Political Economy (GPE) is a relatively new discipline within the more recognised study of International Relations. The application of critical theory towards GPE itself is an even more recent phenomenon, with its epistemological foundation still in its infancy – its aim to date focusing upon providing an alternative stance to those more conventional positivist readings within IPE. In general it aims to demonstrate that the norms and practices, inherent within the global political economy are not pre-determined by 'natural' or 'inevitable' procedures, but are created by ongoing processes, that have been historically formed by human intervention. In this sense critical theory has claimed to be able to 'stand back' from the debates of political scientists, economists and policy-makers alike, who base their assumptions from within the boundaries of current traits of the global political economy, and assess activities from a theoretical point outside of these parameters. This collection of essays aims to build upon the foundations within this critical tradition, while at the same time examining and forwarding ways in which critical theory can develop. In this sense it aims to open up further possibilities and directions that such an approach needs to consider, so that it can increase its onto-logical and epistemological value.

As commented upon by many of the contributors in this book, some of the original groundbreaking work that encouraged a more 'critical' mode of thinking to IPE came from Robert Cox. It was Cox who quite categorically stated that critical theory should fundamentally differ from the methodological realms of 'problem-solving theory', which dominated debate within International theory. For critical theories, problem-solvers operate their studies within a particular historical structure, which they interpret as non-historical or ahistorical. Critical theorists, in contrast, place their studies within a changing historical reality, allowing space and time to continually change and adapt their perception in tandem with the environment that they are studying (Cox, 1981). Therefore the main merits of critical theory rest upon the principle that societal norms and practices have been historically formed through a series of contested dialectical processes. Its critique of 'problem-solving theory' includes the charge (which is commented upon by Farrands in this collection) that it can never apply any real form of value-free theory. This arises from the observation that, as its main aim is to solve the problems within the historical order that it is working from, it is consciously committed to ideologically strengthening and consolidating the status quo. All claims of objective knowledge are therefore rejected, as they always appear to be '*for* someone and *for* some purpose' (*ibid.*, p. 128).

Since the work produced by Cox in the early 1980s, critical theory in IPE has taken certain turns and produced works that have provided certain avenues for students to explore. However some of this work has often lacked the vision and articulation to firmly build upon the ontology that Cox outlined. In particular how critical theory can be developed to adequately fit a criterion that can be applied to IPE/GPE. For, as mentioned by Farrands in the first chapter of this book, the application of a 'critical' edge is often not defined and not conclusively applied to actual political economy. It has found a more distinctive role within International Relations theory as a whole with its terms and objectives seemingly mapped out as an enlightenment project, that draws distinctly from the Frankfurt school of critical theory (Linklater, 1996).[3] Although Cox's 'guidance' is sometimes recognised in such work, it is only used in terms of reference and little if any mention is given by Frankfurt school-inspired International Relations[4] theorists to the theory and practices of international political economy (Wyn Jones, 2001). It has instead been left to Cox's follow-up book, *Power, Production and World Order* (1987), the insights of Susan Strange (e.g. 1983, 1988, 1991) and an edited collection from Murphy and Tooze (1991) among others, to broaden critical approaches to IPE, at a time when the discipline of the subject itself was still placed well within the confines of International Relations as a whole. The more critical perspectives in

IPE have thus grown up at a time when the subject itself was finding its feet as a separate area of study.

One philosopher whose work has greatly contributed to the growth of critical theory is Antonio Gramsci. Since the first extensive translations of the *Prison Notebooks* (1971) were made accessible in several languages, Gramsci's work has been influential in several other disciplines (notable Cultural Studies and Inner-state Politics) and his influence in the development of critical theory in IPE became evident immediately, with Cox's 1981 essay. His theoretical enquiries on hegemony, consciousness and civil society hold great relevance for critical development today. Indeed, a number of edited collections have placed neo-Gramscian thought as the central emphasis for the growth of critical discourse in IPE (Gill, 1993; Gill and Mittelman, 1997). Despite, working from a selection of Marxist texts that were predominately materialist and determinist, and which focused largely upon the stability of the economic base,[5] Gramsci demonstrated that the relationship between base and superstructure was more complex in its nature, and that an adequate critique of political economy needed to adopt a more vigorous sociological understanding of the role of institutions and re-examine questions of class-consent and culture, in order to provide an effective form of criticism (Gramsci, 1971). The main achievements of the neo-Gramscians have been to propel these insights and to apply them towards an understanding of social forces and world orders in IPE (Gill, 1993).

Similar to Gramsci, the addition of Polanyi has furthered the study of the stability of the global economy; his work is of particular relevance to those forming critiques of globalisation. Polanyi demonstrated through his case-study of Great Britain in the nineteenth century how there was nothing 'natural' about *laissez-faire* capitalism. Instead government had to regulate the free market into being and destroy the last vestiges of feudalism and mercantilism. However the social costs of this form of economic liberalism gave birth to a 'double movement' against it, evident both in terms of competition from outside the State and from welfare movements within it. This double movement ultimately resulted in *re-regulation* of the economy by government and the origins of the embedded liberal welfare state of the post-war era (Polanyi, 1944). While, it is recognised that the neoliberal form of political economy in the twenty-first century has developed to a level that surpasses any viable comparisons with the nineteenth century form of *laissez-faire* capitalism, Polanyi's observations have latterly added another dimension to critical perspectives towards the growth and acceptance of globalisation.[6]

Also important in the development of historicism within GPE is the influence of the French *annales* school of history and in particular the work of Fernand Braudel (1973, 1984). While Braudel has played a significant role in the intellectual origins of the World Systems Approach[7] and inspired much of the work of Immanuel Wallerstein and Giovanni Arrighi (among others), Braudel also inspired leading historical sociologists such as E. P. Thompson and Michael Mann (e.g. 1986).[8] Whereas the World Systems school did much to popularise the work of Braudel, their reading of his work produced an overly deterministic structuralism largely derived from Braudel's plural conception of time[9] and his conception of world economies. While Braudel's work is clearly structuralist[10] the richness of Braudel's work is also characterised by his attention to historical specificity. Indeed Braudel's conception of the *longue dureé* was of a temporally defined analytical level in which change was slow and almost imperceptible. This was the domain where the relationship to geography, climate and so forth forged the cultures that underlay the development of distinct societies.[11] It is this area of Braudel's work drawing attention to the influences that local cultures have had on the trajectory of the broader economic system that has warranted less attention than to his conceptual grounding of system metaphors. In critical IPE the influence of this latter focus is apparent, both directly in the work of several of the contributors to this collection (Amoore, Langley and Watson) and in the work of Germain[12] and Palan,[13] as well as indirectly through the dialogue with historical sociology that emerged in the mid-1990s.[14] We also see it in Gills' critique of Eurocentric knowledge construction (e.g. Frank and Gills, 1993), and his critical historisation of 'globalisation' and analysis of the 'politics of resistance' to neoliberalism (Gills, 2000).

The work of Joseph Schumpeter plays an important role in the background of critical GPE, and in IPE as a whole. Schumpeter similarly drew extensively on Marxist thinking while rejecting core ideas in the Marxist orthodoxy, and he influences four areas of critical approaches to political economy in particular. First, he points to the importance of business cycles, while rejecting the idea that they arise 'naturally'. Second, he points to the significance of large oligopolistic firms. Like Sraffa[15] and Joan Robinson,[16] Schumpeter points to the tendency of advanced capitalist firms to become dominating actors that collaborate or cartelise as often as they compete. One only needs to open the work of more recent writers on large firms, including Stopford and Strange's *Rival States, Rival Firms* (1991), the work of John Zysman, or Lynne Mytelka, to see the long-running influence of Schumpeter's work. Third, he pointed to the transforming role of technology in at once driving the business cycle and framing the decisions of large firms. Technology remains a relatively insufficiently studied aspect of GPE, though aspects of technology change are raised by some authors in the critical tradition, and these are eluded to in the chapters in this book by Abbott, and Amoore and Langley. The fourth way in which Schumpeter opens a path for critical IPE to follow, is in explaining the relationship between political culture, social structure and economic organisation. His main work on the subject *Capitalism, Socialism and Democracy* (1942) prefigures much of the recent debate on democratisation and the possible link between market failure and the growth of tyrannical or kleptocratic forms of rule. Although Schumpeter's writings here appear dated, they warrant re-visiting. Their influence on diverse authors in the West, such as Cerny and Strange, is matched by the influence on the work of Third World political economists including W. Arthur Lewis and Amartya Sen.[17]

Post-structuralists have in common a suspicion of what they have called foundational discourses. Some are more radical than others in the consequences of this critical position, while some (perhaps those most influenced by Lyotard and Baudrillard) see the conclusion as being that one can do little but 'play'. Others (perhaps more often those influenced primarily by Foucault) see anti-foundationalism as a starting point to radical action and to the opening of emancipatory space. This final group has clear overlaps or at least parallels with many critical theorists, including Habermas. Post-structuralists also reject what they see as the attempt to dictate a power structure in the knowledge claims of a subject by including some questions, excluding others, and closing down the range of debate throughout. In International Relations, post-structuralism entered with a bang in 1989 with the publication of Der Derian and Schapiro's *International/Intertextual relations: Postmodern readings of world politics*. Post-structuralism is always critical in posture, but many post-structuralists reject the marxian roots of 'critical theory' and the emancipatory programme it advances. However this is not always true. While writers such as Ashley and Campbell critique all attempts at 'building' theory in IR, including emancipatory theory, others cross the line and seek to develop a dialogue between post-modern theory and post-structuralism in which each shapes the other at the same time as critiquing it. Rob Walker can be seen as an advocate of such a view, especially in his influential *One World Many Worlds*, but also through his academic leadership in the choices made in the editing of the journal *Alternatives*. In GPE, it is possible to find powerful echoes of these debates in the ways that writers such as Palan and Tooze organise their argument, but it is harder to find explicitly post-structural writing in GPE which rejects critical theory altogether. Apadurai's contribution to Mike Featherstone's *Global Culture: nationalism, globalization and modernity*, which recognises a world system model but writes of it as fragmented and discontinuous rather than as a homogeneous capitalist whole (as world systems theory generally argues), is very much the exception even now, over a decade since it was published.

However, despite the advances that have been made towards building a critical school of thought within IPE, it is argued here that not enough is being done to continually enrich the possibilities, openings, re-evaluations and challenges that are required for sustainable critical thought. There is a general concern, reflected in the subsequent chapters, that the material which has been produced thus far has a) grown towards a certain point in which it is in danger of becoming a new form of orthodoxy – e.g. towards a certain model, in which its main assumptions are uncontested, b) moved to a position that in its theoretical foundation and in its application can at times appear narrow and c) failed to be adequately reflexive in its responses to new academic openings and to the changes of the world that it is studying.

If as noted earlier (see also Wyn Jones, 2001) those critical theorists working on political and normative theory are guilty of largely ignoring the work of Cox and the so-called 'Italian school' of IPE, then the opposite claim can as equally be made. Namely that while the presence of Cox is clear, few adopting a 'critical' position in the study of IPE make reference to the critical social theory of the Frankfurt school, that other principal set of influences on critical work in international relations theory.[18] Those that do are often approaching IPE from within the boundaries of a *related* discipline of social science (particularly cultural studies) rather than from within IPE itself.

Such an observation is more than simply an exercise in academic boundary drawing. Indeed as Farrands argues in Chapter 1, the failure of political economists to reach out beyond Gramscian-inspired analysis runs the risk of neo-Gramscianism becoming entrenched as the orthodox critical/radical position. If this were to happen then critical IPE will have failed to live up to its early promise to break out of the self-imposed disciplinary boundaries to be both multidisciplinary and interdisciplinary in nature. Consequently, this collection of essays emerged as an attempt to address this dialogue of the deaf between IPE and political/normative theory and to suggest answers to several fundamental questions: Where do critical perspectives in IPE go next? How should they continue to take the theoretical epistemology to a new level? And how should they *apply* different forms of critical theory to a broader study of the institutions, processes and structures within the international political economy?

In addressing the key points here, the critical literature produced by the 'neo-Gramscians' to date is accordingly discussed in detail in several of the chapters in this collection. In the opening chapters both Farrands and White argue in different ways that critical IPE has to build upon its neo-Gramscian origins and engage more thoroughly with critical theory as well as with 'critical' traits and traditions in other disciplines. For both authors critical IPE must remain genuinely interdisciplinary. Watson's chapter meanwhile, furthers this by looking at how critical IPE can be galvanised by re-visiting post-structuralism/post-modernism in order to avoid the 'ideological/conceptual imposition of intellectual boundaries'. Drawing on the work of Rob Walker, Michel Foucault and the political ideology of the Zapatistas, Watson argues that only by being at the 'frontiers' can critical enquiry challenge the exclusivity of narratives inherited from the Enlightenment and explore the complex sites and nature of power. Abbott's chapter on the Internet focuses upon how another critical Marxist, Lefebvre, can be used as a vehicle for furthering the progress of critical thought. In particular he argues that Lefebvre challenges both the reification of a limited conception of spatiality in IR as well as the historicism characteristic of much neo-Gramscian IPE. While Lefebvre agrees that space is ultimately socially constructed, he nonetheless maintains that it is conceptualised in a multiplicity of ways by different actors. Space is thus dynamic and in flux rather than a static construct to be understood in a particularly socio-historical moment. Worth, however, in his chapter on the World Health Organisation (WHO) re-engages with Gramsci, arguing that Gramscian theory is a still very effective force within critical theory, providing that it re-analyses and re-applies its overall ontology.

The functional and 'real' meaning of critical theory is also questioned in the opening chapters. A reflection on what 'being critical' actually entails is presented, with different conclusions, by Farrands and White. The former argues that a certain caution needs to be taken when negotiating the real purpose of critical theory, while the latter believes that to develop further as a viable, effective school, greater dialogue is required between critical theorists in IPE and leading theoreticians and scholars from more established disciplines. White also sets critical IPE in the context of the idea of plural forms of knowledge, and multiple epistemologies, drawing on the work of Connolly and Taylor to open up critical epistemological space where many other writers in GPE concentrate more on critical ontologies. This book aims both to invite new interpretations towards some of the practises and key concepts within IPE, while at the same time highlight the necessity of exploring the more marginalised topics and concerns, which need to be included within any study of the global economy, but for the most part have been rather neglected.

In Chapter 1, Farrands provides an overview of the development of critical theory within IPE. By doing this he places it in relation not just to the growth of critical theory within International Relations theory as a whole, but to the principles of 'critical research' itself. For Farrands too many scholars that contribute towards a critical agenda neglect the real aims of what being critical is all about. He argues that not enough has been done to apply the three virtues of *critique*, *knowledge* and *emancipation*, upon which any critical enquiry should be based. What we have seen instead has been a range of material that stakes a claim of being critical, but does not address the real concerns and purposes that critical theory is founded upon. In addition too much literature produced under the slogan of critical theory is narrow in its theoretical base and offers relatively little to any meaningful form of emancipatory action. Farrands concludes by urging students and scholars to be more reflexive in their research and promotes the critical methodology of Bourdieu as a means to bridge some of the gaps that have appeared in the weaknesses of critical literature, so that it can at least remain true to its intentions. White's subsequent chapter replies to the concerns made apparent by Farrands, but argues that critical theory within IPE is too young a creation to start worrying about caution in its development. Rather, he argues that critical IPE needs to experiment more with competing theoretical construction, and cast out its net to attract possible solutions that could more fluently contribute to emancipatory visions. By searching for scholarly advice from other disciplines, much of which does not necessarily have to fit into the neat criteria of 'criticalness', more depth can be added to the application of critique in IPE.

We avoided the temptation to make a sharp distinction between the more theoretical contributions to this collection and those chapters that were more applied. Nonetheless the essays that appear in chapters 3 to 7 are illustrative of how a more inclusive critical and interdisciplinary IPE can be applied to the study of institutions, processes and structures within the international system and global economy. In Chapter 4 Amoore and Langley stress that not enough is being done to critically assess the complex understanding of globalisation. They feel that the concept is often promoted systematically and that various illusions are created that do not do justice to the larger fragmentary nature of the workings of globalisation. For them globalisation should be understood not within the more macro context of socio-economic transformation, but rather in the effects that it has on the more micro aspects of working and living relations. A wider dialogue between the micro and macro demonstrates that globalisation is increasingly becoming more contested, more contradictory and societal relationships have become more polarised and more fragmented as a consequence. Thus, in terms of suggesting possible avenues for resistance strategies to neoliberalism, and for ways of re-applying the political into an area of study, increasingly defined within economical norms, a wider understanding of globalisation and the possibility of transformation can be applied.

One of the perspectives on globalisation that Amoore and Langley identify is the *project* perspective. From this viewpoint neoliberalism provides the ideological rationale by which 'powerful agents seek to strategically restructure the material and institutional bases of the contemporary world order'. Within IPE one of the schools of this project perspective has been the 'national capitalisms school' which privileges the role of state policy-makers and institutions in directing the restructuring processes associated with globalisation. Because such processes are ultimately determined by the distribution of power within and between states, and these distributions are the result of historically specific factors, it is possible to identify different models of capitalism. Consequently within this literature we find reference to the Anglo-Saxon model, the East Asian Capitalist Developmental State, the Nordic 'social democratic' model and so forth.

One of the models that has attracted much interest in recent years, especially in the UK, is the so-called *Sozialemarktwirtschaft* (the social market economy) associated with Germany. Consequently while Amoore and Langley examine the micro impact of globalisation upon the social relations of work and retirement, Burns turns his attention to how the impact of globalisation upon German finance capital threatens to undermine the very institutional structures that underpin the German model.

Burns' chapter examines in particular changes taking place within the German financial services sector and argues that these changes are having a wider impact upon 'the dominant form of accumulation operating in Germany'. While pressures for financial services liberalisation came from German finance capital eager to ensure that Frankfurt remained competitive as an international financial centre, the reform process is having much wider ramifications as liberalisation begins to 'unravel' the bank-industry cross-shareholdings that were once a core characteristic of the German economy.

One consequence is that with the shift away from *intracapital* relationships, German capital is being 'freed-up' to concentrate on the higher returns available through international investment banking. Another is that German corporations are becoming more focused on the equity culture common in the United States and Great Britain, rather than, as in the past, on their role as *stakeholders* providing cheap, subsidised long-term credit. As these corporations become more concerned with the short-term interests of their shareholders, Burns contends that they will be forced to compete for funding on the global capital market.

The overall result of these reforms, he maintains, is likely to result in much wider liberalisation that 'could challenge the concordat between capital, labour and the state at the very heart of the social market economy'. Were this to happen both the German state and the German trade union movement will be seriously weakened by the neoliberal priorities of German capital, signalling the possible demise of the social market economy not only in Germany itself but also as an alternative to unfettered neoliberalism within the European Union.

Watson's chapter shares similarities with Amoore and Langley, as he argues that resistance to globalisation requires a much larger theoretical focus to that currently on offer within GPE. Using the Zapatistas in Mexico as an example, he argues that it is necessary to move beyond the neo-Gramscian, and more significantly the *Coxian* notion, that such resistance can be seen as a form of counter-hegemonic response to the hegemonic project of neoliberalism. Seen through such a lens, the Zapatistas (or EZLN) are too weak, too localised and thus too insignificant to adequately challenge the hegemonic might of the global order.

Watson, however, feels that such a systematic analysis is *inadequate* for a stringent examination of the Zapatistas. Instead, he argues that the reaction of the Zapatistas appears more akin to the form of resistance theoretically analysed by Foucault. Foucault, he explains, identifies social resistance as a process that critically reflects upon the ruling practices, norms, laws etc., engaging alternatives which re-assess the boundaries in which they are applied. Rather than a symptom of dissatisfaction with the global hegemonic order itself, the Zapatistas should be seen more within a micro context, as their objectives focus upon the need for the state to re-assess factors such as democracy, ethnicity and cultural identity that are threatened by the practices of neoliberalism. Watson follows R. J. B. Walker's contention that the processes and application of such diverse social movements not only provide a challenge to the practices of order in the 'real' world, but should also provide critical challenges for *those who analyse* their contribution within academia (Walker, 1988). This re-evaluation thus needs more attention within the critical discourse of IPE.

In response to claims that practices within the global political economy need to go beyond neo-Gramscianism, Worth outlines certain avenues in which its relevance needs to be brought back in. He argues that it is not the development of Gramsci's work itself that has become narrow in its application, but that some neo-Gramscians have not developed sufficient ways in which his work can be built upon. Drawing from both Rupert and Hall's more sophisticated reading of Gramsci (Rupert, 1998; Hall, 1990) Worth argues that the policies of world health and in particular the World Health Organisation can best be examined through its role within a particular historic bloc. Furthermore, he illustrates that the WHO has, within the current project of neoliberalism, presented itself as a 'junior agent' to the more ideological-central agencies such as the World Trade Organisation (WTO), World Bank etc. By developing this argument he identifies how the WHO has moved to strengthen its partnership with these bodies (especially with the programmes promoted by the World Bank), by moving to embrace globalisation and its practices as a means by which health can be developed. He also demonstrates how the WHO's main directive, the 'health for all' policy, has since its foundation in 1977 been restructured so that it is now located within the overall global neoliberal project.

In his chapter, Abbott questions the commonly held view that the unique characteristics of the Internet provide real opportunities for democratisation and political transformation, especially in societies where freedom of speech and expression is constrained by government. Instead he argues that although the Net may provide a new medium for dissent and opposition its impact is offset by two principal factors. First, the existence of marked digital *divides* between genders, levels of educational attainment, wealth and race (let alone the technological gap between north and south) and second, by growing commercialisation of this 'space'.

Drawing on the work of the French philosopher Henri Lefebvre the chapter argues that in order to understand the Internet more thoroughly political economists need to break free of the 'territorial trap' within International Relations and conceptualise 'space' in a much more fluid and dynamic way.

While critical theorists and post-structuralists may have revealed the extent to which spaces are socially constructed, they nonetheless continue to privilege time over space. Lefebvre's work reveals that space should not be regarded as a static arena – within which things take place – but instead an arena of flux. Spaces, including states and economies, may be socially constructed but they have a multiplicity of meanings, with different actors conceiving of them in different ways. In other words space is relational, adaptive and contested. Consequently Abbott argues that the Internet is both dynamic and contradictory at the same time, a space where on the one hand technology reinforces existing patterns of domination (a *representation* of space) but on the other the Internet provides a 'space which the imagination seeks to change and appropriate' (a *representational* space).

This book then is both a review and critique of the 'current state of play' within IPE. While it recognises the importance of the critical turn in the discipline it maintains that there is still much work to be done. Consequently the essays herein hope to widen the boundaries for the further development of critical thought within IPE, to 'open' up the epistemological boundaries that are in danger of being formed as the 'critical school' matures. Globalisation, models of capital, health, the Internet and resistance politics are all discussed within this volume, each aiming to provide new avenues and interpretative directions for IPE to venture down in the future.

Notes

1. We would both like to thank Chris Farrands for his suggestions, comments and the additions he proposed that went into this chapter.
2. Benjamin Disraeli (1804–1881), speech, January 24, 1860.
3. 'Critical theory' here excludes what is often called critical realism, a tradition of writing derived from the work of scholars such as Bhaskar and Elster, not because their work is not interesting or important, but because it really forms a separate field of debate in which ontological and ethical concerns are brought together in an approach that, while it owes something to Marxism, is quite distinct from the problems which this book explores.
4. Normally referring to the work of Adorno, Fromm, Habermas, Horkheimer, Marcuse etc.
5. Gramsci lived during an era when the works of Lenin, Bukharin and Plekhanov were the dominant forces within Marxist literature.
6. See for example, Birchfield, 1999; Cerny, 1993, 1995, 2000; Inayatullah and Blaney, 1999, McMichael, 1997.
7. Culminating in the foundation of the Fernand Braudel Center for the study of economies, historical systems and civilisations at Binghamton University, New York, in 1976.

8. The journal *Past and Present* was set up more or less deliberately in the image of the *Annales* school in the 1940s and 1950s, and for a long time was edited by the Marxist historian Eric Hobsbawm.
9. Braudel divided time into three distinct moments 'l'evenememtielle', 'le conjuncturelle' and 'le structurelle'. The concept of the short term describes the rhythm of the individual time of events, e.g. such as those reported in the mass media. The conjuncture, comprising more regular periodic changes, is the second unit of time he distinguishes (often linked by World Systems analysts to Kondratieff cycles). The third unit of time is the even more encompassing *longue dureé*. This trend extends in time beyond the cycles, and may embrace many centuries.
10. Though closer to the structuralism we find in Piaget.
11. This distinct historical specificity manifests itself for example in the extraordinarily detailed minutiae on different grains and how their cultivation ultimately affected the development of distinct civilisations!
12. In particular his 1997 work on international finance, *The International Organization of Credit: States and Global Finance in the World-Economy.*
13. E.g. Amin and Palan (1996)
14. 'Debate: The "second wave" of Weberian historical sociology', *Review of International Political Economy*, vol. 5, no. 2, summer 1998. Articles by Hobson, Shaw, Halperein and Spruyt; see also Amoore *et al.*, 2000c.
15. One of Gramsci's closest personal friends, Pierre Sraffa used his personal funds and professional contacts in order to obtain the books and periodicals Gramsci needed in prison. Sraffa himself became a prominent economist, brought by Keynes to Cambridge in the 1920s; he became part of the 'cafeteria group' with F. P. Ramsey and Ludwig Wittgenstein (who claimed that it was Sraffa who helped provide the important stepping stones for his *Philosophical Investigations*) and he collaborated with Keynes to critique Friedrich Hayek in debates on business cycles.
16. Pierre Sraffa's 1926 critique of Marshall's theory of the firm inspired Joan Robinson to inaugurate the theory of imperfect competition. He is also reported to be the only man she ever respected! *History of Economic Thought Website*, http://cepa.newschool.edu/het/
17. E.g. 1981, 1995, 1999.
18. One exception is MacLean (1984, 1991).

1
Being Critical about being 'Critical' in IPE: Negotiating Emancipatory Strategies[1]

Christopher Farrands

So much of the literature in IR stakes a claim for its author taking a 'critical' position. But the expression 'critical' is overused. It appears everywhere, and in a promiscuously wide range of contexts: 'critical theory' of different kinds vies with 'critical realism' and 'critical reflexivity', alongside the 'simply' critical. From its earliest uses, in papers such as that by Hoffman (1988), to the most recent (Wyn Jones, 2001), there is a wide range of uses of the term. It is not easy to find writers who want to keep the expression and yet agree that it has become so ambiguous that it threatens violence to the English language. 'Critical' theory was one of the great achievements imagined by Kant and developed in Marx's writing, intended by both – in different ways – to be radical. But it has increasingly often become a form of orthodoxy, as has recently been commented by Hutchings (2001). Alternatively, it may be a code for a kind of radicalism, but a radicalism grounded in a liberal position, as Beate Jahn (1998) has argued, a position indistinguishable from more or less radical internationalist utopianism. And when it retains a radical edge, critical writing often still lacks coherence about its radical purpose: failing to define the conditions for 'emancipation', it is emancipatory in hope more than in substance. Of course, we should note from the outset that claims to be critical in general, to offer a 'critique', in the study of GPE may have very little to do with *critical theory* more precisely defined. But to say so raises questions about the status, as well as the intellectual history, of each, to which this chapter will return.

Perhaps, then, what is really critical in a discussion of IR is to stick a pin in the pretensions of 'critical' claims, and to clarify what is *at stake* in the claim to write critically. This means interrogating the writing practice of relevant authors as much as the content of their output. One might say that to be critical is to take on certain commitments, which may be articulated in different ways, but which amount to more than a 'merely' epistemological position. But, following Bourdieu (1977, 1984, 1991), we might say that the attempt to be critical is always, at least in the longer run, going to be self-refuting: what starts as critique becomes orthodoxy for the next generation as the critics establish themselves and their ideas as the new orthodoxy. There is a concretising logic in how we produce knowledge that continuously tends to subvert critical purposes, unless those purposes can themselves be continuously renewed. So to claim to be critical may equally form part of a professional strategy in which the author places himself/herself in a particular position in a market for publications and employment. But, as Bourdieu also recognises, if this is really the case, it presents the would-be critic with an apparently impossible dilemma. His work also suggests strategies for escaping the consequences of this logic and finding a possibility of more effectively emancipatory research.

The first part of this chapter looks at the very different kinds of ways in which research in IR and GPE describes itself as critical. The second part asks what conventions and ideas of conventional knowledge lie behind these claims. The third part takes this further, to interrogate established bodies of writing in GPE. The central argument is not that it is impossible or incoherent to make the claims that critical theory seeks to establish, but that there are rules of practice as well as of theory which shape how that might be so, rules which much critical theory tends to neglect.

The chapter thus explores the philosophical debate not very far beneath the claims of critical thinking in IPE. It makes a particular set of claims about the ways in which GPE produces and reproduces itself. Critical theory aims to produce thought, which is itself emancipatory. That concept is often left unexplained in the IR literature, as if there was a straightforward transfer of the idea from social theory, where Habermas and others have spent much time on its definition, to IR, where it is little analysed in major discussions of critical theory such as Gill (1993) and Gill and Mittelman (1997). I shall follow Linklater (1990) in using 'emancipatory'. His view implies a significant but relative (rather than absolute) movement towards a social (not only individual) form of freedom, one which entails three elements: greater self-awareness on the part of the author/student, without which a politics of reflexivity is impossible; greater empowerment for those previously oppressed by structures of domination so as to enable them to resist and transform those structures in their favour; and a recognition that shared knowledge provides a key element in an emancipatory strategy. However, Linklater's criteria delimits what is 'critical' without defining it; or, alternatively, one could say that in proposing necessary conditions for 'being critical', Linklater has offered necessary rather than sufficient conditions. This failure to distinguish necessary and sufficient conditions leaves the discussion incomplete.

The goals of knowledge construction in critical theory follow Marx's Eleventh Thesis on Feuerbach: 'so far, philosophers have only studied the world... [but] the point is to change it' (McLellan, 1977, p. 158). No doubt, Marx would almost certainly have dismissed as utopian at least some of the projects, which have passed as 'critical theory' in the late twentieth century. Habermas has been much concerned over a number of years with the possibility that the goals which critical theory pursues might be contradictory (Habermas, 1999). Emancipatory thought is both more difficult and more provisional than some of its supporters imply. And it is *necessarily* difficult and provisional, if it is to count as 'critical' at all. The 'circus trick' view of critical theory – that after putting on the magic critical thinking hat with one bound you shall be free – is, when stated baldly, a straw man. It may be that no critical or post-modern theorist really holds such a view. But if writers do not hold the 'circus trick' view, many tend towards it in the claims they make. But critical theory is more difficult than this, and more elusive.

'Critical' thinking in IPE

As Susan Strange (1995; see also Lawton *et al.*, 2000) pointed out, the origins of the study of IPE can be found in dilemmas faced by students of IR in the late 1960s and early 1970s as the 'established' but arguably quite exceptional, post-Second World War international economic order seemed to fray into disorder. The Bretton Woods system of fixed exchange rates collapsed between 1968 and 1971, and although initially there were serious attempts to replace it, the structure of floating exchange rates which emerged was much more the result of governments' inability to control exchange and credit markets than it was a consequence of planning. The 1973–4 oil crisis had important effects in fuelling domestic inflation in the West, in creating distortions in transport markets, in concentrating power even more in the hands of major corporations, and, eventually, in driving the debt crisis in the developing world. But its greatest effects included its psychological impact, in creating the sense that 'orderly' Western domination of world markets was under pressure as never before from new players in the global economy. The move away from Keynesian economic policies, where they had actually been followed, and the increased questioning in the 1970s and 1980s of the role of key international economic institutions, also played a part. And while the US retained a capacity to dominate the rule-making process in international trade (as at the Uruguay Round of the General Agreement on Tariffs and Trade [GATT] and in the subsequent creation of the WTO), the increased volume and diversity of trade, the increase in grey or black economic activity, and the rise of private international regulatory mechanisms, contributed to a sense of growing disorder. This questioned whether hegemony in a globalising world economy remained possible or, if it carried costly international management responsibilities, whether it was even desirable. As Strange rightly suggested, the growth of IPE, and the willingness of major institutions to fund this new academic field and use its products, often owed much more to these practical problems than to academic debate (Strange, 1984).

But there was also academic debate, and very often it was framed in terms of a critique of IR. As Strange herself also argued (1970, 1984), IPE could try to make up a gap between the study of politics and of economics in IR, a gap she identified as far from accidental. The mutual neglect between international politics and international economics arose from the particular liberal assumptions of each, and exposed a specific set of liberal biases in IPE represented by Spero and Gilpin, among others, and by a set of immediate policy concerns which drove the agenda at the expense of an understanding of structural and discursive formations and of the variety of actors engaged in shaping IPE. This has affected the vocabulary which is conventionally used: International Political Economy – IPE – is the term used to mean the more established, more practically orientated, liberal-grounded approach to this subject; Global Political Economy – GPE – overlaps the content of IPE in important respects, but denotes a broader agenda. More importantly, it implies a more critical epistemology, what Murphy and Tooze (1991) came to call the 'new international political economy'.

What was lacking here for the most part was an engagement with either political economy or social theory, including critical theory. And it was not until the end of the 1980s that IPE, orthodoxy represented in a sophisticated form by Gilpin's *Political Economy of International Relations* (1987) and Spero's leading text, *The Politics of International Economic Relations*, turned seriously to these questions. Two major steps in the literature, both also published in 1987, were Strange's own *States and Markets* and Robert Cox's *Production, Power and World Order*. Cox himself initially held a mixture of radical (liberal in US parlance) and Marxist views, which were reflected in the Cox and Jacobsen collection *The Anatomy of Influence*. He did not discover Gramsci until the latter book was in the press, and read Gramsci and the Frankfurt school avidly over the next five years. The first fruits of this encounter appeared in two fundamentally important articles in *Millennium* in 1981 and 1983. Murphy and Tooze and their collaborators took this further in their *The New International Political Economy*, to which Strange, previously usually resistant to theory, came out for a broad-based syntheticism, owing a lot to structuralist writers as well as to the Marxist-influenced work of Schumpeter and Polanyi in her paper on a 'new eclectic approach' (Strange, 1991). Most of the other contributors affirmed a loose Gramscian approach to IPE, while also borrowing from feminist and post-colonial theory. In doing so, they defined 'post-stucturalism' as an amalgam of critical theory and post-modernism rather than as a specific subset of the second.

A serious engagement with classical political economy took rather longer, as Razeem Sally has argued (Sally, 1996). IPE suffers because it has grown out of a classical IR agenda rather than a political economy literature. It derives from the agenda of states, diplomacy and war, but adds in economic questions – the 'states and markets approach' – and acknowledges some international economic structures as significant in IR. When Strange first called her classic enquiry *States and Markets* it was intended as an in-joke: the book *attacks* the 'states and markets' approach as too narrow and as neglecting structural power. When students refer to Strange's 'states and markets' approach, they should be automatically failed (as I once heard her say). IPE did not, as it were, grow out of PE, and although there were nods to Weber and Marshall and, at least sometimes, more than nods to Marxism, the failure to integrate the full richness of political economy and to recognise the diversity of economic arguments away from Cambridge and Chicago (especially the diversity of Austrian, French and German approaches, in which Sally specialises) proved vitiating. The more recent encounter with serious political economy, which has only occurred in the last decade or so, associated with journals such as the *Review of International Political Economy* and *New Political Economy*, as well as with authors such as Palan and Sally, has automatically brought a different influence from critical theory back into IPE (Palan, 1996; Sally, 1996). This has been because of the strength of influence of Marxist and Marxian thinking among political economists and economic historians, even if that influence is sometimes only implicit. In short, the contribution of political economy to IPE has been important, but Sally's project remains incomplete, as he admits himself, and there remain important exchanges which IPE needs to develop with both the classical and critical PE literatures.

All this in turn suggests that IPE came face to face with critical theory rather late, in the work of John Maclean (see especially Maclean, 1988), Roger Tooze, Ronen Palan and Justin Rosenberg as well as the Canadian-based colleagues and students of Robert Cox. This was even later than the encounter between IR theory and critical theory, which became important to mainstream IR in the late 1980s (and, despite an often repeated but rather lazy construction, before rather than after the end of the Cold War). Critical theory mainly influences IPE through the impact of the 'neo-Gramscian turn' which has come to dominate much of the field in Europe and Canada, partly because of the excellence of the work of Cox and his colleagues. But outside quite narrow circles, neo-Gramscian writing has quite a shallow reach into both IPE and IR, especially in the US. Impressionistically, one might look at US approaches to IPE and conclude that they are still primarily dominated by an orthodox IR agenda, by the search for positivist theory, and for a 'neo-neo' synthesis, by the rage for constructivism (which is treated more cautiously and less positivistically in European IR), and by a tendency to neglect post-Marxian and post-structuralist critique. But above all, US approaches to IPE (allowing that this is only intended as a broad generalisation, and that there are specific individual exceptions) tends, because it retains its roots in IR, to neglect both political economy and social theory as resources for theorising and for finding more deep-laid patterns and more critical ways of judging knowledge claims.

Gramsci and critical theory in GPE: towards a genealogy of Gramscian thought in GPE

Although there are other kinds of critical theory not directly connected with Gramsci (cf. Geuss, 1982), this chapter takes Gramscian studies as the central element in contemporary critical theory in IR. This is partly simply because of the history of critical theory in IR in particular. But also, Gramsci provides an especially important resource and a starting point for emancipatory thought. His work is not without problems, and has sometimes been too easily translated into a kind of key which can be turned uncritically; for the claim to write 'critically' is itself no guarantee that anything critical or emancipatory is actually going on in a text. One particular question is immediately raised by the ways in which Gramsci is used in IPE: was Gramsci a critical theorist? Although this may seem an odd question in view of the extensive use made of his work, it is in fact an important question because it has an important, simple and at first unexpected answer. No: Gramsci was *not* – and I say this quite categorically – a critical theorist. The first reason for this is demonstrable on a reading of his work. For Gramsci was, as Germain and Kenny (1998) have already argued, more of a materialist and an orthodox Marxist, than he is sometimes portrayed in the literature. What he says is interesting, and perhaps significant; but not only has he not read the Frankfurt school, Schumpeter or Polanyi, or even the *Dialectics of Enlightenment*, for the obvious reason that none of this work was written during his lifetime, but he also had not read the young Marx, whose manuscript and draft work was beginning to become available in German in the 1930s, but which did not appear in Italian (or English) until after the Second World War, and long after Gramsci's death. Furthermore, Gramsci retained an optimism about the possibility of a scientific socialism which is little muted by the trajectory of communism in the USSR in the 1920s, when the now often fruitful ideas of Luxemburg, Bukharin and Trotsky basked in a range of dismissive epithets from 'left-infantilism' to 'right-reactionary' without ever gaining serious consideration as a basis for an emancipatory alternative to orthodox Marxism-Leninism. Critical theory, by contrast, develops through a critique of Marxism-Leninism as much as of liberalism. It scrutinises especially the accounts in Marxism-Leninism of social action, social being and subjectivity. It also makes a comprehensive ontological and methodological attack on simplistic forms of historical materialism. Gramsci was less unorthodox than he is often portrayed, although no doubt where his arguments are unorthodox they did contribute to the emergence of critical theory. But critical theory, I would argue, is better understood as a post-war Western Marxist debate which engages a particular *problematique*, one which is precisely concerned with how to make sense of the world and of our consciousness of the world and our being-in-the-world, of our capacity for subjectivity and agency, against the background of enormous political forces and structures which appear to render us without voice, agency or critical reflexiveness. These debates, which were first taken up, rather inadequately, by Sartre and Lukacs in (respectively) *Existentialism and Humanism* and *History and Class Consciousness* in the late 1940s and 1950s, started to point towards a more open sense of human potential which critical theory imagines. For critical theory needs to be understood against the background of these debates, of the German, subsequently the US, and later the European (but predominantly French) intellectual context of the questions it asks and the methods of reasoning it employs. One issue it recognises, but leaves for later writers to explore satisfactorily, is the question of the relationship between consciousness and subjectivity in a material culture. Gramsci has some insights into this question, which remains a critical and insufficiently clarified issue in how we deal with post-communist Marxian theory. But it is an exaggeration to think that he takes this question very far or any very systematic way in the *Prison Notebooks*, while the letters are too fragmented a source, and the *Pre-Prison Writings* do not recognise this at all (Gramsci, 1971; 1994). In short, Gramsci is an important precursor of critical theory in some, but only *some*, ways. To read him as a critical theorist is to read political theory in an ahistorical, but also in an inadequately theorised, way. He contributed powerfully to critical theory; but he was *not* a critical theorist.

This brings us closer to a definition of critical theory in terms of a set of debates and images which are historically specific to the post-war world, however much we might find evidence for some of the positions it adopts in the young Marx or anywhere else. For it is not in 'being critical' alone that critical theory has its identity, nor in the epistemological critique which that embodies (Geuss, 1982). Three other things alongside this epistemological critique define critical theory. This is important because a tighter definition of critical theory helps to make more sense of what it can and cannot be expected to achieve. First, it is the attempt, especially in Marcuse (1964; 1969) and Adorno at Haskheimer, to engage seriously with psychoanalysis, something that starts while the Frankfurt school is still based in Germany, as evidenced especially in Benjamin's aesthetic criticism, but which only attains a coherence after exile in the US allows a series of contacts with psychoanalytic practitioners. Second, the experience of the Holocaust and the beginnings of a rethinking of social theory are of great significance. And here, writers somewhat on the margins of 'mainstream' critical theory (especially Arendt, as well as those not usually associated directly with it at all – Husserl, Koestler, Sartre, Merleau-Ponty, Piaget, the gigantically obscure presence of Levinas) contribute to the construction of debates in the 1970s and after. Critical theory since 1945 has followed the *Dialectics of Enlightenment* in its recognition that, although one can find critique in Kantian ideas of knowledge or Nietzschean scepticism alone, this will have little of the practical and theoretical force which are acquired through a recognition of the potential of instrumental reason and an image of human supremacy over nature to abuse power beyond inhumanity; warnings always necessarily present in post-Holocaust thought. Third, although critical theory is first of all an attempt to give an account of modernity, it wrestles from the start with the question of how our consciousness can grasp any kind of reality critically if we are gripped by structural conditions which forestall a radical apprehension of the world around us. Whether in individual form or in a more collective form (the 'sociology of knowledge' question), critical theory has to give an account of its own possibility before – or while – it gives a coherent account of itself. It is here that Gramsci's writing on consciousness is important – and far more emancipatory than the tepid step Lukacs made in the same direction. But Gramsci's writing on consciousness is also problematic. It is still highly materialist, it seems to owe more to Plekhanov than to the young Marx (whose manuscripts, unknown to Gramsci, were one of the bases of Frankfurt-school innovation), and where it strays from materialism it is shaped by a nationalistic idealism (drawn especially from Croce) that is a different kind of diversion. What Gramsci does is to frame new questions, and with hindsight and further on we can see that these are questions of great importance to the opening up of Western Marxism after the 1950s. As Wright Mills was later to argue, and as Rosenberg suggested with respect to IR in particular, he allows the informed imagination to open possibilities which a more conventional writer would not dare to suspect (Rosenberg, 1994).

Critical theory has a specific place in IPE, which has evolved a particular role, the critique of IR as a whole, as well as providing a framework for research and debate in IPE. But scholars with their roots in postmodernism also lay claim to a 'critical' label, even though they might well reject all or part of the critical theory prospectus. In addition, critical realists such as Sayer (2000) influence the debate in post-Marxian critical social theory even though with the exception of a very few examples this does not have a strong presence in GPE.

At this stage, it is worth separating different strands of thinking in Gramscian IPE. For the different authors who have acquired authority in the field do not come at it from the same assumptions or with the same intellectual strategies. A genealogy of Gramscian thinking would need to identify *at least* four main strands. The first would be Cox himself, who writes at a more general level than some others, and who acknowledges the primary influence of Marx in his work. Gramsci's influence is strong, but it is refined for a purpose, and Cox borrows from Gramsci to fit that overall, classical (but not orthodox) approach. Mittelman shares Cox's general position, and also his tendency to approach Gramscian thinking at a level of generality in terms of world systems and global patterns. But Mittelman looks more at power relations between rich and poor, and at how patterns of globalisation reproduce patterns of domination, in his own writing (e.g. his contributions in Gill and Mittelman, 1997). Stephen Gill, by contrast (see Gill, 1990, 1993; Gill and Mittelman, 1997) is much more concerned with developing an accurate textual interpretation of Gramsci's writing. Gill's interest seems to focus on getting others to read Gramsci carefully and to repudiate readings, which seem to 'fit' Gramsci too closely to a post-modern position. This is fair enough in the sense that Gramsci is no more a 'post-modernist' than he is a 'critical theorist': both readings are ahistorical and do damage to Gramsci's thought. But there are, all the same, many ambiguities in Gramsci's own writing, and the apparent attempt to dictate a single reading overlooks both the uncertainties in these ambiguities and their potential to inform a much wider discussion.

Third, a younger group of writers, of whom Rupert (1995, 1998) is the most distinguished, have taken Gramsci's work to address questions raised by other debates in IPE. This touches especially on the debate between neorealist or liberal institutionalist ideas of global hegemony – how it is caused, what its effects are, how it is managed by a hegemon – and Gramscian readings of hegemony. Here, the agenda is derived from a debate between positions where there seem to be some overlaps, and where orthodox interpretation of Gramsci's writings is less important than the construction of arguments which criticise orthodox political economy effectively. This is not to say that Rupert and others, such as Neufeld (1995), do not take Gramsci seriously, but that their priorities and research agendas are different from those of both Cox and Gill. At the same time, they engage with the detailed working of power relations, with questions such as how corporations reproduce patterns of cultural as well as managerial and financial power, and with the detailed character of domination between different parts of the developed world. Augelli and Murphy have looked at patterns of power in international institutions in a similar vein. Contributors to Lawton *et al.* (2000) and Gill and Mittelman (1997) also look at dependent relations in some respects. Perhaps the greatest current gap in the neo-Gramscian literature is to explore how these ideas can be focused in detailed studies of developing or semi-peripheral countries: general arguments can be found in abundance, but specific, careful studies of the quality of Rupert's work are needed to take the agenda forward here. This would also open a more theorised dialogue between neo-Gramscian authors and world systems theorists who have stuck with a more classic structuralist approach, a dialogue one looks for both in the literature and in conference debate without much success.

The fourth way in which Gramscian ideas have been developed in GPE is in the analysis of ideas and culture. This is closer to a tradition identified in the UK with sociologists and social theorists such as Raymond Williams and Stuart Hall. This debate is potentially important for IR and GPE for three reasons. First, it has evolved in cultural studies, against the climate of a very critical reception, to give an account of the place of culture in political struggle, and of the character of cultural conflicts, not least including issues such as identity and nationalism. Insofar as both IR and GPE acknowledge the need to recognise the importance of what happens at the culture-politics interface, it would be foolish to ignore what specialists in a related field have achieved. Despite this, there is actually very little input to date from this branch of cultural studies into IR. The second reason why it would be important to draw on this cultural-studies strand of thinking is that it has the most sophisticated sense of the way in which history, memory and the weight of the past play a role in framing and defining the debates of the present, which is to say both epistemological debates and 'real politics' (Callinicos, 1995). In IR, Gramscian writers, including Cox (1987, 2001), draw the importance of the specific historical circumstances in which ideas and actions operate. But their historicism is often only of a general kind. One looks to the writings of historical sociologists, such as Braudel, Mann or Tilly, to give a detailed long-term perspective on how contemporary ideas and actions can be framed. But the distinction between historical sociology and neo-Gramscian GPE is pretty much totally false. The divide between the two owes a lot to the distinctive intellectual histories of each. But both take up the same questions, each makes similar value judgements, and both relate in similar ways to the material they study. They also have very similar vocabularies. In short, it is long overdue for historical sociology and Gramscian social and cultural theory to talk more constructively to each other than they have managed so far. The third reason why this nexus of thinking about culture/politics/history is important is because it offers so much to the discussion on identities and identity formation. This influence is already present in much of the critical literature on identity, although the fact that its roots lie partly in Gramscian social thinking is often ignored or unrecognised. But the importance of arguments about social solidarity, about identity and changing patterns of identity in the face of globalisation and social change have come to play a significant role in the study of IR as well as in area studies, and have an equally important impact in the ways in which we think about state-society relations and power networks in GPE.

This analysis of Gramscian influences in global political economy neglects a lot of possible sources, for there are other strands of Gramscian thought in political theory and cultural studies which might potentially contribute to IR. But within IR and GPE the influence is relatively focused, limited for the most part to those influenced by Cox and his colleagues, by Habermas and the debates around his work, or, in a very few cases such as Murphy, by 'members' of the so-called 'Italian' school of IPE. There is a much greater scope for critical thinking about Gramsci's influence looking at ideas of information knowledge, post-Fordism and history and memory in IR, as well as in studies of identity and consciousness, and in methodology. One such influence, which I shall discuss shortly, is that of Bourdieu, who also owes something of a debt to the climate of Gramscian ideas as well as to the Frankfurt school, although in his casè much of that influence may be as a reaction against them.

Critical and practical thought

At the heart of the debate over critical thought in IPE is the distinction between practical and critical reasoning. The distinction, like so much of this debate, has its roots in Kant's political philosophy and his critical idealism. More recent writers, including Cox and Habermas (cited above), but also influential figures at the intersection of social philosophy and practical politics, such as Hannah Arendt have held out the 'suspicion' that politics, especially political action, is always incompatible with the search for truth (1993, p. 239). But, in this section, I want to argue that this distinction is at once mistaken and harmful. Indeed, its consequences are potentially catastrophic, although most scholars who want to be critical and practical at the same time get round the problem simply by ignoring it and carrying on as they wish. In *Knowledge and Human Interests* (and elsewhere), Habermas (1987) argues for a strong distinction between that *practical* knowledge which tends to serve the interests of established orders and a more *critical* knowledge. Habermas points out that this is not a superficial distinction. Critical knowledge is grounded in a *reflexiveness* which practical knowledge lacks, as well as in specific explicit values. Some practical knowledge, in Habermas account, might be critical or might at least not serve the interests of an established order; but if it does so it is by accident. Critical knowledge uses theory to seek self-understanding, and from self-understanding finds a leverage point to stand outside existing knowledge practices in order to critique them. This Archimedian ambition reflects an ontological revolution –

that such a position exists and can be mirrored in our consciousness and language use at all – as well as an epistemological challenge.

GPE – and IR – needs to be both critical and practical at the same time. Of course this uses the distinction between critical and practical knowledge rather differently from the Frankfurt school's usage, and reflects a part of the strategy of creating ideal speech situations within which, according to Habermas, emancipatory thought and action can be combined. But Habermas stands as an unreliable witness in his own defence, and the formulation raises serious practical and conceptual problems.

Cox's formulation of the critical-practical dilemma is a much more effective, and perhaps more honest, solution. It is worth underlining its importance. Cox points out that 'all knowledge is for someone and for some purpose' (1981, p. 128): there is no such thing as disinterested knowledge, which is to say that all knowledge claims imply an orientation towards the matter studied; 'objective knowledge' is impossible. This is a well recognised principle of much social science (which is not to say it is automatically sound). But it is not the same as the claim that knowledge cannot be critical unless it actually rejects attempts to be practical. And Cox reminds us, although the reminder is rather implicit, that all knowledge claims *commit* the claimant (Cox, 2001). This commitment, one might say, is an ethical commitment of a kind; but it is also an ontological, epistemological and practical commitment.

Bourdieu: the discriminatory role of the expert

Bourdieu has proposed a series of arguments not usually associated with narrow definitions of critical theory. But his work contributes to our understanding of the critical project, of knowledge building, of the role of experts and of the difficulty of reaching some form of critical/practical knowledge. The case for a critical theory is strengthened by drawing on his work, even though it may at the same time induce a sense of discomfort, of insecurity, about what it is possible to claim while remaining 'critical'. Roger Tooze has drawn attention to the potential value of Bourdieu's work in IPE, and especially of the hermeneutics of practice, which evolve in his account of the relationship between theory and practice. But Tooze himself has never developed this argument in writing very far – the most developed account is in *Strange Power* (Lawton *et al.*, 2000), but this does not go far beyond the mention of Bourdieu in his writing in *The New International Political Economy* (Murphy and Tooze, 1991) ten years earlier. Following the argument he points towards, however, and using the wider range of relevant Bourdieu texts, our ideas of what properly counts as critical thought do become sharper. In particular the temporary, contingent nature of the critical element in any critique as well as the relationship of theory to practice (on which Bourdieu builds on Foucault), and the necessarily temporary, processual character of any emancipatory thought, appear much clearer. Whether we see the resulting image of knowledge, consciousness and the potential for a radical political economy as closer to a Maoist or Trotskyist image of 'continuous/perpetual revolution' or to the contingencies and temporary, always to be renewed, always to be reviewed, character of what can be said or suggested in Levinas's use of language, is an open question, not least since Bourdieu would acknowledge at least some influence from both.

Bourdieu points out the extent to which social interaction is grounded in definitions of taste and judgement. These definitions are 'managed' by those who are able to establish themselves as arbiters of taste. The act of 'discrimination' is socially constructed, and, for Bourdieu, fundamental to the exercise of any form of social power. The exercise of social power takes place through the arbiter's ability to manipulate symbolic forms of knowledge (Bourdieu, 1982; 1999, pp. 336–40). Hence, for Bourdieu, symbolic power is inscribed in social relations as a fundamental form of power, analogous to, but not the same as, the power ascribed to discourse by Foucauldians. This defines the special role of 'experts' and 'professionals', including academics (Bourdieu, 1984). The rise and rise of experts and of expertise is, for Bourdieu, a central part of the history of the redefinition of symbolic power in the emergence of modernity and then in the shift from modernity in the later twentieth century. But this also presents a dilemma for Bourdieu, who recognises his own status as an academic. Bourdieu is an intellectual whose powers of discrimination and taste, exercised through his academic and journalistic writing as well as through television appearances and public 'performance', give him an extraordinary status, especially in France (Bourdieu, 1999). His critique of symbolic power and his own position within the symbolic power structure appear to contradict each other. Bourdieu claims that he is able to overcome this contradiction through the exercise of 'reflexiveness', a strategy open to others in this position. However one has to be wary: this explanation is not wholly convincing given that the exercise of reflexivity itself involves the deployment of that elite, priestlike discrimination which is being scrutinised. One might add here that discrimination is being *scrutinised*. It is not being rejected altogether, not least because, as Bourdieu himself acknowledges, there is no independent (*contra* Habermas, above, '*Archimedian*') standpoint outside discrimination from which we can view it:

through reflexivity, we may be aware of aspects of our own discriminatory position, its history, its language, its implications, but nonetheless we cannot stand outside that framework.

If this reading of Bourdieu's work is sound, it provides a starting point to reassess the drive for more 'critical' thought in the study of IR and IPE. It suggests that the growth of IPE and GPE as alternatives and as possible sources of critique of the body of expertise in International Relations fulfils a function for the role of scholars as experts in control of the permissible boundaries of knowledge. What can be known, what questions we are allowed to ask, how we should use our powers of discrimination, characterise a power discourse within the academy. This was not necessarily an original point for Bourdieu to make – we can find the same in Nietzsche, Sorel and even Hume. But in the context of the specifically post-structural and post-communist intellectual debates in which Bourdieu, and neo-Gramscian political economy, situate themselves, it is an important and compelling argument. The dangers of professionalisation in the ossification of fragile and provisional forms of understanding, and in the institutional embedding of what can perhaps only be said in more oblique or temporary forms if it is to retain its emancipatory potential, remains an equally important – if controversial – strategy for setting out how we can refine our take on the possibility of critical thinking in a society in which knowledge is widely consumerised or commodified, and so trapped into more hegemonic conventions. But (as I shall discuss shortly) the problem is not the conventional nature of knowledge here – since all knowledge is in some senses conventional – but the tendency for slippage into more hegemonic, less genuinely critical modes.[2]

We can relate the conventionalism in Bourdieu to a more thorough-going, and in some ways more carefully thought out account in the writings of Ludwig Wittgenstein on social conventions and language. It is hard to think that Bourdieu does not draw directly on Wittgenstein, as well as from Gadamer (cf. Harding, 1992). But he does not acknowledge their influence in any systematic way. Wittgenstein demonstrated that both knowledge of 'social facts' or social meanings and, indeed, all claimed empirical knowledge, is founded in conventions which are social practices rather than objectively 'true' mirrors of a reality or rationally worked out chains of logical argument (Wittgenstein, 1975). In making this argument, Wittgenstein undermines the particular claims to foundational truth which most Western thought has relied on since the Enlightenment. Wittgenstein's argument here owes much to phenomenology, and it is a mistake to read him as a 'British' philosopher. The

British philosopher he is closest to in some respects is Hume, although it is worth adding that one would not recognise it if one read quickly through his work looking for mentions of Hume's name. What he shares with Hume, as with Foucault, Bourdieu and with 'mainstream' critical theory, is a powerful scepticism about positivist or empiricist knowledge claims. That scepticism is used to interrogate the use of language and to point out that deeply embedded ideas nonetheless reflect socially con-structed conventions rather than 'natural' objective truths. In Bourdieu, the argument that all uses of language are politically and socially loaded takes the form of a detailed analysis of the forms of symbolic power, which they embody. This is also of importance in GPE, where a sense of the ways in which material forms of power and symbolic forms of power interact needs to be elaborated. Gramscian thinking touches on this – the *Prison Notebooks* in particular make extensive use of ideas about language, consciousness and ideology as elements in symbolic power plays both by dominant players and by those who would resist them. But in Gramsci, the ideas are not developed as they are in Bourdieu. This is not the least reason why critical theory in IR needs to take Bourdieu seriously.

Negotiating emancipatory strategies

Habermas' work has moved into an increasingly liberal mode as it has evolved in the 1990s. His work on liberalism, democracy and constitu-tionalism is theoretically interesting but conservative by the standards of critical theory, although he would still claim to be a 'critical theorist'. Certainly, some ideas from critical theory remain important in his writing, including the idea of dialogic discoveries of truths and the resist-ance against a very fragmented sense of what counts as truth which we find in Foucault and much Foucauldian work, although Foucault's own slide towards an increasingly liberal position parallels that of Habermas (Marks, 2000). The idea of the ideational dimension of power, of the role of language and of symbolic power, seems to have more in common with Bourdieu, and the parallels here are not only general ones.

If emancipation starts with the creation of the possibility of alterna-tives, as Foucault (1997) proposes, and if that is the essence of critical thought, then that is an important position for a critical GPE. But it is also woolly and inadequate in itself. One reason why emancipatory thought tends to be woolly, we might hazard, is because when it has sought to be specific it has failed. What is the more useful model here? It is not Strange, whose theoretical inconsistency was legendary, and shows no-where more sharply than in her *The Retreat of the State* (1997), where she spends most of the time imagining ways in which the state has declined, using the broadly structural approach she had developed in *States and Markets* (1994) and elsewhere, only to overturn the logic of her own argument in a much more liberal conclusion which re-asserts the role of the state. Both arguments are plausible; but they cannot sit together, and their methodologies are at war. This is not a coherent face of eclecticism. Murphy and Tooze, and Strange in the same volume, suggest a more open eclecticism and underline a radical purpose for the opening up of epistemological debate in GPE away from liberal-realist orthodoxies (Murphy and Tooze, 1991). But the image of critical thinking that seems to make sense in terms of maintaining a consistency, offering a way of avoiding some of the traps identified here, remains the approach that Cox adopts. The importance of neo-Gramscian thinking is not that it solves all of the problems it faces, but that at least it remains true to its own intentions, and it has a sense of its own contingency. Gramscian critical theory and Bourdieurian reflexivity can accommodate each other; and, we might conclude, they need each other.

Conclusions

As knowledge in the study of global political economy has moved on, has it moved 'forward'? The Foucauldian sense of emancipation discussed above, that emancipation is immediately present when we can imagine alternatives, has a powerful ring to it. But it is also designed to conform to a worldview in which 'progress' is always to be viewed with deepest suspicion. Critique is possible without progress, as much of the argument around Foucault's own work suggests (cf. also Lynch, 2000). Possible, yes; but is it worth anything without some sense of possible change? This does not need to mean 'progress' in the liberal or social democrat sense. But the work of a variety of scholars from Habermas to Castells on communications, Judith Butler and Kristeva on identity and change, Held, Laclau and Mouffe on democratisation, or writers as diverse as Amartya Sen and James Manor on development, continues to articulate a need to find transformatory possiblilities in the process of knowledge creation. If knowledge is for something, for someone, it *can* make a difference. Or so many would want to believe, including this writer. The suggestion in the literature, which this chapter has tried to underline, is that there remains a possibility of transformation, or at least of radical improvement or development (even if both these words are tainted by some of their past uses). This possibility is found, among other places, in Pels's (2000) defence of reflexivity. In the study of GPE, including neo-Gramscian uses, it can be defended providing that some of the more stringent criteria (for example those outlined by Germain and Kenny, 1998) are observed. But this approach, which is grounded in a particular set of values and epistemologies, is still insufficient in itself.

This search for emancipation is *negotiated*. That is not to say that it is negotiated as a liberal strategy or as a compromise with its detractors, but it is negotiated in four absolutely vital senses. First, it is negotiated in the sense that it is part of a dialogue, for dialogic understanding reduces the risk of hegemony or enforced dominance. It leaves knowledge as provisional in that it may change, but also in the sense that it is provisional within an evolving conversation: there is no absolute truth, but there is a tendency in the dialogue to separate truth from error or mistake. If we repeat ourselves in that conversation, we can learn iteratively. Second, it is negotiated in the sense that it questions its own discourse and is open to questions from others: this is part of the 'dialogue'. Third, the dialogic community to which it contributes to represents an attempt to agree standards of knowledge, the conventions within which arguments can be justified or refuted. Fourth and finally, it is reflexive in the sense that Bourdieu asks us to be. We debate with ourselves in our writing, and we need to write with self-suspicion (Bourdieu and Wacquant, 1992) if our knowledge claims are to withstand the test of reflexivity. In these ways, we are in a continual dialogue both with ourselves and with others to maintain the standards of a critical, non-hegemonic but practical knowledge.

Does a continuous search for critique take us where we want to go? If knowledge is only provisionally so, and if there is no foundational criterion for truth, or even for validity, we have one possible path sketched by the Frankfurt school and marked out by Habermas which enables us to engage with a 'real world', although in philosophical terms the realism here is a weak version, tentatively held and always under threat. We also have a different path, one rooted in Foucauldian discourse analysis. We could, of course, also just stay in the garden and merely play, as some versions of post-modernism might encourage. Or we might, more seriously but not more purposively, conclude that we (academics, people in positions of power, especially Western ones) do not yet know enough, and perhaps cannot ever know enough, to found knowledge claims sufficiently firmly to constitute grounds for actions which are not, if only implicitly, imperial, oppressive or ineffective.

Hannah Arendt's assertion of the importance of the search for a single identifiable truth, and of the dangers of searching for truth in the inimical waters of politics, is well made even if her more classical ideal of the ultimate unity of that truth does not hold (Arendt, 1993); indeed, in a plural world, a continuing sense of critical purpose is if anything even more important, as Chris White suggests in the following chapter in this volume. But I have to admit my own concerns – values – here. It seems to me that the actual conditions which people face in the global political economy do not allow the luxury of inaction, even if we run the risk of mistake. As Rosenau and Durfee argued in their introduction to a special issue of the journal *Millennium* in 1996 on Poverty in Global Politics, there are questions which we cannot ignore unless we are willing to accept existing power structures and forms of exploitation which do very obvious harm to many people. GPE is still founded, as it has always been, in questions, which Cox raised: knowledge for somebody and something in a given context. This imposes a responsibility that we cannot shrug off in play, in an assumed impotence, or a retreat to inward contemplation. It also returns to what I have argued are fundamental questions in critical theory – the attempt to bring together accounts of symbolic and material forms of power and domination, the impact of the interaction of the aesthetic and the political in ordering the economic imagination, the problem of giving an account of consciousness and of the sociology of knowledge. In particular, how is an emancipatory knowledge – or subjectivity, or any kind of agency – possible at all in the 'real' world of globalising structures and their powers? This puts an emphasis in turn on the need for reflexive thinking, for reflexive imagination, in research. In addition, it underscores the need for practical and critical knowledge to be grounded in a common project; the two are not separate, nor are they possible if one is securely grounded and then the other is tagged on as an afterthought.

Critical knowledge is fragile, and the conventions that encode it are always, and unavoidably, in danger of being taken away or co-opted back to an orthodoxy. That critical/practical knowledge is possible we cannot doubt, which is to say that we cannot allow ourselves to doubt, although the lived experience of writers such as Gramsci and Benjamin might help us to recognise the struggles involved. But that it is, while possible, always difficult, always provisional, always fragile, is vital to understand the ways in which we might approach it. Much that claims to be 'critical' is interesting; some of it is repetitive; but relatively little seems to appreciate the commitments involved in the claim to be critical. To be critical, properly so-called, is to engage in a commitment to a certain mode of working in which we cannot expect definite, permanent results. There is no continuous unfolding *telos*; but the results obtained, albeit temporary and negotiated, are significant not just because they are all we could expect, but also because they are sufficient to ground a critical, elaborated radicalism. Bourdieu does not solve the intellectual problems about emancipatory knowledge that we inherit from Habermas. But he helps to establish the ethical and epistemological conditions which enable us to build on Cox, Gramsci and others, and on which a critical understanding can be elaborated. A respect for Bourdieu's work locks us into an acknowledgement of the importance of reflexivity in research and in writing practice, and it recognises the importance of the writing process itself, something which every PhD student knows but which is easily forgotten – because it is taken for granted under the welter of deadlines – by more experienced colleagues. In short, to be critical and effective in the study of global political economy, we have to take more notice of Bourdieu and at the same time to remain positive about what our research practice and our writing can potentially achieve.

Notes

1. This chapter draws extensively on conversations with a number of colleagues and PhD students in Nottingham Trent University, and owes much to them as well as to exchanges in the NTU Faculty of Humanities Research Student Seminar, including Jason Abbott, Richard Johnson, Eleanore Kofman, Stephen Chan, Heikki Patomaki, Christopher May, Roger Tooze, Neil Turnbull, Chris White and Owen Worth. An earlier and similar working draft of this chapter was presented at the ISA 41st annual convention (2001) with Worth and Abbott.
2. On reflexivity, see Pels, 2000, and Lynch, 2000, for a debate on the significance of this widely discussed notion, and Harding, 1992, for a valuable and perceptive take on Bourdieu's relationship to methodology in the more positivist US context.

2
A Case for IPE Theoretical Plurality
Chris White

Introduction

This chapter is written in an effort to illustrate and explain a rather different approach to the building of International Political Economy (IPE) theory. Within this relatively young discipline a case will be made for an opening-up of receptivity towards aspects of theory from other disciplines, that we might appreciate the potential for more accurately, more pertinently, theorising on the modern (or indeed post-modern!) world. At its inception this chapter was not intended to occupy a particular space in this book; however, I do find myself in juxtaposition to some of the points (or their spirit as I perceive it) raised by Farrands in Chapter I. This is contained simultaneously on a number of levels. The principal project in this chapter is a call for the further opening of dialogical spaces in IPE, with one of the prime aims being to dispel fears, such as those expressed by Farrands, of the appearance of critical experts in IPE; parties whose range of influence would, or could, determine the themes and sites of critical debates.

Neither should we fear, in my view, the diversity of opinion in relation to our emancipatory visions. The great danger in some of this preceding chapter is that it can be seen as offering a degree of support for some consensual vision of emancipatory efforts. For now, perhaps, we would be better to recognise that this thing IPE is still too young a creation to wrestle with emancipation without the outside help of more mature disciplines. It then has the space it needs to wrestle and experiment with theoretical constructs, and its interpretations of actualities, as a prelude to truer, more solid contributions to the wider social science cannon. Far from Farrands' urge for caution and a re-examination of what it means to be critical, this chapter calls for further progression of thought and writing in the critical regard, with extensions of imagination and visions being encouraged and included as worthy in and of themselves, provided they are seen as worthy within the caveats explored below. Critical IPE theorists do seem (as Farrands implies) to have generated a critical industry for themselves, so there is no call here for writing for the sake of it. Rather, in accord with Farrands, let us recognise the need for a return to a certain stringency in our revisionings of emancipation, while at the same time pressing on with the project of ever widening the academic scope of IPE. I fear in the context that Farrands, and other theorists describe, both these elements are not necessarily satisfactorily accommodated.

One of the fundamental premises here is that IPE pays too much dogmatic attention to its visions of what the discipline is/ought to be concerned with. Indeed, there appears to be what can only be described as an overwhelmingly conservative attitude in IPE theoreticians as to the degree of conformity that must exist before any theory or theories are seen as within the purview of any given discipline. It is in the cause of challenging these attitudes that this has been written. The purpose is to attempt to energise recognition of the value of the development of our theoretical and disciplinary imaginations, though this is by no means the first attempt to achieve this!

Karl Marx famously urged us all to go one better than philosophers in trying to change the world for the good. How, in IPE (or any other 'social science'), is this possibly to be effected within the climate of conservatism referred to above? No discipline could hope to do this alone, not even (or perhaps, 'especially') one that espouses to theory at the global level. If it is too much to expect within any single discipline, why do theorists in IPE appear so loathe to concede the necessity of spreading their nets further, in order to more faithfully rise to Marx's challenge? Or, more specifically, what difficulties/issues are generated by a greater inclusiveness of theory from alternative sources, embraced as helping to contribute to the development of the IPE cannon? The initial quest here is for a case for broadening of descriptions of the world(s) we inhabit, in order that an agenda for more meaningful change should be arrived at.

As will be shown, this appreciation has been demonstrable for some decades now in other social disciplines. This is to give voice to the frustration that results from IPE's apparent inertia or lack of insight into these issues. A browse through the major publications (books, journals) reveals it as a discipline awash with brilliant, imaginative commentators and analysts. What does seem in short supply however, are visionary theorists who would propel it to the forefront of social research; who, merely by their approach, are willing to confront current theorising practice, which will insist that the scope and range of IPE's inclusiveness becomes boundless by current comparison.

Even at this early stage, one can feel the hot breath of '*les tricoteuses*' of IPE, fanning the fragile neck of another inexperienced theorist. Indeed it would not be unreasonable to fear that the argument thus far is merely a call for intellectual anarchy, with 'anything goes' as the implicit (or explicit) message. However, this is definitely not the intended message. Nothing written here is intended as a justification for reducing IPE to a catch-all discipline, indeed the most strenuous efforts ought to be expended to ensure that this does not happen. The need to maintain academic standards while expanding the range of usable theory need not be incompatible and this case will be illustrated below.

This view has historical precedent. In the 1950s, Wright Mills (1959) proposed the same thing as a reaction to the predominance of positivist/ behavioural approaches in the social sciences. Forty-five years later, Justin Rosenberg (1994) took up the Wright Mills challenge specifically in relation to IPE. Following Wright Mills' 'classic social analysis', Rosenberg urges us towards both a more positive position and state of mind. As stated above, these combine in the sense that 'good' theorising (as specified by Rosenberg) should always find room in IPE, regardless of its academic source, in pursuit of the 'international imagination' vis-à-vis that which the theory attempts to address. The potential issues this view generates will be approached here from a significantly different angle. This is centred mainly around a critical analysis of the concept of *consensus*, in the hope that forward movement can be produced by criticising implicit and explicit presuppositions on this theme, in current IPE theorising.

In this work philosophers and theorists will be compared and juxtaposed with the intention of promoting the case for seeing the need for greater theoretical pluralism in IPE. One of the writers (Connolly) directly relates his work to IR issues, and so is readily applicable to this context. The other two main featured theorists (Habermas and Rescher) stand in direct relation to one another. This chapter is sited within the discussion of what it is to be critical; therefore one of the most prominent Frankfurt theorists, Jürgen Harbermas, was an obvious candidate for inclusion here. He is considered, it must be said, only in relation to one of his more recent (and accessible!) works. Alongside this, Rescher provides a withering attack on many of the notions upon which Habermas founds his critical notions in his 1979 work *Communication and the Evolution of Society*, and provides colourful and interesting (if inconsistent) alternatives to many of the aspects of Habermas' thesis in the book. Taylor, the final writer for consideration, threatens to disconnect the critical project from its Marxian roots. His criterion for inclusion revolves around the strong case he makes for theoretical pluralism. His is a subtle, nuanced call for this form of progress, a direction that this chapter attempts to strongly lean towards.

The process of discussing the authors will be broadly historical though, obviously, there may well be periods of chronological deviation in the pursuit of particularly salient points or the uninterrupted exposition of concepts. In relation to Habermas, one of his more recent publications will form the basis of consideration; particularly, his writings on the centrality of consensus, and the societal achievement of this, thus his *Communication and the Evolution of Society* will be the site of attention.

As a direct counterpoint to this, Rescher's 1993 work *Pluralism – Against the Demand for Consensus* will be used. In this Rescher is frequently critical of Habermas' ideas on how consensus could be achieved and effected within the societal setting. Indeed, he feels that his interpretation of Habermas' vision of a consensual world would be both a dangerous and undesirable realisation. He prefers his own brand of 'acquiescence' as a more honest, transparent example of how disagreements on points of principle (in individuals) can be married to common agreement on action and/or policy within the societal setting.

Connolly's argument (1995), from a stance sympathetic to a teleological approach, tries to establish pluralism's place in the new 'modern' social/academic order. This revised order is somewhat of a curate's egg for Connolly. He rejoices that we appear to be emerging from the dark ages of the 'transcendental violences' that were the norm, when our IPE theorising was cosseted in the erroneous moralities of the traditional Realist agenda(s). However, as support for the aims of this chapter, we are still too bogged down in unnecessary theoretical conservatism to be too pleased with any progress we have made. A fundamental problem arises with the prima facie case that Connolly makes in this regard however, in that his use and application of Nietzschean theory appears inconsistent. This has to be borne in mind here; as one of the mainsprings of this paper is that theoretical pluralism and maintenance of 'academic rigor' are mutually compatible aims.

The book on Charles Taylor for primary consideration here is more difficult to summarise alongside the others (Tully, 1994). The structure of the book is, in itself, dialogical and we see Taylor going through a process of re-fining (though just as often re-affirming) his earlier positions on the case for plurality as the result of critical analysis from colleagues. He too enters the enactment aspect of the issues of plurality, which form the focus of the Rescher/Habermas differentiation in this. His comprehensive vision of the concept and implications of theoretical plurality mean that expositions on reality, government and the natural/ social science differentiation are also present in the book. Necessarily these are somewhat truncated discussions; nonetheless, they are extremely useful and illuminating for the purposes of this work. He is sure of his support for epistemic pluralism and he is equally keen to at least flag up that this support is 'real' in the senses of its depth of consideration and 'real' in terms of the world into which he would try to introduce it.

The chapter will follow a rigid and, hopefully, easily identifiable structure. Its main structural purpose is to have the theme of the case for plurality as a constant thread. Within this, the case made by each analyst will be briefly described and the tensions (and issues raised by these tensions) between their various views will be explored. This will highlight long-standing inconsistencies in the pluralist position that will have an airing here. However, the more significant ambition here is to propose the case for optimism in indications for de-emphasising, perhaps even pointing in the direction of resolution of these areas of concern. The crux of the case here is for a willingness to accept the present, somewhat conservative theoretical status quo in IPE, to problematise this and to call for a renewal of visions of the future. Central to this will be an implicit insistence that what there is that is already good is preserved and that the 'better' world aimed for in this project has its roots in recognisable worlds. 'Sovereignty still gets people killed' was the insistent reminder of a renowned theorist (Robert Walker) at a conference in June 2000.[1] This unpalatable truth is yet another facet of the burden of responsibility that we all share in IPE endeavours of whatever source or nature.

Habermas and consensus

Habermas occupies a paradoxical position in this work (1979). In the book as a whole he uses a mixed methodology that would obviously be supported here. He demonstrates this in the illustration of his vision of society emanating from a broad array of psychological and sociological theorists, ' . . . basic psychological and sociological concepts can be interwoven because the perspectives projected in them of an autonomous ego and an emancipated society reciprocally require one another' (*ibid.*, p. 71). He then goes on to harmonise and develop concepts derived from this combination by adding and describing conditions of ethics and morality, which should also impinge upon individual and societal behaviour.

Later, he agrees with another basic premise above: that Marxism is a theory in need of revision in many respects but whose potential for stimulation still has not been exhausted (*ibid.*, p. 124). His major revisions are to restructure and further emphasise the cultural ramifications of historical materialism. He is much more explicit about the inclusion of normative structures in his Marxist analysis. He goes further, citing religion ('mythical world views'), and offering anthropological slants in his views on the development of the origins of class in societies. He ends by reinforcing the necessity of inclusion of Naturalist (positivist), scientific approaches in our quest for greater comprehensiveness (Rosenberg's 'international imagination'). Thus, the position supporting the basic tenet of this chapter is outlined.

However, this is not to imply that all is well in relation to Habermas' pronouncements in the book. Some of the theorising, and his vision of its teleology, is problematical for our purposes. First, there are some practical problems with Habermas' view of participation in his society. Second, and perhaps more fundamentally, other writers (as we shall see below) do not share his opinions on the development of 'consensus' as a means of societal progress. Both these dimensions have ramifications for IPE theorising and this will be particularly addressed around the work of Rescher (1993).

Habermas' theorising in *Communication and the Evolution of Society* principally revolves around certain central tenets that he has made his own. For him, certain rights are undeniable: free speech, voting in elections and a detectable level of welfare state, as examples. All these are seen as forms of desirable universal provision, and it is in the use of the word 'universal' that a serious potential problem lies in considering the practical application of Habermasian theory. It is a term he uses principally in other areas of his theorising in the book – 'universal ethics of speech'. Both these universalisms beg the question as to how these would be applied in the societal setting.

This is not an issue which Habermas discusses in any detail. He constructs a vision of fully participatory processes at both the global and domestic levels. This will be most fruitfully achieved, mainly drawing upon the theories of developmental psychology, through the individual attainment of psychological and sociological 'maturity'. However, the concept of universalism can be seen to come somewhat unstuck in its practical examination.

This lack of cohesion springs from at least two areas. Historical templates for participatory democracy at the 'global' level bode poorly. The League of Nations and the United Nations seem, for many, to have achieved little more than institutionalising current, unequal status quos. However, this does not seem a particularly fair criticism in many aspects, subsequently it will not be afforded much room here as it contravenes directly the Habermasian spirit (and letter) of trying to construct a new global order. Second, a Universalist view seems to contain some disputable, even potentially dangerous, assumptions as central to its realisation. Principally, it contains an implicit generalisation of highly contentious, Western, culturally bound principles: 'development' and 'maturity' as examples. Even more grievously, it skates over difficulties in matching relative values and views on participation, democracy and leadership – to mention but a few, either on cultural, religious or any other social grounds one may wish to identify.

Crucially, the whole thing seems to be suspended around a rather simplistic notion of 'right'. Habermas does not seem to view right (as in correct/truth) as a fixed entity; indeed, its shifting quality according to group negotiation is a central plank of his vision of the participatory process. However, while not having definite, fixed properties, his descriptions tend to assume that the reader will be happy with a consensual, one-dimensional view of 'right'. He draws a picture of the unstoppable force of the 'rational' argument, which will guide us all to a simultaneous and identical vision of the 'right thing'. As we shall see, this is too comfortable for other analysts. It contains a representation of the process leading to a recipe for getting at the 'right', which appears outrageously simplistic. Habermas freely transposes this societal process to a level where it would be, necessarily, reflected in the outlooks, policies and procedures of our global institutions.

Unfortunately, we are now left with two neat, sequential illustrations, ('development' and 'right') which are extremely problematic for other analysts. Before reflecting on this in detail through a consideration of the work of Rescher, it behoves this writer to indicate some of the starker criticisms/weaknesses of the visions Habermas offers us. His efficacy in arguing for a pluralist mode of social theorising is hamstrung (paradoxically) by the very disciplines he tries to use in order to reinforce his arguments. Not for some time, in psychology and sociology, have sequential taxonomies of development (such as Habermas offers us more than once in his book) been seen as the most pertinent form of theorising, in terms of representing the holistic development of self, personality and/or experience.

Nonetheless, Habermas does provide some vital facets of the vision of how plurality can be logically justified and realised. The words are chosen carefully here, as the need for justification is a serious responsibility. The project at issue is far from being a case for the ushering-in of a new mode of theorising *per se*; it is also a call for more recognition of a multiple paradigm attitude in IPE theorising. Unfortunately, it can be seen that the Habermasian approach does not quite get us there in its own right. It needs the support of other approaches. In the following sections, the shortcomings of the Habermasian vision will be elucidated with a series of alternative dimensions offered. The first alternative for consideration is the work of Nicholas Rescher.

Rescher – the case *against* Habermas and *for* plurality

Rescher (1993) is involved with a broader project, both relevant to the overall discussion of the chapter and feeding into the analysis of Habermas above. He makes a case for pluralism, and argues strongly against the idealisation of consensus, as both a philosophical desideratum and a pragmatic goal for global/local basis of governance. His philosophical stance is opposed to the 'indifferentist relativism' of scepticism and it also is against opinion from the other extreme – 'dogmatic absolutism'. The former (scepticism) sees pursuit of the rational or truthful as pointless, there is no rational, enforceable consensus; there is no 'fact of the matter', but only mere opinion or arbitrary decision.

The latter position, generating opposition from Rescher, is syncretism. The desperate policy of accepting all the alternatives, of seeing all avenues of choice as equally appropriate. The sceptic rejects all available options, while the syncretist goes to the opposite extreme and endorses the whole lot. His attempt is for a middle ground solution in which the quest is for 'acquiescence', the book's aim being to outline a framework for dissensus management.

There is much to consider here. Before contrasting the Rescher and Habermas approaches to consensus, the case Rescher constructs for theoretical plurality will be analysed. Pluralism is the basis of 'sensible empiricism' for Rescher. In his words, '[m]any problems are most effectively handled when different lines of inquiry are pursued by investigators who are committed to different theories and hold different opinions on relevant questions' (*ibid.*, p. 57). This is the doctrine that any substantial question admits a variety of plausible but mutually conflicting responses, there is a plurality of versions of the answer(s).

He is quite definite on some of the characteristics of this pluralism: it sees everyone's rights to hold a different view as valid; it works on the logic of individual rationalism. However, not all bases of judgement are equally valid, analysing how people arrive at their judgements is of importance. These conditions are stipulated, and are attempts to isolate principles that will guide us as to how pluralism can be ethically, morally, philosophically, academically and pragmatically achieved. Truth is ontologically and epistemologically pluralistic and morally, we must stick by our opinions if we view them as rational.

How then, in the societal setting, are we to address issues that it is felt require action at some level? Here Rescher introduces his concept of acquiescence, '[t]o acquiesce in a situation where others think differently from oneself is neither to endorse their views nor to abandon one's own' (*ibid.*, p. 123). He goes further, in his subsequent chapter, towards sweetening this somewhat bitter pill. He reminds us that our experiences (ergo actions) are not the exclusive domain of the empiricists. Affective elements are also a significant part of our experiences and our epistemologies and ontologies should reflect this. He ends by reminding us that value disagreements are not necessarily 'communally incapacitating', i.e. they do not totally preclude us from 'getting on'. On reflection, in support of the case for theoretical plurality, this passage is a mixed blessing.

First, behaviour as an element of study, and an integral element of experience is neglected here. This is most sharply brought into focus in the consideration of acquiescence above. Misleading as it may be, acquiescence (especially where that is expressed behaviourally, i.e. 'going along with') has the very real potential to be seen as an endorsement. What 'getting on' means is also in need of much greater explanation. If it is merely taken to mean coexistence (while recognising other's differences) then it is of little use in the argument for theoretical plurality. On the other hand, if it is taken to mean that theoretical approaches (though reflecting differing values) can still mutually contribute to the big picture, then this needs to be more explicit. In these circumstances, there is an argument for there being no such thing as complete value disagreement; as here, all stances must value their combination in the cause of overall, greater 'totalising' (Rosenberg, 1994) theory. This would be seen in direct conflict with Rescher's vision of how plurality is pragmatically accommodated, while remaining consistent with the philosophical support for it. As we leave Rescher's explicit case for plurality we recognise that the argument does not escape his clutches intact. A central difficulty arises pragmatically from his philosophical grounding.

For Rescher, consensus is a multifaceted concept, which does not bring with it the cure-all properties that other theorists have attributed to it. In his view consensus equals a support for the truth. It is a process, a journey, of approaches to the truth, rather than an end goal that, as for others, is something that should be seen as synonymous with truth itself. Crucially, in the case for pluralism, he sees consensus as turning on what people think rather than on objectivity – on what is actually so.

Aside from the degree of dispute, which is possible with this sentence, Rescher feels that a fundamental error of Habermas, in relation to his regard for consensus, is that he (Habermas) is forced to see steps leading away from consensus as necessarily regressive, and steps towards as always progressive. Rescher feels that this ignores the possibility of exactly the opposite being the case in both instances. The difference crucially turns on the representations of consensus as a process for Rescher, and an end stage for Habermas. However, with a little more thought, these representations become simplistically problematic – this will be given more space below. For now, a greater exposition of how consensus is constructed by Rescher, philosophically and pragmatically, is necessary.

His opening in relation to it as a pragmatic proposition is categorical, '[w]e have to be prepared for the fact that a consensus among people, be it global or, local in scope, international or familial, is in general un-attainable' (*ibid.*, p. 4). Crucial in this pronouncement is the representation of consensus on offer here. He has many reservations regarding the philosophical and pragmatic ramifications of Habermas' propositions in this regard. He couches these in a stern warning on the dangers of Habermasian 'idealisation' of consensus as a desirable end goal in rela-tion to structures of global and local decision-making, stating that, '[a]bove all the consensus-downgrading position articulated here op-poses a utopianism that looks to a uniquely perfect social order that would prevail under ideal conditions' (*ibid.*).

For Rescher, 'contemporary partisans' of consensus seriously overesti-mate both its use and desirability. He reminds the reader that rationality does not guarantee consensus, which, in turn, does not necessarily lead to truth. Thus, Habermas has rationality and consensus in the wrong order. This is not as simple as it appears, to illustrate the point we need to delve into why Rescher sees consensus as not necessarily desirable. He cites historical political excesses, for example Nazi Germany of the 1930s, as evidence of a certain form of rationality resulting in bad, 'evil' consensus. This does not seem fair to Habermas – he is often cited as a member of the Frankfurt school of social theorists, who were only too well aware of the censorial excesses of the Nazis to the point that most of them felt it necessary to flee Germany. With this experience as part of the recent history of his theoretical foundation, it would appear reasonable to assume that Habermas would be very well aware of the propensities for ethically/morally questionable consensus. Thus, the neat view, presented by Rescher, that Habermas is writing in favour of consensus at any/all cost, and that any move away from this project is a societal regression, deserves criticism. The other major facet that Rescher criticises in Habermas' work, as indicated earlier, is his perception of consensus as an endpoint, rather than a constant procedural concept; again, in reading this latter work of his, Rescher's criticism seems untenable. While consensus may have been presented as a panacea for all our practical and idealistic difficulties in Habermas' earlier works, e.g. 'Theory of Communicative Action' (a moot point in itself), it certainly has a constantly developing aspect to it as presented in *Communication and the Evolution of Society* – the criticisms of this work (outlined above) notwithstanding.

Both these theorists have their place here in supporting the case for greater theoretical pluralism. Habermas, as he has done for many decades now, adds to the emancipatory vision of the project. He also acts as a case-study for devising theory derived from diverse (if epistemologically similar) ranges, and formulating a robust schema whose potential for stimulating debate, like Marx (his theoretical forefather) is still evident. Rescher, while wishing to tread a similar path to Habermas, urges us to proceed with caution. All that we think we should wish for is deserving of critical analysis. Consensus, as with any current model of group decision-making, requires some form of analysis, even management, if we are to be confident of avoiding the worst excesses that history illustrates. At the philosophical level too, Rescher warns against easy logical progressions (rationality = consensus = truth) as our starting point.

While contributing to the argument for theoretical plurality both writers also generate cause for concern upon a particularly pertinent and complex issue area for IPE. This is the need for our theorising to more faithfully address our individual increasing sensitivity/awareness to the multiplicities and complexities of modern identities. It is with this particularly in mind that we turn to the next major theoretical source in this discussion, W. E. Connolly (1995), whose opinions are much more directly related to the specific subject areas pertinent to this chapter – international studies.

Connolly – extending the range?

Connolly adds extra dimensions to the issues involved in building a case for theoretical plurality; before looking at this in detail some more general foregrounding of his approaches needs provision. He supports a 'teleological' position with a variety of philosophical nuances provided by some of the great names of philosophy in support. This teleological approach is described in *The Ethos of Pluralization* as a combination of approaches derived from Plato, Aristotle, Kant and Hegel. In Connolly's view, they all believe (in one way or another) that the universe, or history, or the structure of human reason can, when properly understood, yield a pattern that makes sense of life and human aspirations.

His other philosophical influences include Nietzsche, whom Connolly draws upon regularly, perhaps most significantly in his support for Nietzsche's view of modernity. They both feel that we have now developed further than the medieval times, particularly in our view of God. This 'god of signs' has faded into obscurity, his place being taken by an electronic/media/techno deity, who foments and funds political campaigns of late modern fundamentalism.

The other immediately apparent influences on Connolly's writing are Foucault and, to a much lesser extent, Heidegger. In order to build a more inclusive picture of Connolly's orientation a longer look will now be taken at his rationale for the Nietzschean and Foucauldian elements of his writings. His general view is that these two sources form the most effective basis for a theorising approach dedicated to breaking free of the constraints of the matrix he illustrates in the book. This framework has resulted from a combination of many of the great philosophers of history and, in effect, is used to define the range, scope and rules of what can be viewed as valid theorising today. His challenge of the validity of the matrix arises from the following conviction:

> There is too little emphasis, within this matrix, on the positive value of maintaining contending positions in a relation of restrained contestation, maintaining such relations because no unified model of the world is likely to marshal sufficient evidence to establish its certainty and because an ethic of care for the very differences that made self-identity possible realises itself best through the institutionalisation of relations in agonistic respect between contending perspectives.
>
> (1995, p. 21)

His post-Nietzschean elements (especially the view that 'nothing is fundamental' – see below) are particularly important in relation to IPE theorising, in his view, as they are the best forms of both defence and attack on previous theories' limitations. He charges these with having committed 'transcendental violences' against previous, alternative theorising enterprises; they were lodged for too long, in comfortable, erroneous moralities of 'god, home, rationality, territory and country' (*ibid.*, p. xxx). At least part of his project here is an attempt to redress the injuries that resulted from this conservatism.

He acknowledges the inherent weaknesses indicated by other analysts of some of Nietzsche's positions. These include comments that he supports a 'will to power' approach, that he is anti-rationality and, finally, that he opposes morality because he points to the 'immorality of morality', and because he resists every attempt to ground morality in something necessary, automatic or final. Connolly persists in the value of his approach, not only for the value of his theoretical reflections but also he sees the potential for the construction of a viable political alternative. As he comments, 'I merely want to suggest here that such a stance provides an appropriate terrain for exploration among those who would disrupt established regimes of political thought and cultivate an ethic of critical responsiveness' (*ibid.*, p. 30). This is part of the clarion call of this chapter! Here, we have the erudite case for the maintenance of the critical project, while (as we shall see below) Connolly feels that we must also maintain a radical, imaginative edge.

Connolly, as previously stated, also has sympathy for aspects of Foucauldian analysis and insists they can be included in a case supporting theoretical pluralism. For him, Foucault is seen as the most efficient way of challenging academic hegemony, especially as, in the political realm of IPE, the academic conservatism is arguably visible in many actual social structures. In this respect, Foucauldian *genealogy* particularly interests Connolly. It is an essential component in an 'ethico-political' orientation that both asserts that the fundamentals of being are mobile and that in the ordinary course of events, social pressures accumulate to present particular formations of life as if they were intrinsic, solid or complete (*ibid.*, p. 34). Hence the title of the chapter from which this quotation is taken – 'Nothing is Fundamental'.

This is not to say (as with Nietzsche earlier) that he buys wholesale into the principles of genealogy, or more specifically, Foucault's illustration of its application. Indeed one of his reservations on this matter is in direct contradiction to the inclusion of Nietzschean principles above. Connolly feels that Foucault is, if anything, not radical *enough* in his application of genealogy. He (Foucault) seems to assume that genealogy can proceed by bracketing 'ontopolitical assumptions' into already established perspectives. As noted earlier, a significant feature of Connolly's enterprise is to prise apart these perspectives, and exploit the gaps this generates as a source of insistence that we spread our theoretical net, and imaginings, across a much broader scope. Early in his academic career, Foucault also fell victim to an insistence of his critic's approaches towards dualism. People thought that as he was detaching himself from one set of presumptions that, by extension, he was automatically attaching himself to opposing arguments. Visker (1992) cites Habermas as one of these offenders, who felt that Foucault described too stark a truth/falsity differentiation. In fact, Foucault's focus was what makes 'truth' true, rather than the true/false dichotomy. Only later did Foucault realise the full implications of this and attempt to deal with it. How he did this will be outlined as a more general argument for transcending the power emanating from the matrix Connolly devises in his book. In closing this section on the philosophical origins of his position, there is a passage in the book where the essential rationale for the combination of the 'post-Nietzschean' and Foucauldian elements is provided from which I will quote at length:

> Partial detachment from established modes of realisation, insistence, and closure is the first and most difficult task set within a post-Nietzschean problematic. This is the route through which enhanced care for the strife and interdependence of identity/difference can be cultivated. It is hardly likely to be achieved completely. It then slips into that (nearly) vacant space between modern theistic devotion and secular doctrines of rational principle and moral instrumentalism. Such a nontheistic gratitude for the rich diversity of being provides an ethical source from which a modified version of pluralism might emerge, one which a larger variety of identities strive to find to coexist on the same territory, combining together from time to time to support the general material and spiritual conditions of this very cultural diversity. For it is when a genealogical sensibility is mapped onto the pluralist imagination that both perspectives achieve their highest degree of attainment.
>
> (*Ibid.*, p. 31)

For Connolly, efforts to extend the academic range are, in themselves, inherently worthy. This particularly relates to American theorising, which he accuses of being too confined in its range. He had in mind particularly US sociological theorising, with its preponderant positivist character. He is strident in calling for an extension in this range and attitude towards theorising; in particular, he wishes for a greater US generosity in pluralist imagination/ethos, and a giving of priority to possibility over probability within this. This chapter is an exercise in transatlantic empathising, a call for global academia to hear Connolly's plea.

Developmentally, one of the prime causes for concern that is addressed by his approach (via Nietzsche and Heidegger) is a differing form of the duality debate to which the early Foucault fell victim. In this instance, he co-opts Heidegger as a response to the previous, limited, truth/false dichotomy by which theories' validity can be measured. Connolly uses both the philosophers above to expand the vista of possibilities by examining the concept of 'untruth'. The standard US practice of giving primacy to epistemology obscures a sufficiently full exposition of this.[2] This adds extra force to the urging here for us to expand minds, imaginations and agendas. We are left with a moral imperative to deal with the issues generated by these views once aired.

We are not there yet. The most faithful way of addressing the moral obligations above are at once attitudinal and reflective of the need for a transformation of the academic ethos. This is not to imply that Connolly feels that the lack of fresh air within the academic atmosphere has been a deliberately constructed phenomenon. Rather, he feels that as an attempt to embrace the 'critical' approach (as, with Rescher, Habermas cited as the prime example) an undesirable degree of homogeneity has resulted. This returns us to his view that, especially in North American theorising, 'ontopolitical' discrepancies are overlooked in favour of epistemological considerations. A second group also exists – those who seek to reduce the gaps between man and his doubles. This was highlighted by Foucault, who felt that each time a new analysis of itself is brought back to the subject it is moved; it never reaches the solid ground it seeks to stand upon. The other aspect of this second group is that they treat the quest for rational consensus, self-consciousness and freedom as intimate allies. They fear that if no such basis is found for morality, the web holding society together will become unstrung. This is the major basis of his criticism of Habermas whom, Connolly feels, has a paradoxical relationship with the foundationalism his alternative model seeks to supersede: 'In general, I share Foucault's doubt that any transcendental argument in the late-modern context can foreclose the ontopolitical contestation as severely as Habermas, Taylor, and others sometimes hope. Certainly, none has succeeded in doing so yet' (*ibid.*, p. 15).

Far from this deleterious situation being a source of concern or regret for Connolly however, it is instead a source of stimulation and motivation and allows space for laying the principles of the reform of the academic ethos referred to earlier. It provides food for thought and an occasion for rejoicing. In Connolly's own words, *'It provides the launching pad for pursuit of a political ethos in which alternative perspectives support space for each other to exist through the agonistic respect they practice toward one another'* (*ibid.*, p. 16, this author's emphasis).

The restrictive epistemological matrix that he outlines (and then, as here, forms the major basis of his alternative vision), leaves too little room for differing positions to maintain a relationship of 'restrained contestation'. The institutionalisation of relations in an atmosphere of agonistic respect remains the call from Connolly: 'In the near future perpetually stretching before us, the indispensability and contestability of fundamental presumptions hover over interpretation; the irony of interpretation; the joyful ambiguity of "man" and his doubles; the indispensability of contestable ontopolitical projections' (*ibid.*, p. 39). In combination with this overall philosophical perspective, Connolly also has specific words for IPE. The 'nostalgia' for a time past, when the politics of place formed a coherent agenda for the future, has had its day. He supports a more cosmopolitan, multidimensional imagining of identifications across multiple sites (including the State) to be seen as the way forward. His vision of democracy insists that, as a crucial part of it, we recognise these multiple sites, theoretically and pragmatically. Surely, this would be too much for any one discipline's ontology or epistemology?

Connolly provides support for theoretical plurality far beyond the rationale he constructs for its desirability. Part of his project is to blow away the cobwebs that have developed in the realms of social science conservatism. Habermas may, meritoriously, be seen as one of the first sites of resistance to this conservatism; but now, in relation to the fundamental idealism of many of his central tenets, can be seen as having relinquished many aspects of his 'critical' mantle. There is room for perceiving threads of liberalism in his visions, especially in relation to seeing consensus as an endpoint rather than a process by which a more fulfilling life schema may be realised. He provides new impetus for the struggle towards more inclusive approaches and, perhaps most significantly of all, reminds fellow academics that they may have left the site of ontopolitical considerations too early, in favour of the more popular epistemological debates, which seem in current vogue. Unfortunately, Connolly does not deliver all he promises. In particular he does not sufficiently explain his attitude towards teleology. He freely proclaims himself a 'teleologist' early in his book and then later does little to square his liberal use of Nietzsche in his own formulations, whom by Connolly's own admission has been validly analysed as anti-teleological in his approach. This surely calls into question the validity of his use of Foucault's views on man and his twin. Those sympathetic to a teleological approach surely would have little use for this simultaneity of experience that Foucault describes.

However, usefully for our purposes here, Connolly remains strident about two things; firstly that his views have very real, direct bearing on IPE theoretical approaches, in terms of both orientation and approach; second, that the more traditional philosophical foundations for the rationale of plurality no longer have the force of argument that they once had. Specifically for him this relates to Habermas and the next writer for consideration here – Charles Taylor.

Taylor – pluralism re-visioned

The main source of Charles Taylor used here provides us with a number of valuable insights across many levels of philosophical opinion. In 1994, Tully edited a book called *Philosophy in an Age of Pluralism* in which various contributors offered chapters critically interpreting Taylor's views. The work then goes even further, the final section of the book consists of a series of replies by Charles Taylor to the points made in the preceding critical chapters. In common with the previous commentators, Taylor is cited as a supporter of the pluralist mode of theorising.

According to Berlin in the introduction, Taylor is a Christian, teleologist and Marxian, who shares with Berlin the idea that a sense of belonging to a society is a fundamental human need, forming the basis for his opinion of the desirability of pluralism. An odd mix indeed! (Tully, 1994, p. 1). Yet, perhaps not so, as we shall see. In relation to this outline of Taylor, Berlin's view is anti-teleological, in that he believes that purposes are imposed upon the world by human beings (in direct contrast to the teleological position described above) and anti-Marxian, in that he does not share Taylor's view that if human society is liberated from oppression, exploitation and domination (which are inevitable consequences, even embodiments of modern capitalism), only then can it hope to achieve full its potential. As Berlin remarks:

> I wish I could believe this but I do not ... I believe in a multiplicity of values, some of which conflict, or are incompatible with each other,

pursued by different societies, different individuals, and different cultures; so the notion of one world, one humanity moving in one single march of the faithful . . . is unreal.

(Ibid, p. 3)

Now, as to how comprehensive a degree of rebuttal of Marxism is contained in the passage above, is something best left to the individual reader, but what it does illustrate that is interesting for our purposes is the insight into how close pluralists sail to a wind of criticism that can drive them onto the rocks of an idealised form of consensus, the charge levelled at Habermas by Rescher. Taylor does not respond on this point.

In a following chapter, 'Taylor on truth', Rorty takes him to task for his superficial 'the way things are' view of truth:

> I see two ways of interpreting 'in virtue of the way things are'. One is short for 'in virtue of the way our current descriptions of things are used and the causal interactions we have with those things'. The other is short for 'simply in virtue of the way things are, quite apart from the way we describe them'. On the first interpretation, I think that true propositions . . . the desirability of respect for our fellow human beings, and about everything else are true 'in virtue of the way things are'. On the second interpretation, I think that no proposition is true 'in virtue of the way things are'.
>
> *(Ibid*., p. 22)

Taylor takes exception to this analysis as an oversimplification of what he has said (*ibid.* p. 219). In his response section, he illustrates his view of the need for differing schemas of thought, language and perception (amongst others) in order that we may more fully approach differing forms of reality. Indeed, Taylor uses the very term 'reality' as a token of his support for elements of a perceivable external reality as a viable target of our examination (*ibid.*, p. 220). He goes on then to explain that we need (and are equipped with) very different analytical schemas for the consideration of things more 'causally related' to us (*ibid.*).

This opens the door for Geertz's charge, in a subsequent chapter, that Taylor, while undoubtedly pluralist, retains an undesirably rigid dualistic view of the universe. Specifically, for Geertz, he maintains too wide a division between the social and natural sciences in his visions of schemas. This allows scientists to continue to consider themselves the best judges of science and, frequently escape the need for public ethical and moral monitoring:

> We need to set ourselves free to make such connections and discon-
> nections between fields of enquiry as seem appropriate and product-
> ive, not to prejudge what may be learned from what, what may traffic
> with what, or what must always and everywhere inevitably come –
> 'reductive naturalism' – from attempts to breach supposedly un-
> breachable methodological lines.
>
> *(Ibid.*, p. 89)

Taylor's response is essentially to concede this point made so passion-
ately by the writer (*ibid.*, p. 234). He proclaims himself 'no friend' of
those who falsely separate nature and mind, and describes his mission as
trying to re-introduce the mind back into nature (*ibid.*). However, his
original confusing stance was well intentioned, he explains, as it was a
reaction against theorists who have reinforced the mindlessness of natural science with claims for a bogus, 'unified' scientific approach, for
example the proponents of 'social physics' (*ibid.*, p. 85).

An ideal example of the essence of Taylor's point has recently emerged
in the field of IPE. Mark Rupert's recent exposition on the phenomena
involved in the vexatious concept of 'globalisation' provides an ideal
case-study for Taylor's opining (Rupert, 2000). In the book Rupert
professes his belief that there is evidence of a series of globally interconnected processes that can be labelled globalisation. Particularly significant for our purposes here, he sites the evidence for his conclusions from
a wide array of disciplinary sources. As might be expected, much of the
source material has political, economic and political economy eman-
ations, however many cultural theorists, well known in global academic
fora are also used as fundamental supporters of the arguments and
evidence presented; among them particularly noticeable are Turner,
and more prominently, Stuart Hall. This is precisely the approach that
it is part of the project of this chapter to encourage, but it is interesting
for more than this reason. The book can also be seen as the next point
on the chart of academic development of a previously prominent,
Gramscian, critical political economy analyst. This may be seen as a
move made out of necessity, in the sense that if (international) political
economy is to further its project of self-sustenance as a credible analytical discipline, then it must maturely recognise the need for more inclusive (in terms of other disciplines) theorising, such as that which Rupert
engages in.

Thus far, some writers have been shown to delve deeper into the practical ramifications of their pluralism than others. In Tully's book, as with
Connolly above, Taylor's visions about how we would govern the new

pluralistic society are outlined. In the final chapter for consideration here, Weinstock feels that Taylor is unfairly critical of liberal philosophy, particularly in relation to his scepticism of the centrality of the liberal notion of the neutrality of government. He takes issue with this interpretation of his work (Tully, p. 249). For him, neutrality is desirable up to a point (*ibid.*, p. 260). He does not see it as desirable in an absolute sense however, as democratic political freedom often boils down to the privileging of some views over others, 'Neutral liberalism as a total principle seems to me here a formula for paralysis; or else for hypocrisy, if one tried to occlude the real reasons. It is at this point that it begins to appear more than costly; in truth, inapplicable' (*ibid.*, p. 253).

An overview of Taylor's thoughts on pluralism compounds some of the sources of optimism above as to how it can be achieved and sustained, while echoing notes of caution against it as a blind ambition. On balance, the case that Taylor tries to sustain for pluralism may be in trouble. He is not particularly active in the defence of the 'Marxian' elements of his views (*ibid.*, p. 25), insists that there is an objective reality medium for our analysis (*ibid.*, p. 234) and allows that his work can be interpreted as perceiving too definite a difference between the varying forms of epistemological investigation (*ibid.*, p. 247). In plurality's enactment, absolute neutrality is an anathema to him; he prefers the 'real' world where, in the final analysis, choices have to be made that will prioritise one alternative to another (*ibid.*, p. 250).

Does this render Taylor a closet empiricist, or are his differences with the other analysts above more fundamental than this? In this sketched outline of his views, he begins to look more like he approaches the whole matter from a critical realist stance in the mould of Roy Bhaskar (1991). This is his escape route from the same charges that Bhaskar leaves at Rorty's door. Bhaskar feels that Rorty, in his 'pluralism', has rendered himself a hostage to fortune on epistemological grounds. Taylor may well be seen to be reacting to the dilemma that Bhaskar feels catches Rorty: 'I now return to Rorty... His contrast between epistemology and hermeneutics is drawn without regard to the difference between the natural and the human sciences (he is hyper-naturalist)' (Bhaskar, 1991, p. 143). Taylor appears to have insight into the subtle analysis of the essentials of the epistemological and hermeneutic inconsistencies within other works of this nature and indicates that, in his awareness, another, deeper consideration of these issues may offer a way out (*ibid.*, p. 222).

A proposal that vaunts the place of critical realism in any meaningful analysis of the discipline of IPE is something that should not be taken on lightly (or briefly!). Obviously, that is not the intention here. Rather, its existence is used as a signpost in two senses here. First, it is significant that Taylor indicates his sympathy towards it, especially as one route of response to criticism of his own work by Rorty – a central figure of criticism in 'Philosophy and the Idea of Freedom'. For him, there is much more work to be done in refining pluralistic concepts before we should be happy with the case we are making. Second, critical realism's use here can be perceived as a source of comfort for those worried that a bi-product of pluralism will be 'academic' compromise, in any or all its facets. This returns us to the potential criticism of pluralism identified in the introduction to the chapter. There is no case being made here for lowered standards of rigour, or for meaningless attempts at synthesising of approaches within IPE. Indeed, if some of the roots of real truth lie in the density of critical realism (as its proponents suggest), then we shall have earned our academic corn well.

Conclusion

The project of this chapter has been to illustrate the roots of a *many worlds* (ergo many ontologies and epistemologies) approach to future IPE theorising. Crucial in the case has been the insistence that this would not of necessity lead to denigration of academic standards in any, or all, its aspects. This has two major facets: first, that the case built should be theoretically congruous; second, the vision of the alternative social and academic community that results should be described and problematised. Habermas is credited here with providing the first vision of both these elements, without any claim to historical accuracy in this claim. *Communication and the Evolution of Society* provides us with a neat, sequential vision of how both the ethos of theoretical tolerance and the system of societal governance can be structured. For him, the pursuit of consensus is our aim; this should happen within a developmentally mature society of free-thinking and free-speaking individuals.

Rescher presents a different version of our course. We must be anti-sceptic and anti-'dogmatic absolutism', with sensible empiricism as the basis for our pluralism. He has two fundamental problems with Habermas' idealisation of consensus. First, he profoundly mistrusts it, refusing to see it as an automatically positive notion towards happiness. He produces powerful historical precedent in support of this view. This is compounded by a fundamental re-envisioning of the concept of consensus as a whole. Contrary to Habermas, consensus is not the process by which we are transported to happiness. Further, he would wish to replace the whole notion of consensus with his vision of 'acquiescence'.

This more nearly reflects the reality of choosing to cooperate, rather than the comfortable notion of fully committed agreement that can be an interpretation of Habermas' faith in the weight of the most rational argument as always forming the basis of eventual action. He believes that we should be open about the potential situation we would find ourselves in, and that we should recognise that, regardless of the system of governance, it will require management.

Connolly adds more detail to the actual mechanics of this scenario. The ethos of all exchanges should be restrained contestation, arising from mutual respect. He feels that current societies and academic communities are either victims of (or a means of) the continuance of current façades of solidity, which are primarily reflective of our societal power structures and processes. His analysis of this is illustrated in an explanatory text and in diagrammatic form and owes some debt to Foucault. This represents a new configuration of the principal structures of the debate and the contextual rationale within which it happens.

For Taylor, this project is more intricate than a 'mindless' call for some form of epistemological constructivism. We do see a common reality in many of our worlds, regardless of their definition and/or regulation. The requirement for full apprehension of these subtle, interesting complexities is a variety of 'mindful' epistemological approaches. Geertz reminds him to be sensitive to the need not to be too rigid in his natural/social epistemological divide. Taylor not only concedes this point but also develops a view that indicates the path towards truer epistemological sophistication. We are thus set upon the theoretical emancipatory course as the trajectory the foreword to this book promises.

In other words, there is much to do before the emancipatory vision in critical IPE is restored. It was 'easier said than done' from the beginning, and has remained a thorny issue ever since its inception, even in the groundbreaking works of Cox. While having sympathy for many of the points raised by Farrands in this regard, I would still urge different courses of action. I see the problematic of his analysis as the dilemma of the critical being in danger of appearing as the orthodox. This oversimplifies the critical project, in my view, and submits it to the false binary oppositional stance that was seen earlier to dog the early Foucault writings. The more fundamental message of this chapter is not to lose faith in the continued pursuance of the critical cause, for there is much at stake here, especially in relation to the discipline of political economy.

Principally here then, the argument is accepted that the 'Italian school' IPE theorists, and their wellspring – the writings of Antonio

Gramsci – were too easily labelled *critical*. The main objection to their critical title can be seen at a relatively early level of analysis. They were (quite rightly) readily critical in the sense of providing insightful critical analysis; however, their shortcomings are highlighted by the absence of the creation of a coherent, truly emancipatory vision, as an alternative to the various inequities/injustices of the present.

However, as has been illustrated here, this insight does not get us much further in relation to our 'criticalness'. One of the foremost living Frankfurt writers (Habermas) is seen to have blatant shortcomings in the application of his principles for our purpose. Of course, the degree to which Habermas is seen to remain within any recognisable bounds of the critical realm (another important issue raised by Farrands' exposition) is a moot point to be left to one side for the time being. Political economy, by nature of the very name, projects an image of mixed methodologies, and, more crucially in this context, mixed epistemologies. At once then, we can illustrate at least two directions in which political economy may fruitfully proceed. In a three-dimensional image, these would be seen as simultaneously pursuing broadening and deepening projects of the critical political economy project.[3] The depth being provided by the continuing pursuance of rich veins of theoretical sources demanding that we constantly pursue more sophisticated ontological and epistemological formulations. That we also continue to ever more complexly problematise the dynamics of their interaction, that we may more faithfully represent the world we strive to explain and/or illustrate.

The breadth would be developed by the responsible continuance of the transdisciplinary theorising outlined in the early stages of this chapter. There are many disciplines with more experience of the critical agenda in relation to the world(s) they attempt to explain. It would be an exercise in futility not to reflect on these, both in terms of our expectations of the knowledge structures of our discipline (loosely regarded here as political economy) and as active elements of our theorising and theoretical structures, along the lines of Santayana's oft-quoted maxim 'those who do not learn from history condemn themselves to repeat it';[4] alongside of this attitude, is the respect the continuance of this practice would show to those pioneering theorists (especially Robert Cox) currently regarded (with, or without, their approval) as critical. We should serve this pioneering potential best by remaining equally fearless in relation to *inter*-or *intra*disciplinary criticism and/or overly pedantic considerations of our degree of critical-ness. There is time enough for this issue later; indeed an answer may emerge organically from our increasing experience of grappling with the issues involved. As we have seen above, at least one political economist has recognised this opportunity and actively applied many of the principles encouraged here – Mark Rupert.

Notes

1. 'Democratizing Global Economy and Culture', Cosmopolis Conference, University of Helsinki, 2–3 June 2000.
2. ' "Untruth" is deeper than truth and falsity, then: untruth is that which cannot receive sufficient standing within the terms of discourse of a time without stretching contemporary standards of plausibility and coherence to their limits of tolerance. Untruth is the foreign not up for debate and reflection within a temporally constituted register of the true and false; its very absence enables the historically constructed division between the true and false to sustain itself...In Heidegger's thought, then, giving primacy to the question of truth does not mean giving primacy to epistemology. It means exploring the historical conditions in which the question of truth became reduced to the pursuit of reliable criteria of knowledge.' Connolly (1995), pp. 5–6.
3. After Archer (1999).
4. Often incorrectly attributed to Winston Churchill.

3
Process, Project and Practice: The Politics of Globalisation

Louise Amoore and Paul Langley

> Globalisation can be grasped in the small and concrete, in the spatially particular, in one's own life.
>
> (Beck, 2000a, p. 49)

The mood is shifting in the contemporary globalisation debate. Only a few years ago, talk of a societal engagement with the politics of globalisation would have been met with scepticism at the underestimation of the sheer economic power of globalising forces. Indeed, even Group of Seven (G7) governments themselves popularised the rather convenient image of globalisation as a powerful economic and technological 'bulldozer' about which mere politicians and citizens could do very little (*Economist*, 1995). The very discourse of the 'competition state' (Cerny, 1990) effectively sanitised the globalisation process, removing the messiness of politics and leaving only the 'right and necessary' policy measures. As the millennium turns, the picture is changing and we begin to see partial glimpses of a restored attention to a politics that was, in truth, always present. Now, the news media is popularising debates about the power of multinational corporations and the plight of the global economy's 'new slaves', bringing uncomfortable images to our armchairs (Klein, 2000; Bales, 1999; *Guardian*; BBC; Channel 4). At the same time, scholars from International Relations (IR), International Political Economy (IPE) and sociology have called for the 'political' to be studied as an inclusive arena encompassing both public and private spaces (cf. Davies and Niemann, 2000; Marchand and Runyan, 2000; Hay and Marsh, 1999; Bauman, 1998; Beck, 2000a).

From within the field of IPE, this chapter seeks to develop further existing efforts to restore politics to the globalisation debate. The chapter is critical of the early neoliberal images of globalisation as an imperative-driven, inexorable and de-politicised bulldozer – what we term the *process perspective* on globalisation. We also mark a *critical* departure from what has emerged as the principal politicised image of globalisation, that is, the *project perspective*. Under the project perspective, the bulldozer of globalisation is viewed in strategic terms, politically driven by either conflicting national capitalisms or transnational capitalist classes that encounter 'road blocks' of protest and resistance organised at the national and global scales. For us, however, the politics of globalisation is not limited to the policies of G7 national governments, the IMF, or the corporate boardrooms. Nor can it be captured solely by attention to resistance by social movements (old and new), for these occupy distant and inaccessible spaces for too many. Rather, we develop a *practice perspective* on globalisation. Globalisation becomes viewed as experienced, given meaning, reinforced and/or challenged in the everyday structured social practices of individuals and groups, such that globalisation is marked by political contestation over the reality and representation of social change. While we welcome the insights provided by the project perspective, we contend that arriving at a comprehensive and nuanced understanding of the politics of globalisation also requires attention to the tensions, contradictions and resistance present in everyday social structured practices. We illustrate our argument through a 'first cut' empirical engagement with the everyday social practices of work and finance in developed state-societies, both of which tend to be presumed to have been subject to significant changes in line with the process perspective of globalisation.

Part I: process, project, practice

Our starting point here is to recognise that the theory and practice of globalisation are contested (Scholte, 2000; Amoore, 2000a; O'Brien *et al.*, 2000). In much of the globalisation literature the primary focus has been on outlining the various aspects or dimensions of transformation in, for example, finance, production, culture, the state and technology, that combine to constitute an identifiable process of globalisation (Waters, 1995; Jones, 1995[1]). At first blush it would seem quite sensible to begin by addressing the question 'What is globalisation?' However, it is clear that the different aspects of globalisation are selected, defined and explained in divergent ways. As such, the answer to the question 'What is globalisation?' can only be 'It depends how you look at it.' Our first order question, then, must be 'How is the problem approached and understood?' In this way, various perspectives on globalisation in general, and the politics of globalisation in particular, are given an epistemological and ontological context. Below we advance a three-fold typology of perspectives on globalisation: process, project and practice. Each of the process, project and practice perspectives on globalisation provides a contrasting route into, or lens on, the study of globalisation, and each has particular implications for the relative visibility or invisibility of politics.

Process

Under the process perspective, globalisation is the metaphor that is used to describe the processes of material and institutional change across contemporary economy, politics and society. The process perspective forms the orthodox view of globalisation, tending to be shared by national governments, international organisations and media commentators alike.[2] Globalisation is cast in teleological terms, not dissimilar from an enormous bulldozer that effortlessly shovels up mere states and societies (Amoore *et al.*, 1997). Informed by the triumphalist assumptions of neoliberalism, the processes of change are viewed as the inevitable outcome of the expansionary ambitions of a global market economy and transborder technologies. In this vision states, societies and firms have no alternative but to conform and compete amidst the processes of change that occur above and beyond them, embracing convergent forms of organisation. The social costs of globalisation are commonly presented as temporary by-products of adjustment to the imperatives of change that do not detract from the assumed longer-term benefits.

The orthodox neoliberal process perspective presents an inherently *de-politicised* reading of globalisation. Politics tends to be regarded as interrupting inevitable change and to be avoided at all costs, ultimately incidental to the processes of change (Ohmae, 1990). Understood as practised in and through sovereign state governments, politics becomes cast as largely outmoded as the salience of the nation-state wanes under globalising pressures. For instance, under this perspective it is not only that a central bank's independence is perceived as the best way to maintain monetary stability, but also that political interference is regarded as a fruitless and foolish attempt to buck the financial markets. Elsewhere and in conjunction with others (Amoore *et al.*, 1997), we have outlined the misleading and ideological nature of the process perspective on the politics of globalisation. Indeed, for many IPE scholars, the central purpose of inquiry has become to overturn the common sense orthodoxy by restoring a pivotal role to politics in the course of contemporary global change. It is to this work that we now turn.

Project

For the project perspective, globalisation forms a close relationship with neoliberal economic thought and provides the ideological banner under which powerful agents seek to strategically restructure the material and institutional bases of the contemporary world order.[3] From the field of IPE, two broad schools of thought are distinguishable within the project perspective. On the one hand, what might be termed the 'transnational school' identifies the role of transnational state and social forces in consciously driving the shift from an international to a genuinely global economy. Those that Gill (1994) terms 'globalizing elites' become a 'directive, strategic element within globalizing capitalism' (p. 179). Key state and societal forces are viewed as acting through multi national corporations (Stopford and Strange, 1991) and a range of international organisations such as the IMF, G7 and the Trilateral Commission (Gill, 1990; Overbeek, 1990). On the other hand, what might be called the 'national capitalisms school' privileges the role of state policy-makers and institutions in directing the course of restructuring that is determined by the distribution of power within and between divergent and competing nation-states (Albert, 1993; Zysman, 1996; Weiss, 1998). Significantly, the national capitalisms school denies the shift from an international to a global economy. The mythic and ideological character of globalisation is held to obscure the 'real' continuation of an essentially international economy, with the restructuring that is underway generating not a global economy, but the formation of regional economic blocs in Europe, North America and Asia (Hirst and Thompson, 1996).

The project perspective has served to illustrate the extent to which powerful actors have driven and continue to drive the bulldozer of globalisation. Furthermore, adherents to the project perspective are united in normative terms by both a 'progressive politics' (Radice, 2000a+b) of anti-neoliberal globalisation, and a search for political space for resistance amidst seemingly prohibitive structural constraints. However, the divergent understandings of material and institutional restructuring offered by the transnational and national capitalisms schools feed different strategies for resistance. Following from their assertion that the world economy remains essentially *inter*national, the national capitalisms school stresses the continued scope for strategies that are undertaken within the political space of state institutions (Ruigrok and van Tulder, 1995; Hirst and Thompson, 1996; Zysman, 1996; Weiss, 1998). Progressive but somewhat 'technicist' resistance through state policies remains, in turn, highly feasible. Meanwhile, adherents of the transnational school have identified the potential for resistance strategies (Gramsci's 'counter-hegemony' and Polanyi's 'counter-movements') advanced in the political space of 'global civil society' (Lipshutz, 1992, 1996; Cox, 1999; Falk, 1999). For both schools, then, politics is restored to the understanding of globalisation and to the development of strategies of resistance that seek, at a minimum, to forestall the worst eventualities of change.

The challenge to the process perspective made by those who have contributed to the project perspective is clearly an essential element of confronting the common sense orthodoxy. However, the politics of globalisation is presented by the project perspective as coherently designed and directed by rational collective agents. Radice's recent critique of 'progressive nationalism' (2000a, p. 7), for example, highlights the problems associated with the assumption of a static 'endurance of state power'. The state as agent is imbued with a cohesive and unitary identity that significantly underestimates the tensions that may emerge amongst and between social forces over the direction of state policy. Not dissimilarly, the transnational school's view of collective agency tends to ascribe a unity of interest and purpose to political actors operating across borders. Within many of the identified agents of globalisation and/or resistance – states, firms, international organisations, trade unions, social movements – there exist conflicts and contests over the form of the globalisation 'project' itself. Yet these tensions tend not to be explored by the project perspective. Politics remains largely confined within a promotion-resistance struggle between collective agents.

Practice

We contend that a more comprehensive and nuanced account of contemporary politics than that currently on offer requires the development of a third perspective on globalisation. A limited number of scholars have sought to advance a practice perspective that draws attention to the emerging social relations of globalisation and the structured social practices that make these possible (Sklair, 1991; Germain, 2000; Jones, 2000). However, the existing work that comprises this embryonic perspective has focused almost exclusively upon the social practices of elite groups. Developed along these lines, the practice perspective becomes akin to the project perspective by another name. In contrast, the practice perspective advanced here views globalisation as experienced, given meaning, reinforced and/or challenged in the *everyday* structured social practices of individuals and groups, such that globalisation is marked by political contestation over the reality and representation of social change.

Our attempt to re-value everyday structured social practices as part of understanding the politics of globalisation is underpinned by a diverse body of thought which asserts the significance of the 'everyday'. For instance, scholars have stressed the need to consider the 'micro-macro dynamics' (Rosenau, 1997, p. 59) of the contemporary transformation, 'drawing links between ordinary lives and major structural change' to bring about 'an international political economy of the commonplace' (Sinclair 1999, p. 165). Similarly, others have called for greater attention to be paid to 'the concrete production of internationalised social relations in the daily practices of workers, families or consumers' (Davies and Niemann, 2000, p. 6). The work of feminist scholars has encouraged us to reflect upon our own concrete everyday experiences in order to make sense of the 'abstract structure known as the international political economy' (Enloe, 1989, p. 4; see also Marchand and Runyan, 2000). Others remind us that constitutive relationships bind the knowledge of globalisation that we realise in the field of IPE with social practices in the contemporary period (Burch and Denemark, 1997). Furthermore, we would equate the 'everyday' with what Bauman characterises as 'the near', '. . . primarily that which is usual, familiar and known to the point of obviousness; something seen, met, dealt or interacted with daily, intertwined with habitual routine and day-to-day activities' (1998, p. 13). The near contrasts directly with its obverse, the far, that is, the unusual, unfamiliar and unknown to the point of obscurity and extraordinarity. By the very nature of globalisation as 'a real or perceived intensification of global interconnectedness' (Held *et al.*, 1999, p. 2), it is increased real and perceived interconnectedness with the far that marks the restructuring of contemporary everyday social practices. What constitutes the far will, of course, be considerably differentiated across different sets of social practices.

Considered through the lens of the practice perspective, the politics of globalisation becomes characterised by contests over the reality and representation of social change. Such contestation can and does take the strategic and organised forms highlighted by the project perspective. However, the oppositions that distinguish the politics of globalisation are also present 'at the centre of people's lives' (Beck 2000a, p. 73), in their everyday structured social practices including work, leisure and consumption. Tensions permeate the juxtaposition of near and far, as established everyday structured social practices confront demands for change based upon perceptions of unfamiliar 'good practice'. Such tensions are exacerbated as the restructuring of everyday structured social practices brings into being new patterns of inclusion and exclusion that are subject to challenge. Changes to everyday structured social practices also entail contradictions that themselves undercut more significant transformation. Everyday social practices may further occasion 'silent resistance' (Cheru, 1997, p. 153), as the social practices of subordinated groups become informed by a collective consciousness that serves to challenge common sense understandings of real and perceived structural forces (cf. J. C. Scott, 1990). Capturing these tensions, contradictions and forms of silent resistance in everyday structured social practices offers the potential of a significant advance in our understanding of the politics of globalisation, complementing existing efforts to restore politics to the making of globalisation.

Part II: globalisation and the everyday practices of work[4]

The process perspective on globalisation has done much to inform dominant 'common sense' understandings of transformation in the everyday practices of work. So, for the Organisation for Economic Cooperation and Development (OECD) 'the globalisation process requires economies to be more adaptable and workers more willing to change' (1996, p. 13). A similar vocabulary of globalisation and imperative change in the form and nature of work can be found in G7 government policy documents, IMF structural adjustment programmes, management journals and corporate strategy documentation. Here the message is that in order to respond effectively to globalisation it is necessary for production costs to be reduced through the removal of barriers to the free market in factors of production – predominantly in labour. Globalisation is cast as an indomitable process, equated with a shift to new forms of work organisation in line with lean production, just-in-time (JIT), teamwork and kaizen. Workers are assumed to move towards more flexible working practices and 'atypical' forms of employment such as part-time, temporary, zero-hours and fixed contracts, outsourcing and homeworking.[5] This reading treats labour as a commodity that must be restructured in line with global logics. The concrete transformation of social practices is not problematised and the whole process is sanitised of politics. Indeed, it is those societies and workers who fail to adapt to the new realities that are perceived to incur the 'costs of inaction' (OECD, 1996, p. 21). A single global 'best practice' of flexibility subsumes all distinctive social practices. Hence, any discussion of politics is confined to an instrumental role in implementing prescribed reforms.

The globalisation process is taken as given and a 'problem-solving' mode of knowledge is generated to 'deal effectively with sources of trouble' (Cox, 1996, p. 88).

Critics of the process position on globalisation and work tend to assert the view that the interests of global or national agents drive transformations in production and work. As in our discussion of the project perspective on globalisation, these coalesce around two broad schools of thought – transnational classes or authorities, and national capitalisms. Thus, change in production and work is variously driven by MNCs as political actors (Stopford and Strange, 1991) or the disciplinary forces of neoliberalism (Gill, 1995). Meanwhile, others point to the competing models of national capitalism, particularly industrial relations institutions and systems of production, that give distinctive character to divergent patterns of change in forms of work (Crouch and Streeck, 1997). Such approaches do go some way to restoring the political dimension to knowledge of change in working practices. However, taken together, the project perspectives focus rather narrowly on states and multinational corporations whilst neglecting workers. In essence the state and the firm are assumed to 'contain' workers but are rarely unpacked to reveal the political and social forces engendered by these workers (Vilrokx, 1999; Amoore, 2000a).

The project perspective can tell us much about the elite actors who may reinforce and sustain a particular view of globalisation and restructuring, but little about the everyday forms of action that give character to that restructuring. Where labour is acknowledged in analysis, this tends to be in the form of organised and represented workers in trade unions. This is highly problematic at a time of rapid de-unionisation and when MNCs are fragmenting into hived-off contractual relationships to maximise their flexibility and cut costs so that many people do not work in a space that is organised and identifiable.[6]

There is currently, then, a relative invisibility with regard to the meanings and concrete experiences that workers, and particularly unprotected workers, themselves ascribe to the pressures and transformations of globalisation at work.[7] In order to restore and capture the political nature of contemporary change in the workplace it is necessary to address the articulation of conflicts, tensions and compromises in everyday social practices. Informed by the practice perspective developed above, and underpinned by an ontological commitment not to view labour simply as a factor of global production, 'work' is explored here as sets of structured social practices that may enable or contest the emerging social relations of globalisation. The practice perspective as it is applied to the workplace has developed out of a series of studies undertaken into the restructuring of production and work in engineering and electronics MNCs. The contemporary study of MNCs must confront the problem that new 'flexible' working practices do not sit neatly within the firms studied by IPE scholars (Hoogvelt, 1997). Indeed the very process of restructuring itself serves to fracture the firm into a myriad of loosely connected or contracted fragments. Thus, as a MNC outsources some of its core and most of its non-core activities, understanding the social practices of the workplace extends to the practices of homes, workshops, sweatshops and *ad hoc* and unprotected sites of production (cf. Bales, 1999; Klein, 2000).[8]

Contradictions at work

The route into the transformation of work provided by the practice perspective reveals a series of contradictions that serve to undermine the essentialistic framing of restructuring by the process perspective. First, at the heart of process-centred accounts of workplace transformation there is an assumption that a failure to respond to globalisation with deregulation and new forms of work organisation will result in rising unemployment and declining competitiveness. In this sense flexibility and security are viewed as mutually reinforcing and jointly achievable. The US, UK, Canada and New Zealand are widely offered up as examples of the success of deregulatory flexibility strategies. By contrast, Germany, France, Belgium, Denmark and Sweden, among others, are highlighted for their failure to implement prescribed reforms to ease general constraints on atypical forms of work (OECD, 1997). However, a focus on the tensions between flexibility strategies and everyday social practices reveals that general deregulation and new forms of work organisation simply replace one problem of poverty (unemployment) with another (income inequality and insecurity) (ILO, 1995). Indeed, implicit within OECD figures there is a correlation between those state-societies that have 'implemented the jobs strategy' and those that have high drop-out rates from education, widening income inequalities and a growing disadvantaged social group (OECD, 1997). Studies of workers' experiences of new working practices confirm the apparent contradictions between flexibility and security, suggesting that the low-wage, low-skill 'low road' serves the longer-term interests of neither workers nor corporations (Milkman, 1998; Pollert, 1999).

Second, there is a contradiction between processes of de-unionisation and levels of contestation. The restructuring of working practices along UK/US-style neoliberal lines is widely associated with an assault on traditional industrial relations practices. Direct admonitions to deregulate collective bargaining to the level of individual firms assume that the contests of centralised industrial relations can be eradicated. However, an exploration of the ways in which concrete industrial relations practices are challenged by restructuring reveals a different picture. The loss of formalised channels of collective bargaining in the 'radically restructured' workplaces does not result in a diminution of contestation and dissent.[9] Rather, the traditional channels are replaced with less organised and more fragmented tacit forms of resistance and challenge. Equally, where unions and other civil society groups are involved in negotiating the shape of further forms of work, such as in the German Standortdebatte,[10] the result has been a focus on skills and job security rather a direct standoff over pay. Industrial relations studies do much to demonstrate that the social configurations of employment, family and welfare play significant roles in defining the parameters of transformations in working practices (Rubery, 1995). As formalised traditional forms of industrial relations practice are diminished, it is important that we open up our analyses to reveal new contests that emerge within the firm and extend into less conventional workspaces (Anderson, 2000).

Finally, there is a contradiction between the global image of empowerment and the concrete realities of increased control. Images of empowerment abound within global blueprints for new forms of work and work organisation. In an elite group are the 'symbolic analysts' whose new 'weightless' portfolio careers offer flexible alternatives to traditional structures (Reich, 1991; Coyle, 1997). Then, there are the workers for whom teamworking, quality circles and working time flexibility are said to offer empowering alternatives to Fordist/Taylorist scientific management. The disparities in social groups' experiences of work in a global era will be explored further below. Here the purpose is to emphasise the patterns of control and power that lie behind the images of empowerment. In terms of everyday working practices globalisation has come to be associated with a hiving off of peripheral activities into branch-plants, microfirms, households, or the informal economy. This is an image that is far from the promise of a flexible and productive global workforce. In a very real sense production has exploded into a galaxy of stratified, loosely connected workspaces that are, nonetheless, closely controlled by the MNCs at the centre. In the example of teamworking, presented as a potentially autonomous and innovative experience, workplace studies demonstrate a reality of monotony, repetition, diminished skills and increased surveillance and control (Danford, 1998; Pollert, 1999).[11]

At the heart of expressions of change in everyday working practices is the experience of increased individualisation, intensified risk and heightened tensions between individuals and groups. The image of empowerment emerging out of globalisation and flexible forms of work is just that, an illusion that is not borne out in concrete experiences.

Divisions at work

Alongside the contradictions outlined above, the practice perspective also reveals patterns of inclusion and exclusion that are significant to the restructuring of work. New forms of work organisation and the rise of flexible and mobile forms of work imply challenges to past practices and a reconfiguring of working relationships. An emerging 'global consciousness' (Scholte, 2000, p. 85), though, is not a unifying characteristic. Indeed it is based on an association of globalisation with increased risk and short-termism, the intensification and speeding up of work, and feelings of individualisation and acute competition, as Beck argues, '[f]lexibility means a redistribution of risks away from the state and the economy towards the individual' (Beck, 2000b, p. 3).

If workers come to know and recognise change in the global economy through the lens of their own experiences then there is a need to explore the stratified social practices of different groups and individuals. We discuss these here in terms of *insider, intermediary* and *outsider* practices. Though, of course, many groups cut across these ideal-type boundaries and there are important patterns of inclusion and exclusion within the groups.

Insider groups are those who participate in defining the terms of new forms of work and work organisation, and whose social practices reinforce a global image of flexibility and mobility. These 'portfolio people' (Handy, 1995) represent a managerial elite, to include business analysts, marketing and advertising agencies, and media and academic commentators. The intensified risks experienced by these groups are matched by the potential rewards – stock options, bonus-led pay structures and performance-related pay. We can see the extension of these practices as the 'worker-stockholder' emerges in Europe along US lines. As Coyle argues, there is a stark contrast between those working in the 'weightless industries' who can use the new flexibility to 'turn themselves into stars', and those people for whom flexibility 'boils down to being exploited' (1997, p. 91). For the insider groups an increasingly mobile and flexible lifestyle serves to reinforce their own security. Indeed, as Beck (2000b) suggests, the security and mobility of these groups rests upon the relative insecurity and immobility of other groups who are excluded from a defining role. Stability is not experienced by insider groups in terms of a single workplace, but in terms of the ability to enter multiple workspaces, as consultants, commentators and managers of change. In this way the 'far' and the 'near' are more comfortably and readily interchangeable for insider groups than for those working in the spaces they seek to transform.

Intermediary groups can be understood as those who enable the insiders to remove themselves from responsibility for the fallout from the reorganisation of work. Often, for short periods of time, intermediaries perform insider functions that are directly designed to transform existing working and production practices. Currently, for example, there is a trend towards the use of British consultants on short contracts to oversee the privatisation of industries in Continental Europe. In essence, the intermediaries provide a 'buffer' function at the interface between the demand for flexible labour and the need for work. Intermediary groups can take radically different forms, from the proliferation of employment agencies and consultancies, through legal, audit and accountancy practices, to the individuals and 'gangs' trading in the supply of illegal, unprotected, or even slave labour (Bales, 1999). Then there are the firms that establish themselves in a relationship with a large MNC with the precise role of 'taking up the slack' in a lean production system.[12] These firms, usually small and medium enterprises (SMEs), but also large MNCs producing for multiple brands, actively absorb the risks of globalisation on behalf of MNCs. The growth in outsourcing and contracting out production and services effectively reduces the responsibility (or perception of responsibility) the customer firm has for work done in its name. In terms of working practices, outsource plants demonstrate a higher instance of poor pay and intensified work loads, and greater use of temporary, unprotected or illegal labour than the MNCs they supply (EIRO, 2000; Klein, 2000).

Outsider groups are those who are excluded from a role in defining the terms and nature of new forms of work and working practices. This is not to say that their social practices do not play significant roles in shaping or contesting transformation. Indeed, within the outsider grouping there are distinctive patterns of consent, dissent, collaboration and contest. The overwhelming trend is towards a fracturing of common working identities, these being replaced with 'a series of contracts between a customer firm and a mass of labour-contracting firms, temporary agencies or individual providers of labour services' (Crouch, 1997, p. 375). Thus, the nature of work in a global political economy becomes 'a patchwork quilt characterised by diversity, unclarity and insecurity in people's work and life' (Beck, 2000b, p. 1). A focus on those who grapple with the implications of globalisation for their everyday working practices can raise questions as to the concrete meanings of global change.

First, global change at work is expressed in terms of a consciousness of individualism and 'hypercompetitiveness' (Vilrokx, 1999; Sinclair, 1999). The use of human resource management (HRM) techniques such as the 'benchmarking' of the performance of production plants, coupled with the 'storming' effects of JIT production,[13] leads workers to feel that the greatest threats exist within the corporation itself. Thus, the volatility and irregularity of production that is commonly associated with demand in global markets, is understood by workers to be created by the manipulation of orders to fit JIT and to suit shareholders' reports. Similarly, outsider groups associate the use of quality circles and teams with attempts to encourage them to compete with one another, and this is resisted via tacit and non-direct means (Rubery, 1995; Danford, 1998; Moody, 1997).

Second, and a related point, outsider groups widely associate globalisation with a diminution of their representation as a group (Towers, 1997). This is, of course, a phenomenon that is widely documented by industrial relations scholars in their studies of de-unionisation. However, the changing practices of the unions themselves reveal much about the character of contemporary change in the workplace. UK and US trade unions have responded to challenges by becoming individual service providers for their 'consumers', thus reinforcing individualisation. Stabilising and protecting core workers has the effect of further destabilising the already precarious contract workforce. For a flexibility-seeking corporation, a protected and stable core of workers increases the incentives to create a buffer of temporary or outsourced working practices. This contributes to the polarisation of a core group of predominantly male workers who are 'inculcated into a culture' and whose social practices reproduce that culture, and a larger group of predominantly female workers in contingent, outsourcing or homeworking roles whose practices may contradict the culture (Crouch, 1997).

Finally, the social practices of paid work are perceived to become increasingly similar to the social practices of unpaid work in the home. For the most 'flexible' workers the twenty-four-hour instantaneous demands of care and household work are contemporaneous with the demands of production for the global economy. These 'precarious workers' (Cox, 1999, p. 87) convey acute experiences of what one woman working in electronics assembly termed 'knife-edge flexibility' in paid working practices and absolute rigid constraints in unpaid family work. Overall, this 'multi-activity society' (Beck, 2000, p. 42), characterised by competing sets of structured social practices gives rise to new political questions and potential sites of political organisation.

Politics at work

The global restructuring of work cannot be effectively understood, then, as either an automatic response to economic and technological processes, or an elite-driven project. A focus on the contradictions and divisions that arise from flexibilisation strategies demonstrates that work and workers need to enter the globalisation debate on a level that reveals the political nature of changing practices. Is it possible to sketch the terrain of an emergent politics of transformation in working practices? At one level the most visible political contests could be said to be the strategic activities of nationally or transnationally organised trade unions. Here the contradictions of globalisation may create the pressures and opportunities for 'global social movement unionism' (Lambert, 1999), and extend IPE inquiry into the political economy of labour (Harrod and O'Brien, forthcoming). The roles of trade unions in forming alliances with non-governmental organisations (NGOs), monitoring MNCs' labour codes of conduct, suggest for some that the voices of organised labour represent the sole coherent political mechanism for a global civil society (Somavia, 1999; IILS, 1999).[14]

However, at the level of social practices the study of firms, unions and organisations as primary sites of political activity in the global political economy is problematic. Put simply, the fracturing of traditional sites of production leads us to question the representativeness of trade unions and other institutionalised political bodies. Mechanical and organised forms of solidarity tend to be imagined and constructed in ways that are historically particular (Thompson, 1963; Hyman, 1999). As production is actively shifted into unprotected domains, programmes of restructuring have rendered past myths of solidarity more difficult to sustain, raising the need for 'organic' solidarities based on 'direct experiences, immediate milieux and specific patterns of social relations' (*ibid.*, p. 96). Challenges to existing workplace political institutions have broken open past patterns of solidarity and allegiance. There are clear dangers but also opportunities here. The dangers lie in assuming that the workplace has become de-politicised, thereby reinforcing emerging disparities in working practices. The opportunities lie in a recognition of the common challenges within these diverse practices. The form and nature of change in work and its organisation remains politically open, contingent and contested.

Part III: globalisation and the everyday practices of finance

World finance tends to sit at the heart of common sense representations of globalisation, where 'global finance' is understood as the emergence of an integrated, twenty-four-hour capital market. Such an image of contemporary finance is present in the statements of the International Monetary Fund and the Organisation for Economic Co-operation and Development, the policy pronouncements of the leading states and the business literature that seeks to promote successful corporate financing in a perceived global era. International political economists (e.g. Strange, 1998), economists (e.g. Allen, 1994; Ghosh and Ortiz, 1997) and economic geographers (e.g. Leyshon and Thrift, 1997) also often concur with this popular representation of restructuring. The received wisdom emphasises trends towards disintermediation, the benefits of liquidity and transaction cost reductions associated with integrated global capital markets, the securitisation of formerly illiquid assets (e.g. mortgages) into tradable secondary market instruments and the associated growth of market-orientated risk management strategies through the use of derivatives and futures.

In line with the dominant process perspective on globalisation, the inclination is to view the innate expansionary tendencies of markets (carried forward through developments in information technology) as driving the emergence of an integrated global capital market (e.g. Cerny, 1994). This de-politicised orthodoxy has been challenged by IPE scholars who take what we term the project perspective on globalisation. Given the 'design capacity' (Vipond 1993, p. 187) of states over financial market structures and the inherent instability of financial markets, some IPE scholars have stressed that restructuring rests upon both the liberalisation and deregulation policies of the major states, and interstate cooperation to manage the ensuing financial crises (Strange, 1986; Underhill, 1991; Helleiner, 1994; Pauly, 1997). Relatively little attention, however, has been paid to the relationships between world finance and everyday financial practices, with the consequence that significant political dynamics involved in world financial restructuring have been left largely neglected.

Everyday financial practices are taken here to be those sets of structured social practices through which individuals and households undertake saving (i.e. accounts, insurance, investments and pensions) and borrowing (i.e. loans, mortgages and consumer credit). While guided by the practice perspective on globalisation, a concern with everyday financial practices is also rooted in a theoretical understanding of finance as comprised of social relations and practices that arise from the very nature of credit as 'promises to pay' (cf. Ingham, 1996; Woodruff, 1999). It follows that understanding the restructuring of contemporary finance requires attention not only to the marketised organisation of actual promises to pay themselves (e.g. credit instruments, loan agreements, etc.), but also to the field of social relations and practices that make these possible.

The general failure to consider what we might call 'global finance in the everyday' is largely a consequence of the widespread and deeply entrenched orthodox dichotomy between global-wholesale finance on the one hand, and national-retail finance on the other (see OECD, 2000, for a recent re-statement). Everyday financial practices are designated as retail finance. Given the continued national-orientation of retail finance,[15] everyday financial practices become at best only of indirect significance to the changes in wholesale finance that are usually labelled 'globalisation'.

In contrast to the orthodox global-wholesale/national-retail dichotomy, the common sense image of an integrated global capital market is suggestive in an ideal-typical sense of a transformation in everyday financial practices once it is viewed through the lens of the practice perspective. The emergence of an integrated global market is not simply constituted by the issuing, buying and selling of credit instruments at a global scale institutionalised within investment banks, stock exchanges, fund managers and institutional investors. Rather, the promises to pay and social relations of global finance also incorporate and rest upon a restructuring in everyday saving and borrowing practices in line with the 'far away' image of twenty-four-hour integrated markets.[16] Given that the social relations of finance have been traditionally different in their institutional configurations across state-societies, including state-led (e.g. France), bank-based (e.g. Germany) and capital market (e.g. USA, UK) arrangements, such a restructuring of everyday financial practices is likely to follow divergent trajectories in contrasting contexts (Zysman, 1983; Vogel, 1996). The importance of everyday financial practices for world finance becomes re-valued in terms of both the shared understandings that inform them and their material significance. The image of global integrated capital markets may come to frame understandings of what constitutes 'good' saving or borrowing practice, while restructured everyday financial practices may contribute capital for global investment or draw down credit from global markets.

Everyday pensions practices

In order to illustrate the linkages between everyday financial practices and contemporary world finance in more concrete terms, the remainder of this part of the chapter will focus on the everyday saving practices of occupational pensions. Pensions provision in developed state-societies tends to combine three principal 'pillars': state-based 'pay-as-you-go' (PAYG) social security schemes, occupational schemes; and personal pension plans. Complex relationships have been identified between a discernable shift away from dependence upon PAYG towards an increased supplementary role for occupational pensions practices on the one hand, and the globalisation of finance on the other (Marden and Clark, 1994; Minns, 1996, 1996a; Picciotto and Haines, 1999; Clark, 1999). Several sets of related factors have contributed to this shift in pension practices. First, state-based PAYG provision has, alongside social expenditures in health, education and social security, become perceived as problematic since the 'fiscal crisis' of the early 1970s (cf. O'Connor, 1973). A shift to pension practices organised through private institutions has, then, tended to be promoted as a matter of state policy.[17] Second, demands to supplement state-based PAYG have received further and considerable impetus amid more recent perceptions of the so-called 'demographic time-bomb' (cf. World Bank, 1994). Ageing populations undermine PAYG provision, which is reliant on current taxation of the working population to fund current payments to the retired. Third, writers from the French regulation school highlight that the roots of shifting pension practices lie broadly in changes to socio-economic relations (Aglietta, 2000; Boyer, 2000). If the central personality under Fordist socio-economic relations was the organised worker, then the central personalities under contemporary post-Fordism are the flexible worker and the professional investor who manages the former's occupational pension plan.

Finally, and perhaps most significantly for the formation of linkages between everyday pension practices and global finance, the shift to private pension practices tends to be couched in Anglo-Saxon, neoliberal terms. It is not simply that public PAYG is discouraged while private occupational pensions are encouraged, but that the Anglo-Saxon variant of occupational pension practices is promoted as 'best practice' and a key component in the creation of integrated capital markets.[18] Clark (1999) terms this the promotion of 'pension fund capitalism'. The capital saved under Anglo-Saxon occupational pension practices is invested in stock and capital markets by institutional investors and fund managers. This contrasts with, for instance, German occupational pension practices. In 1996, 57 per cent of German occupational pension practices were organised under the 'book reserve' system that ensures that employee's pension contributions are invested within the firm for which they work (COM, 1999, 134, p. 21). Not only do such practices mean that the volume of pension capital invested in national capital and stock markets is reduced, but also that foreign investment is also heavily circumscribed. In our terms, then, the emergence of an integrated global capital market entails, in an ideal-typical sense, a transformation in everyday pension practices along Anglo-Saxon lines as a significant contributory dynamic.

The material importance of occupational pension practices to world finance is clearly apparent. By the end of 1993, pension funds held investment assets (stocks, shares, bonds, cash and property) to the value of $10 000 billion with the expectation that this figure would grow to $12 000 billion by the year 2000 (OECD, 1994, p. 9).[19] Not surprisingly, Anglo-Saxon pension practices contribute the majority of the capital for the purchase of such assets. $6 000 billion and $750 billion of the $10 000 billion worth of pension fund investment assets at end of 1993 were owned by US and UK pension plan holders respectively (Minns, 1996a, pp.385–6). In terms of the emergence of global finance, it is the extent to which pension investment portfolios are diversified that matters. While around 30 per cent of UK, Dutch and other 'small economy' pension fund assets are foreign, the figure for US pension funds is around 10 per cent or $600 billion. Given that the total value for cross-border-owned tradable capital and equity market instruments in the mid-1990s was $2 500 billion (Eatwell and Taylor, 2000, p. 4), occupational pension practices can be seen as making a meaningful material contribution to the emergence of an integrated global financial market.

Key to the prospects of a restructuring of occupational pension practices along Anglo-Saxon neoliberal lines is the extent to which the far away image of an integrated global capital market comes to dominate the shared understandings that inform practices. Popular awareness of the linkages between global finance and everyday saving and borrowing practices has clearly increased since the 1980s, prompted in particular by the growth of a specialised financial press (Leyshon, Thrift and Pratt, 1998). However, while significant to the creation of individual financial consumers, the relevance of this specialised press to occupational pension practices is less certain. The everyday experience of occupational pensions tends to be an automatic electronic transfer of funds that appears on a worker's wage slip. In contrast with the likes of mutual fund practices, occupational pension practices are largely a 'passive' investment (Harmes, 1998, p. 113). Therefore, central to whether occupational pension practices become, *de facto*, framed by the image of an integrated global capital market is the extent to which they are institutionalised within Anglo-Saxon-style pension funds. While pension plan holders may *own* the investments made on their behalf, they do not *control* the criteria for investment (Minns, 1996). As Harmes (1998) highlights, it is through the collective investment decisions made by institutional investors that occupational pension practices serve to contribute towards the neoliberal restructuring of world finance.

The politics that infuses pension reform is important, then, in determining the extent to which occupational pension practices either reinforce or challenge the creation of an integrated global financial market. In many continental European state-societies in particular, PAYG and occupational pension practices that do not conform to the Anglo-Saxon model appear unlikely to be swiftly transformed. PAYG pension practices continue to account for around 90 per cent of pension benefits across the EU (OECD, 1994, p. 8). Considerable political tensions are associated with the juxtaposition of familiar embedded practices with real and perceived forces for change. For instance, those leading the recently renewed efforts of the European Commission to drive forward pension reform across Europe are clearly aware of the tensions which caused their earlier efforts at the beginning of the 1990s to flounder (COM, 1999, 134, p. 25). Alongside continued strong political support for PAYG practices, organised interest groups appear likely to mobilise in an effort to retain the investment ceilings and currency matching requirements which, at present, largely constrain the investment of occupational pension funds to national assets.

The tensions that permeate the juxtaposition of existing everyday pension practices with real and perceived forces for change are further exacerbated by both the prospect of new patterns of inclusion/exclusion, and by contradictions inherent to Anglo-Saxon practices themselves. State-based PAYG pension provision has tended to be grounded in principles of universal coverage. Occupational pension practices, meanwhile, largely exclude not only those who are unemployed, but also employees in small companies, the self-employed, part-time and temporary workers, and women (Minns, 1996a, p. 389).[20] Even in the US where occupational pension practices are most developed, only 48.8 per cent of families currently have an occupational pension plan (Federal Reserve Board, 2000). Such exclusionary dynamics appear likely to heighten everyday opposition to an Anglo-Saxon-style transformation in pension practices, with the consequence that the creation of an integrated global financial market is challenged. Furthermore, contradictions present within Anglo-Saxon pension practices themselves serve to undercut change. On the one hand, occupational pension practices encourage cooperation between capital and labour as the capacity of workers' pension plans to deliver depends upon the performance of the economy. On the other hand, with institutional investors controlling the criteria for the investment of funds, short-term demands for high returns on investment are privileged ahead of long-term productive investment. Such short-termism, in turn, encourages the creation of the very part-time and temporary employees who are excluded from occupational pension practices.

The current restructuring of everyday pension practices would seem, then, not to be characterised by an unproblematic shift to Anglo-Saxon occupational pension practices. The creation of the social relations and practices of Anglo-Saxon occupational pensions that could potentially do so much to reinforce the making of an integrated global financial market remains subject to considerable political tensions. Equally, however, the grip of institutional investors over the investment process serves to limit the potential restructuring of occupational pension practices in support of alternative credit instruments (i.e. ethical and 'green' investment funds) that would directly challenge the making of an integrated neoliberal global financial market. Two implications follow. First, the restructuring of everyday pension practices is likely to continue to be marked by considerable contestation, an important field of politics within the restructuring of world finance. Further and ongoing research into the restructuring of everyday saving and borrowing practices is required if we are to broaden and deepen our understanding of the politics of contemporary world finance. Second, the common sense far away image of 'global finance' unravels if a practice perspective is taken. Contemporary world finance is not characterised by the emergence of an integrated global market, the Anglo-Saxon neoliberal model writ large. Rather, integration is far from complete. The sets of transnational financial practices that are emphasised by the common sense (e.g. disintermediated, securitised, risk management) are only partially linked to everyday financial practices.

Concluding remarks

Our starting point was to recognise the essentially contested nature of the theory and practice of global restructuring. Rather than ask 'What is globalisation?', our first order question was 'How is it understood?' At a time when IPE scholars have called for the 'P' to be restored to IPE (Hay and Marsh, 1999), our concern is with the ways in which the 'P' becomes *removed* by the dominant process understanding of globalisation. Under the process perspective, politics is viewed, at best, as incidental to the course of change and, at worst, as anathema to the management of change. Research in IPE has done much to direct attention to the political drivers and resistors of change, whether national governments, transnational elites, or old and new social movements. However, paradoxically the emphasis placed by this project perspective on the organised promotion-resistance of globalisation has reinforced the neglect of *everyday* forms of politics. We contend, therefore, that there is a need to focus on the structured social practices through which people experience and apprehend globalisation in their everyday lives.

Re-valuing *everyday* social practices makes visible the political contestation that takes place over the reality and representation of globalisation. Our exploration of the everyday practices of work and finance illustrates that the politics of globalisation is not adequately captured by the 'drivers versus resistors' formulation. Rather, the oppositions of the politics of globalisation are present in everyday practices, arising from the tensions, emergent divisions and inequalities, and contradictions inherent to restructuring. Hence, real and perceived demands for change in work and finance realise tensions between the 'near' and everyday, and the 'far' and unknown. The juxtaposition between 'near' and 'far' takes on multiple forms, with increased security for some matched by intensified risk for others. Thus, for the 'portfolio person', an insider worker who holds an occupational pension plan, the near and far may be reconciled comfortably. Meanwhile for the most 'flexible' contingent worker, reliant, at best, on state-based pension provision, the far intensifies the risk and insecurity experienced in the near. Such tensions and divisions are not just the politics of transition. The contradictions present within the process prescriptions for restructuring themselves ensure that the everyday politics of globalisation will continue to give character to contemporary social change.

Notes

1. See also Editorial, 'Forum for heterodox international political economy', *Review of International Political Economy*, vol. 1, no. 1, Spring 1994.
2. So, for example, at the closure of the Fujitsu Corporation's plant in north-east England, the British Prime Minister, Tony Blair, announced during a BBC television interview that 'regrettably there is little a government can do

about the twists and turns of world markets in a globalised economy'. Under the heading of 'globalisation', a recent International Monetary Fund (IMF) (2000, p. 6) paper concerned with the former Eastern bloc noted:

> [t]he last decade of the 20th century has been marked by immense changes in the world economy. The new phase of the technological revolution and the far-reaching internationalisation of capital have changed the patterns of economic performance... Hence, on the eve of the new century, there are not only mounting old structural problems, but several new issues that must be addressed properly.
>
> A similarly 'globalist' statement is made by Jonathan Freedland for whom'the economy has moved ahead of politics... vast global corporations influence every aspect of our day-to-day lives. Our only weapon is national governments – and these have proved themselves all but powerless. (*The Guardian*, 1 December 1999, p. 21)

3. While the key elements of a project perspective have been discernible for some time, there are now analyses that explicitly refer to a globalisation project (cf. Rupert, 2000, ch. 3; McMichael, 2000).
4. The roles of everyday practices at work came into focus during research into the restructuring of production and work in European engineering and electronics multinational corporations (MNCs). The research demonstrated that new forms of work organisation fragment production sites so that it is necessary to explore practices that extend into agencies, microfirms and households.
5. A focus on broad shifts in industrial and workplace relations in ideal-type neoliberal and neocorporatist political economies would indicate that globalisation has indeed been accompanied by transformation in forms and modes of work. The 1998 British Workplace Employee Relations Survey reports that 47 per cent of firms located in Britain had no union members, a figure that has increased from 36 per cent in the 1990 survey (Cully, 1999). The number of part-time workers grew by 5.4 per cent over 1999 to total 24.9 per cent of total employment (European Industrial Relations Observatory [EIRO], 1999). Ninety per cent of British firms use subcontracting, 44 per cent use fixed-term contracts and 28 per cent use agency workers (EIRO, 1999). Figures for Germany show that trade unions lost 30 per cent of their membership between 1991 and 1998 (Institut der Deutschen Wirtschaft, 1999). Part-time working accounted for 18.3 per cent of total employment in Germany for 1999, whilst temporary work accounted for 10.8 per cent (EIRO, 1999). Eurostat figures suggest that the use of non-standard (temporary, part-time, fixed-contract) employment has increased in all EU member states over the last decade, though this has been accompanied by varying degrees of legislative protection in different states (Eurostat, 2000).
6. 86 per cent of US workers and 67 per cent of British workers in paid work have no form of recognised representation at work (Towers, 1997). This trend towards unrepresented work has led some industrial relations scholars to question the representativeness of trade unions in such circumstances (Hyman, 1999). This, of course, raises questions regarding the focus on unions in the analysis of the effects of globalisation on workers.

7. Jeff Harrod's (1987) work on the significance of the unprotected worker for production in a global economy has laid the foundations for those who wish to take seriously the 'workers' eye view' of globalisation. It is now possible to point to an emergent International Political Economy of Labour that seeks to explore the roles of unionised and non-unionised workers in contemporary world order (Harrod, 1997; Harrod and O'Brien, forthcoming, 2001).

8. ILO (2000, p. 114) reports rapid increases in the numbers of homeworkers providing 'optimal flexibility' in the industrialised and developing countries. The clothing industry, electronics and assembly sectors, together with 'noncore' activities such as catering and repairs have found their way into homes. As sites of production homes are predominantly low paid and unprotected, based on piecework with no formal contract of employment. The use of unprotected labour in production for the global economy has led scholars to focus on the increased use of child labour and bonded or slave labour (Bales, 1999; Klein, 2000).

9. During 1999 the UK lost twelve days per 1 000 employees due to industrial action. In Germany, where trade unions remain central despite declining density, one day was lost per 1 000 employees (EIRO 1999).

10. The German Standortdebatte is the debate between the social partners surrounding the competitiveness of Germany as a location for production and investment.

11. The 1998 British Workplace Employee Relations Survey reveals that though two-thirds of workplaces report using teamworking, only 3 per cent of these actually devolve decision-making autonomy to the level of teams.

12. As one production worker for an automotive component supply firm commented, 'In a lean system, someone somewhere has to take up the slack. It is usually the weakest link in the chain.' Naomi Klein argues that trade liberalisation and labour law reform has enabled large MNCs to 'no longer produce products . . . but rather buy products and brand them' (2000, p. 5). The result in terms of working practices is an arms-length relationship between the brand and the workers producing for a contractor.

13. Just-in-time (JIT) production implies a reduction of slack or buffers in the system, requiring minimal materials and labour inventory, and an electronic data system, linking the customer to the firm and the supply chain. For large electronics MNCs this commonly manifests itself in weekly or bi-weekly estimates of production runs, necessitating instantaneous responses in working practices.

14. Clean Clothes Campaign and ITGLWF.

15. See, for instance, a recent OECD (2000) report that highlights the limited cross-border trade in retail financial services. Germain (1996, pp. 214–15) has highlighted three main reasons why retail banking practices remain largely nationally orientated. First, a lack of profitability in retail banking due to low returns and large fixed costs of creating and maintaining retail institutional networks discourages new market entrants. Second, national cultural differences continue which prevent the emergence of a uniform, transnational approach to retail banking. Third, even in Europe where attempts have been made to codify European law into national law, legal institutional barriers persist. In addition to these reasons, instances of national banks utilising

their domestic political power to obstruct foreign competition are also apparent. For instance, Barclays Bank's attempt to introduce an interest-bearing account in France in the early 1990s was thwarted by collusion between the major French banks and their domestic regulators (*The Economist*, 1994, p. 33).

16. This view is informed by Gill's (1995) notion of 'market civilization', that is, the way that global capitalist norms and values become embedded in everyday social practices.

17. The extent to which so-called 'pensions reform' has come to be a common policy objective across the states of the developed world is illustrated by their attempts to learn from each other's implementation experiences. For instance, the OECD recently formed its 'Working party on Private Pensions', and on 11 October 2000 the European Commission made a proposal for a Directive on Occupational Pensions to form part and parcel of the development of the internal European market (COM, 1999, 134).

18. A statement by the European Commission's Internal Market Directorate is broadly representative of this position:

> By operating freely in capital markets, pension funds can optimise their investment policy and help accelerate EU capital market integration. Increases in pension fund investment returns will benefit employers (decrease in pension contributions) or employees (increase in pension benefits). This can be achieved without compromising pension security. In the context of the ageing population, this can help Member States preserve the long-term financial stability of existing pension systems and provide risk capital to promote jobs and growth. (http://europa.eu.int/comm/internalmarket/en/finances/pensions/index.htm, October 2000)

19. To give some kind of context, the value of pension fund investment assets is broadly equivalent to the total combined value of the assets quoted on the world's three largest stock exchanges (Minns, 1996, p. 43).

20. On the dynamics of financial inclusion/exclusion more broadly, see Leyshon and Thrift (1995).

4
Germany Unlocked? Globalising Capital and the Logic of Accumulation

Gary Burn

At the end of 1999, undercover of Christmas and buried away among the minutia of proposed personal and corporate tax changes issued by the German Ministry of Finance, a single sentence announced what could mean the end of Germany Inc. and the Rhineland model of capitalism. For, it was in this way that the Schröder government announced new legislation would be passed through the German lower house, the *Bundestag*, so that by January 2001 German companies would be able to sell any equity they held in other German companies without incurring capital gains tax.[1] Two days later the DAX share index showed financial sector stocks had risen by 4–5 per cent. Within six months, Germany's big commercial banks, by utilising the simple device of deferring these transactions in their accounts until the following tax year, had already begun to divest themselves of their substantial industrial holdings.[2] It would seem, then, that German financial capital, which has been traditionally tied tightly to the German manufacturing base since the time of Bismarck, is breaking free at last.

In Germany itself, this announcement has gone largely unnoticed by the general public, while political opposition has seemed oddly unfocused – with the left complaining of tax handouts to big business and the right peeved that small business was not getting the same generous deal (Lutz, 2000, p. 165). Yet, the significance of these tax reforms for the Rhineland model can not be exaggerated. For the unravelling of these bank-industry cross-shareholdings, bringing to an end the *Konzerne* (the quasi-*Keiretsu* structure of interlocking equity ownership) would seem to presage the rapid demise of Germany's intermediary-based financial system, and the death of organised capitalism.[3]

Before, German industrial and financial capital formed what Coates (2000, p. 64) describes as *'intra-capital* relationships'. As such they were, to a great extent, mutually dependent sinking or swimming together. If German industry was unsuccessful and the rate of accumulation low, there would be an inadequate share of the surplus due to German capital. Now and in the future, as the big German commercial banks concentrate on 'higher returns' in their core business of international investment banking, German capital will be able to maximise profitability and pursue liquidity preference on a global basis, largely free from domestic social and economic 'frictions' which might compromise these aims.[4]

If German industry has to learn to live without the line of cheap, subsidised long-term credit it has relied upon for most of the last hundred years, then it will be forced to compete for funding on an increasingly global basis, via Germany's rapidly expanding external capital market. Here equity culture and the interests of shareholders, which overwhelmingly centre on the short-term optimisation of share value, take precedence over any conflicting interests of the other stakeholders, including, if necessary, the long-term well-being of the firm itself. A movement away from a 'bank-based' towards a 'securities market-based' system of corporate finance, from bank debt to equity financing, is, in itself, a loosening of the institutional ties between both ownership and management and capital and production, to form what are described as 'market', or more aptly, 'arms-length' relationships. Taken together, it should not be surprising that, as a recent *Financial Times (FT)* survey on German banking and finance made clear, 'th[is] tax reform is certain to generate pressure from shareholders impatient to see hidden wealth unlocked' (Barber, 2000b). In the euphemistic language of shareholder culture, this means, for the most part, trading future profits for more immediate returns.

The question that needs to be asked, however, is whether, taken together, these structural-institutional changes will result in Germany mutating into a true Anglo-Saxon-style capitalist economy. A taste of what might be to come was predicted by Walter Seipp as long ago as 1990. Speaking for the Commerzbank, he saw an unwinding of bank-industry cross-shareholding leading directly to Jimmy Goldsmith-style asset stripping of Germany's industrial base.[5] Deutsche Bank's Alfred Herrhausen, though speaking mostly from a fear of foreign takeover of German industry, predicted that moves to 'force' banks, as he saw it then, to dispose of their equity holdings in industry, would result in 'excited protests' Herrhausen (1989).

Ten years on, Mannesmann is in the hands of Vodaphone and there is a new Mergers and Acquisitions law modelled on Britain's takeover code in the offing. Yet, these same banks, having in the meantime actively campaigned to be freed from this institutional marriage, which they now consider synonymous with managerial complacency and poor returns, are delighted. They now want to concentrate on their core activities on behalf of the shareholders. As Deutsche Bank chairman, Rolf Breuer made clear, in selling off its 'historic industrial holdings', the Deutsche Bank was demonstrating its 'commitment to realise maximum shareholder value' (*ibid.*).

However, having said all this, informed opinion as to the significance of these tax reforms is divided. Typically, those working in the financial markets seem most convinced that fundamental changes are taking place. For example, Thomas Weisgerber, securities market expert with the German Bankers Association is certain they will accelerate the opening up of Deutschland Plc.[6] Richard Deeg (1999, p. 3), however, disagrees, believing that despite convergence in the regulation of national financial markets, the distinct shape of Germany's institutional framework will endure. Such a fundamental change in the nature of the accumulation process is likely to have the direct effect of restructuring German industry and the wider economy, both in terms of organisation and control, so as to precipitate the dissolution of the concordat between capital, labour and the state upon which economic governance and the *Sozialemarktwirtschaft* (the social market economy) are based. Should this happen, it can be expected that financial and institutional support for education and training, research and development, and the provision of healthcare, will be radically, if gradually, redefined, in line with the new global priorities of German capital and the weakened position of the German state and the trade union movement (Deeg, 1999, p. 1). According to the *Financial Times* this is a battle being waged by US investment banks in the 'vanguard of global capitalism' who have become the 'shock-troops for a new, essentially Anglo-Saxon corporate culture...in continental Europe'. Sir Win Bischoff, chairman of leading investment bank Citigroup Europe, agrees, although he puts it more prosaically as the 'Americanisation of the financial system' (Pretzlik, 2001, p. 8).

Given this diverse opinion, it is the central purpose of this chapter to critically access the extent and nature of the globalisation of German capital and how this can expect to impact on the future of the German model i.e. the institutional framework that underpins Germany's socio-economic structure, not only in relation to Germany itself, but also to the future development of the EU. I begin by presenting a brief summary of the models of capitalism debate on which much of this analysis turns.[7] I then explain the origins of German industrial development which, essentially, defined the German model, and trace the evolution of the role played by the banking sector, from Germany's rapid industrialisation in the second half of the nineteenth century, to the present day project to create *Finanzplatz Deutschland*, a global financial market centred in Frankfurt. Following that, I present a comparative analysis of the German variant of the Rhineland model and the British variant of the Anglo-Saxon model, in order to demonstrate the concept of the *logic of capital accumulation*, and the socio-economic consequences that can be expected to flow from detaching capital from local and national accumulation and locking it into a global money capital circuit. Then I turn to considering whether changes currently taking place within the German financial services sector can expect to alter the dominant form of accumulation operating in Germany in such a way as to reduce the future provision of cheap long-term investment funding to German industry. I define three distinct divisions that make up the German banking sector: first, the big commercial banks; second, the public savings banks, both the *Sparkassen* at a local level and the *Landesbanken*, at a regional level; and third, the cooperative or mutual banks, i.e. the *Volksbanken* and *Genossenschaftsbanken*. I identify two distinct but complementary processes that are leading to a fundamental restructuring of Germany's capital market. The first is taking place at a national level. The second is occurring at the level of the European Union and at a wider regime level, both of which are emanating from the neoliberal 'Washington consensus'.[8] Finally, I ask the question: 'Is there a future for the German model?'

Germany and the models of capitalism debate

Swept forward on an ideological wave of globalisation euphoria and underpinned by a dominant neoliberal economic orthodoxy, the dynamic growth of the US economy and, to a lesser extent, even the UK economy, in the second half of the 1990s, saw the unregulated, unrestrained market form of capitalism, the Anglo-Saxon model, triumphant. Talk no longer of British economic decline, British prime ministers have recently been busy giving seminars to their continental European counterparts on how to restructure their sclerotic economies. Pride in the superiority of the Germany model has been replaced by doubts as to the essential 'viability of *Industriestandort Deutschland* [Germany as an industrial location]' (Dore *et al.*, 1999, p. 115). Responding to the new reality, Gerhard Schröder, the German Chancellor, after seeing his capital gains tax reforms pass successfully through the upper chamber of the German parliament, proudly announced: 'No longer can anyone talk about the German disease' (Barber, 2000b). Clearly then, whatever else may be happening, the Rhenish model of 'organised' or 'coordinated' capitalism, for so long residing on the laurels of Germany's *wirtshaftwunder*, is under grave threat, from without and within.

Yet, Anglo-Saxonism was not always held in such high regard. The whole 'models of capitalism' debate emerged in the 1960s, first, as a reaction to the waning of the US as an industrial power, pre-eminent in 1945 and, second, out of the wider 'decline of Britain' debate, which had been carried on since the 1890s.[9] Put simply, Great Britain, the first industrialised power, had been on the slide since the 1870s so that by the early part of the twentieth century she had been passed by Germany and the US, and, since the second World War, by first France, Japan and then Italy. In terms of gross domestic product (GDP) per person Britain stood sixth in the world in 1950 but seventeenth and falling by 1994.[10] Meanwhile, West Germany and Japan, the vanquished, had recovered to become the dynamic post-war economies. Until recently, supporters of the more trust-based, regulated, Rhenish model, built on a *concordat* between capital, labour and the state and taking a longer perspective on the accumulation process, have been able to point to a consistently better economic performance than that experienced by the market-led Anglo-Saxon model.

Central to the success of the German model, it is claimed, is the role played by the financial system, regarded as the key institution shaping Germany's institutional framework to facilitate *national accumulation*. Of particular importance here, is the much proclaimed relationship between the large commercial banks and industrial joint-stock companies, whereby the former, through the control of equity voting rights in the latter (both, directly as shareholders, and via the exercise of proxy votes made on behalf of their own customers who are also shareholders) come to sit on the supervisory boards of the latter. In this way the banks are said to play a tutelary role with regard to industry, ensuring, thereby, (a) the monitoring and supervision of the firm in a way that delivers a system of corporate governance that, largely, overcomes the problems of asymmetric information which so worry the investor. Increased transparency and control reduces the risk, and thereby the cost, of providing external finance, so as to ensure (b) a more optimal and long-term allocation of cheap investment capital for both the individual firm and industry as a whole (Edwards and Ogilvie, 1996, p. 428). Finally, banks, by the very fact that they are represented on supervisory boards across and between industrial sectors, occupying a common position within a network of interlocking shareholdings, are able to fulfil (c) a vital coordinating role which facilitates both interfirm and sectoral co-operation and concentration without which the ongoing restructuration and adjustment process necessary for successful development cannot be efficiently achieved.

However, these are contentious issues, as even a cursory examination of the literature on German bank-industry relations makes clear. They feed into a complex debate carried on at an academic, technocratic and political level, posing fundamental implications for policy formation, which are argued back and forth over a 'paradigm choice' between free and social market economies, that ebbs and flows, largely in response to the comparative economic performances of the respective models. This debate is further complicated by the fact that numerous 'models', 'stages', 'varieties' or 'types' of capitalism have been defined, backed by a voluminous literature, which cannot be adequately discussed in this chapter. Yet, essentially, what is important to understand is that, historically, because each state has evolved in its own particular way, unique social structures of accumulation have developed, some of which are qualitatively different to one another. Central to this formation has been the specific nature and form of industrial development each country *initially* experienced, out of which evolved a national institutional framework to support and perpetuate distinct patterns in the organisation of production and commerce.[11]

The German model: from finance capital to *Finanzplatz Deutschland*

Germany was the original 'catch-up' economy when Great Britain was the dominant economic power in the world. The father of German economics was not Adam Smith with his concept of the 'invisible hand', on which the entire edifice of neoclassical orthodoxy remains balanced, but the political economist Friedrich List who, writing in the 1850s, saw liberal economic theory as one based, not on the production of values, but on their exchange. Liberal theory best appealed to those whose wealth came, not from production, but through trade and commerce. British economic policy was designed primarily to further the interests, not of manufacturers, but of merchants, whose income came from, as List explained, 'profits on the commodities which pass through their hands' (Lash and Urry, 1987, p. 9). Britain possessed a *makler*, or 'middleman', economy (*ibid.*). Who made the products and who might buy and ultimately use the products was immaterial. British merchants had no special interest in the national productive economy or restricted domestic sphere, but were, rather, orientated towards the wider international market. For that reason, from the early part of the nineteenth century, they zealously supported free trade. In this way, as List observed, the City of London became the hub of 'cosmopolitan mercantile capitalism' (Ingham, 1984, p. 226).

List, unlike Smith, Ricardo and Marx, fathered an ideology around a national, rather than a liberal international political economy, to suit the need for Germany to pursue a strategy of rapid industrialisation, beginning in the mid-nineteenth century (*ibid.*, p. 156). This process necessitated taking measures to protect Germany's national economy from stronger foreign competition (especially British), by erecting tariff walls. Then, it required the harnessing of national capital to large-scale investment in the industrial process. As entrepreneurial capital was not enough, this could only be done by making 'industrial investment banking...[the] specific instrument of industrialisation' (Gershenkron, 1962, p. 14). For this reason, heavily influenced by the French *Credit Mobilier*, German credit banks, such as the Dresdner Bank, were established in the 1870s to foster industrial development (Whale, 1968, p. 10). The Deutsche Bank became the housebank for newly created Siemens (Harding, 1999, p. 74). At around the same time, the German cooperative banking movement, founded on the basis of mutual liability, began to organise capital for small firms and local production, something which proved crucial in the development of Germany's *Mittelstand* sector of SMEs (Deeg, 1999, p. 35).[12] In this way, German money capital began to become 'integrated' with what would become 'the advanced and export-orientated sections of productive capital' (van der Wurff, 1993, p. 167). In addition, public hostility to bank power and money capital orientated towards speculative short-term ends, that had first broken out after the 1873 Berlin financial crash, helped establish an institutional bias away from investment banking and the power of pure money capital (Story, 1997, p. 246). Taken together, this goes some way to explaining why, in the nineteenth century, German banks operated largely outside the international circuits of money capital, and became directly dependent on the fortunes of German industry, both large and small, to which their capital was tied, rather than on the commissions and fees to be had from investment banking, the financing of international trade, trading in securities or from dealing in international capital markets. While Germany certainly possessed an international banking elite and pure money capital fraction, her powerful bank-industrial oligarchy never allowed it to become hegemonic, as had occurred in Britain (van der Pijl, 1984; van der Wurff, 1993).

Instead, because Germany pursued a strategy of national accumulation centred around the new heavy industries of the Second Industrial Revolution (steel, chemicals and electricity), the high degree of economic concentration and capital investment which this development had demanded, defined a mutually reinforcing process of industrial and financial cooperation and concentration. Such a regime of accumulation necessitated the creation of large cartels, characterised by the fusion of industrial and financial capital, which Marxist theorist Rudolf Hilferding (1981) termed 'finance capital', and saw as central to a new phase in capitalist development – monopoly capitalism. While Hilferding must be read in the context of Marxist theories of imperialism of the first decades of the twentieth century, Gerschenkron (1962) returned, more recently, to the relationship between finance and industrialisation, as pioneered in Germany, and concluded that it was crucial to understanding how development out of economic backwardness could be optimally achieved for a nation-state. It is also central to understanding the nature of West Germany's recovery after the second World War. While the Allies' original policy was to break the institutional support necessary for the German model to be reconvened, the reality of the Cold War determined that Germany's industrial power be rebuilt (Dore *et al.*, 1999). Nevertheless they did naively attempt to deconstruct the national bank-industry structure along federal lines. But by the 1950s, two of Germany's 'big three' commercial banks had regained control of their branch networks (Lash and Urry, 1987).

Germany resumed a strategy of national accumulation built around an export-orientated capital goods sector, which the loss of the eastern agrarian regions after 1945 and the consequent demise of the aristocratic land-owning class, the *Junkers*, made, if anything, even more dominant. With Germany's industrial-orientated finance capital fraction remaining hegemonic into the post-war period, historical continuity was guaranteed, and interest rates kept low; a similar policy to that pursued by the *Reichsbank* before 1914 (Born, 1983). Of course, production's gain was finance's loss, which explains Germany's low-return banking sector; at least low in Anglo-Saxon terms. Possibly even more important to German industry, an undervalued exchange rate policy was pursued throughout the 1950s and 1960s which, effectively, subsidised the export sector and protected and rewarded domestic capital. This was a mirror image of Britain's experience over the same period, where the power of international financial/commercial capital in the City demanded an overvalued pound and in the process made Britain's manufacturing sector internationally uncompetitive (Hall, 1986). In addition, the German 'national accumulation' model, where investment funding was driven by the need to develop the productive economy, was institutionally less inclined to experience inflation than the British internationalist model which was, largely, detached from Britain's industrial base. In Germany credit expansion was more likely to be coordinated with the expansion of industrial capacity, consequently reducing the risk of credit booms. The German economy was therefore inherently less volatile than the British economy. The British model, on the other hand, had no way of coordinating the expansion of credit and production and was more likely to experience an expansion of liquidity, which fuelled an increasing demand for existing (and imported) goods rather than an increase in industrial capacity and more domestic production. This was translated very quickly into credit-led inflation and balance of payments crises. This explains why the Keynesian compromise was essentially flawed and ultimately failed.

Clearly then West Germany was eminently more suited than Britain to the development of Fordist production methods introduced in the 1950s. For these required a sufficient supply of cheap and long-term investment capital with which to pay for the required industrial infrastructure, the establishment of a level of demand high enough to warrant large-scale production runs, and price stability. That West Germany was more able to exploit export markets than Britain delivered to her the greater economies of scale necessary for Fordism to operate successfully. Furthermore, the rationale for 'going for market share' was reinforced by the fact that the existence of a *Sozialemarktwirtschaft* determined that German firms regard labour as a fixed cost (Story, 1997, p. 248).

Fordist production methods had been pioneered in the US in the 1930s in the New Deal, consequent to a corporate liberal synthesis between money and production capital, as a way out of the Great Depression. However, unlike the US (and especially Britain) where this arrangement remained an unstable and temporary compromise between different fractions of capital, in Germany it evolved out of the adaptation of the dominant finance capital concept to the increasingly international orientation of accumulation which accompanied the successful re-establishment of a multilateral international trading system around the lines set out at Bretton Woods (van der Wurff, 1993). This explains why the use of counter-cyclical Keynesian demand management techniques, so central to the economic strategy of successive British governments from the late 1950s to the late 1970s, as they struggled to maintain a commitment to full employment in the face of a declining manufacturing sector, were unnecessary in West Germany until as late as 1967, when the first post-war recession occurred. It also explains why German corporate liberalism was able to withstand the monetarist counter-revolution and wider neoliberal offensive of the 1980s, which as Overbeek (1990, p. 202) points out, was perfectly 'correlated with the resurgence of money capital domination'. Thus, while paying lip service to the neoliberal orthodoxy which swept Keynesianism and embedded liberalism aside in the US and Britain in the 1980s, Helmut Kohl's Christian Democratic Government (CDU), mindful of the still hegemonic position of a productive capital fraction which continued to operate largely in terms of national accumulation organised on a regional level. Kohl was reluctant to follow London's example and instigate a fully blown 'Big Bang' opening up of the German financial services industry. Although, significantly, in an attempt to keep international financial markets onside, something which became increasingly urgent with the rise of government debt (especially after German reunification), it did conceive the slow-burning fuse – the *Finanzplatz Deutschland* concept, which I will discuss below (Story, 1997).

However, having said all this, the exact nature of the relationship between industry and finance on which the German model is based, especially the extent to which the former relied upon and was controlled the latter, is hotly contested. While Hall (1986) claims that, as late as the 1980s, German banks controlled 70 per cent of the shares of Germany's largest 425 firms, Deeg (1999) maintains that large German corporations were never as heavily reliant on bank capital, nor so in the thrall of bank power, as the German model suggests. Either way, one factor is not in doubt – the last two decades have witnessed a dramatic decline in traditional bank lending, as German corporations became increasingly self-financing and began to turn to the domestic and foreign securities markets when they did need to raise external finance (Deutsche Bundesbank, 1997). This, in addition to the declining margins to be earned from this type of corporate lending has, in turn, made the commercial banks' move into international and investment banking more inevitable, as they search for alternative and more attractive opportunities to make profit (Lutz, 2000b). Clearly then, pressures to unlock Germany are being brought to bear, not only exogenously, via the impact of an integrated global financial market, but also, increasingly endogenously, as Germany's corporate sector itself, gears up to go global. Not surprisingly, Germany's big commercial banks got behind the project to create *Finanzplatz Deutschland*, and make Frankfurt a leading global financial centre to compete with London and New York. This, however could not have taken place until Germany's financial system began to 'approximate the structures, products, and especially the regulatory rules of the US and UK financial systems' (Deeg, 1999, p. 87).

More controversially, in pursuing this strategy, the banks have been able to rely on the enthusiastic support of the German government, which, Deeg (*ibid.*) points out, began as long ago as the mid-1980s, when the use of new financial products, such as deutschmark currency swaps, were first permitted.[13] To get an idea how far Germany had to come before Frankfurt could even begin to resemble a global financial centre, it was not until legal changes made in the 1990s that German investment funds were allowed to trade in derivatives, that a market in deutschmark commercial paper (CP), long opposed by the Bundesbank, was set up, and that trading in money market funds was permitted; a restriction which had previously limited the use of short-term corporate debt instruments as an alternative means of raising funds to bank finance. Also, an effective DM futures market (DTB), a prerequisite for the operation of a global equity market, was opened in 1990. In total, seven new laws have been passed which together have precipitated the rapid development of Germany's capital markets, where total share issue capitalisation grew from DM 170 billion in 1982 to DM 1,034 billion by 1996 and volume traded increased from DM 40 billion to DM 1,940 billion over the same period (Lutz, 2000b).

Setting the parameters to allow Germany's big banks and industrial firms to move nearer Anglo-Saxon corporate culture appears to have been government policy in Germany as long ago as 1984, when the Banking Act (KWG) first introduced incentives to induce banks to sell their industrial holdings (Deeg, 1993). Yet the banking sector had begun to divest even earlier, when, in the 1970s, the Deutsche Bank began selling off their cross-shareholdings, in response to public fears that banks were becoming more powerful (*ibid.*). It seems, then, that big business and the big commercial banks have been going their own way in Germany for some time now. Yet, despite this, the German model still appears to be, largely, intact. For it was not the performance of the big German corporations that engendered German post-war economic dynamism and the success of the German model in the first place, but that of the SMEs that make up the *Mittelstand*, and which together account for the lion's share of Germany's industrial output.[14] And the development of this sector, which continues to depend heavily on traditional bank finance, has actually reinforced the bank-based system, as the big commercial banks, their big business lending in decline, have begun to move in and take up compensatory equity holdings.

Yet, the big commercial banks are but minor players in the provision of capital to the *Mittelstand* in comparison with that made available by Germany's two other banking sectors, the private cooperative and mutual banks, i.e. the *Volksbanken* and *Genossenschaftsbanken*, and the public savings banks, i.e. a network of 564 local Sparkassen and twelve regional *Landesbanken*, which were originally established to finance local and regional development (Allen and Gale, 2000).[15] The savings banks specialise in utilising their large pool of cheaply serviced savings account deposits to provide long-term industrial finance to their customers. They were originally organised, unlike the commercial banks, on a local and federal, rather than a national basis, and through an association of interdependent but, essentially, autonomous local and regional state banks, rather than in a hierarchical branch bank system.[16] Publicly controlled, they are used to help pursue the political and economic priorities of the federal state in which they operate, as well as to ensure policy autonomy from the centre. From as early as the nineteenth century, the savings and cooperative banks began to develop a close symbiotic relationship with local small business which ensured that local capital kept close to local industry, unlike the experience in Britain, where, from as early as the 1860s, local savings were swept away to finance international trade and speculative international currency movements (Burn, 2000). Because these German banks do not have to make a profit, nor pay a dividend; because they are not responsible for their own credit rating, but can piggy back on regional state (*Länder*) government's AAA rating and because they can rely on a cheap capital base, the public savings and cooperative banks have been able to expand market share at the expense of the big commercial banks, prompting the latter to decentralise their own organisational structures so as to be better able to compete at a local and regional level.[17] It is this so-called 'artificial competition', as the *FT* recently termed it disapprovingly, that has provided Germany with a low-return banking sector, enabling Germany's local smaller banks and firms to retain the housebank relationship and operate successfully alongside the large commercial banks and national firms, underpinning the success of the *Mittelstand*.[18]

In this way competition between the three banking sectors has been maintained, something which, at least until today, cannot be compromised by mergers and acquisitions between banks in different sectors. Competition, in turn, has guaranteed Germany's SMEs a continued source of cheap investment capital. Significantly, as Deeg (1999) points out, because the public savings banks are under the control of the local state authorities and hence can be and are used as 'instruments of state intervention', this provides the federal states with the means of ensuring that the whole three-sector banking system continues to supply the *Mittelstand* with long-term finance and does not opt for liquidity preference in the circuits of international capital, which would be expected in the market-based model. Thus, while internationally, Germany's large commercial banks have adopted an aggressive mergers strategy in order to compete in the global investment banking market and offer their large German clients the 'know-how' that companies like Goldman Sachs and J. P. Morgan can provide, domestic competition has ensured that the Anglo-Saxon culture of investment banking could not be simply transferred to Germany's domestic market and local German companies (Lutz, 1999a). This was exactly the outcome that the architects of *Finanzplatz Deutschland* had hoped for. However, recently, as I will explain in greater detail later in this chapter, the cooperative and public savings banks have also come under threat from institutional change, which poses a substantial challenge to the survival of the German model.

The logic of accumulation and the globalisation of capital

However difficult it may be to analyse where Germany has been, it is infinitely easier than predicting where Germany is going. In basing my analysis on changes to Germany's financial system, within the context of the models of capitalism debate (the hidden comparator being, of course, Britain's financial system) I must first establish why, of all the dimensions on which the debate could be elaborated along, I regard the nature and operation of a country's financial system as fundamental to explaining its socio-economic structure and not, for example, that of production, trade, corporate governance, business systems etc. It is not enough to simply explain that it is because finance, as Cerny (1993, p. 155) puts it, is 'the "life-blood" of the physical economy'. I need to demonstrate how the institutional relationship between finance and production determines economic performance on the one hand and socio-economic and cultural national variations on the other. For example, I need to relate the following statements:

1. In 1990, fixed rate, long-term loans, accounted for nearly 66 per cent of total bank finance advanced to German firms, whereas in Britain

this was the exception rather than the rule, with funding being provided predominantly on a short-term basis.

2. In 1992, capital stock per worker in Germany was $50 116 compared with $22 509 in the UK.

3. In 1989 West German manufacturing had 30 per cent more physical capital per worker hour than UK manufacturing.

4. In 1985, West Germany produced 38 per cent of total manufacturing output in the EU compared with Britain's 12.8 per cent (cited in Coates, 2000, p. 172).

5. Between 1980 and 1987, Britain's real education spending per capita declined by 1.8 per cent per annum while Germany's increased by 4.8 per cent (OECD, autumn economic studies 1991).

6. In 1989, Britain spent 5.8 per cent of GDP on healthcare, compared with 8.2 per cent in West Germany.

7. Whereas Germany has 9.6 doctors per 1000 people, Britain has 1.6.

Coates points the way when he writes that 'behind the institutional differences of the two systems [German and British] lie different relationships between financial and industrial fractions of each national capitalism class' (2000, p. 176), something which I referred briefly to above in regard to the hegemonic role played by Germany's bank-industrial oligarchy in its initial industrialisation. But, he does not go far enough. He needs to take his analysis one step further, to show that these 'institutional differences' originate in the realm of the accumulation process itself through which capital expands. While accumulation cannot occur without a qualitative transformation of materials in the production process, what classic Marxist theory expresses as M-C-M' (or to be a little more precise, M-C-C'-M') – (whereby circulating money capital is invested in the production of commodities which are then sold for a profit and thereby re-transformed back into circulating money capital – as Overbeek explains, the interdependence of circulation and production 'is not confined by spatial limits ... [and] can take place in quite distinct geographical locations' (1990, p. 25). There is no reason, therefore, why the owners of money capital need rely on domestic industry for accumulation to occur. In any particular country, productive and money capital – industrial and financial capital – can be totally independent of one another. Nor do the *owners* of capital need have anything directly to do with the *employers* of capital in the productive process, if the former, in return for lending this money capital to the latter, are able to 'absorb' a share of the eventual surplus, in the form of interest, fees or arbitrage profit (Harvey, 1982). This, as Overbeek (1990) points out, 'is of course exactly what British financiers have been doing since the last quarter of the nineteenth century'. The capital the City controls is therefore 'abstract' in the sense that it is 'without specific commitments to concrete production' (Harvey, p. 267) and hence 'spatially indifferent' (Lash and Urry, 1987, p. 85).

Thus, although impossible for capitalism as a whole to replace M-C-M' with M-M', it is perfectly logical for an individual capitalist or a group of capitalists, say bankers or financiers, to do so. If, in addition, they can become hegemonic within a particular state, as the City of London merchant banking community was able to be in Britain in the nineteenth century, then the institutional structure necessary to support and perpetuate such a form of tangential accumulation will itself become dominant. For the logic of accumulation is such that it determines the evolution of an institutional structure necessary for a particular form of accumulation to take place; what Screpanti (1999) calls an 'accumulation governance structure' (AGS). Thus, the essential institutional differences between the German and British models are rooted in the differences between the form of accumulation, or AGS, dominant or hegemonic in each country. It is this, which determines the particular relationship each nation's banking sector has with industry and industrial investment.

In the case of Germany, where initial industrialisation determined that accumulation could only be derived nationally and was dependent directly on successful industrial development, the bankers and financiers had no alternative but to accept, as Cox points out, 'that their own future viability depend[ed] upon the long-term performance of the productive sectors of the economy which they must facilitate and defend in their own self-interest' (1986, p. 4). This reality determined the evolution of industrial banking. The longer the term on which the bankers had to supply investment loan capital, the greater was their need to ensure for the efficient, profitable organisation of the production process, something which they could only do by forming a close working relationship with management. It also determined that the banking sector welcomed some degree of state intervention in the market, if this worked to the benefit of industry. They favoured, therefore, an active industrial policy, which might include, for example, export and loan guarantees, preferential interest rates and a low exchange rate regime. Finally, and most importantly for the German people, it rationalised the importance of investing in the training of engineers and other skilled industrial labour, as well as for the provision of an infra-structure and an accommodation with the labour force, without which industry could not operate at an

optimal level. In addition, the extent to which these primary requirements could not be provided without the intervention of the state, did,
to a great extent, define Germany as an 'enabling state' (Streek, 1997,
p. 38).

In Britain, however, the hegemonic position of the City's merchant
banking community, whose interests lay in the wider global economy
and did not rely on 'national' industrial development, determined that
the financial institutions were unwilling to make any unnecessary concessions or take any unnecessary risks in relation to British industry.
Their responsibility was defined purely in terms of their shareholders'
interests, which was to maximise short-term profit and minimise long-
term risk. Given the problems posed by an uncertain future it was
perfectly logical, therefore, for them to want to keep investment capital
as liquid and secure as possible, favouring short-term over long-term
loans and safe investments over more risky ventures. They also called for
an unregulated, as opposed to a restrictive, international financial
market, so that, according to Cox (1986), they could protect their profitability by making requisite international investments whenever optimal domestic investment opportunities were unavailable. This implies
that at least, all things being equal, they gave preference to investing in
Britain's domestic economy. Yet, I would not expect investment decisions to be made on any basis other than on the optimal computation of
profitability vs. risk.

Naturally, the City bankers had no vested interest in involving themselves in industry. They were also suspicious of any investments that
could not be securitised, i.e. traded in the market. Their preference was
for dealing in 'paper' transactions, however ephemeral or 'fictitious' –
from bonds, shares, government debt and bills of exchange to derivatives, such as options and financial futures. Anything, as long as it could
be traded in the market, so that investment capital could, if necessary, at
a moment's notice be reconstituted into circulating money capital.
Logically, it should be no surprise that British financial institutions
were also vehemently opposed to any state role in the market, unless
it was to deregulate unwanted restrictive practices. For example, unlike
their German counterparts, they were opposed to the state offering
industry preferential export loan finance and guarantees. They being,
on the one hand, indifferent to any advantage this might have brought
industry, while on the other, very conscious that this would have the
effect of removing the market mechanism from organising commercial
credit, the very *raison d'être* for the City and the basis on which their
income accrued (Burn, 2000).

Again, as with the German model, in Britain, the extent to which these primary requirements could not be provided without the intervention (or non-intervention) of the state, did, to a great extent, determine the role of the state: for example, Britain's use of 'gunboat diplomacy' to open up and keep open international markets and maintain international peace (something which is surely still determining, to some extent, Britain's present day stationing of troops in various corners of the world). It also defined the ideological credo on which the hegemonic logic of accumulation could be rationally defended. This accounts for Britain's 'night-watchman' state model, especially the evolution within the British Treasury of the rationale of the balanced budget that to a great extent was determined by the loss of revenue from customs duties and tariffs which followed the adoption of free trade. This, in turn defined the 'Treasury view' of non-intervention in the market, which, to be effective, was then institutionalised within government in terms of the control of costs rather than the planning of optimal investment. Significantly, during two world wars when an industrial capability was essential, the Treasury was demoted in government, with the Chancellor of the Exchequer not even getting a seat in Churchill's War cabinet. Britain's dominant internationalism also explains the adoption of the ideological underpinnings associated with a *laissez-faire* political economy, especially neoclassical economics, which, in the last twenty years has reached a level of orthodoxy which has seen it removed from the political arena to become a pseudo-science; its mechanistic, increasingly mathematical rationale, gold-plating the Anglo-Saxon model with unassailable truth. Interestingly, as Phillips (2000) points out, Alfred Marshall, the founding father of neoclassical economics, had an essentially 'nostalgic' view of industrial development. Rather than looking forward to the large-scale capital intensive industrialisation associated with the Second Industrial Revolution in Germany, Marshall looked back to Britain's First Industrial Revolution of small competing, self-financing manufacturers.

As well as keeping capital as liquid as possible, the logic of the Anglo-Saxon model has been to maximise loan income and to promote free trade and keep global markets open, opposing any form of protectionism. The institutional structure that evolved to support this model was designed to do just that and nothing more. Unlike Germany, in Britain the provision of an educated, skilled industrial workforce, and the other accoutrements of industrialisation were unnecessary, as the City's elite did not rely on them to make their fortunes. Education for the City was a private affair, concerned traditionally with teaching the classics and inculcating a culture of 'gentlemanly capitalism', that, by default, instilled a spirit of anti-industrialism. British industry, therefore, as well as being starved of long-term, cheap investment funding, had invariably to do without the latest capital equipment and the highly skilled workforce necessary to operate it. Instead it turned to raising capital in the equity market, institutionalising even further a short-termist logic which works contrary to effective long-term industrial planning and development, and to relying on extracting greater productivity from a relatively under-skilled workforce, by getting it to work longer hours, rather than from introducing more sophisticated technology into the production process. This goes a long way to explaining why, even today, the British work longer hours than that in any other country in Western Europe. That Britain's culture of anti-industrialism persists into the twenty-first century is clear. It is demonstrated by the fact that, unlike Germany, in Britain engineering is still afforded very low professional status (Marsh, 1995). One would not expect British industrial firms to be run by engineers and technologists, as is the rule in Germany. Invariably in Britain, control of costs rather than production efficiency defines business culture. So much so that even engineering firms tend to be run by accountants. More basically, this anti-industrialism is demonstrated by the fact that Britain continues to spend a lower percentage of its GDP on education than most other Western European states and, as a recent OECD report has shown, has one of the worst literacy levels in the industrialised world.[19] Kurt Liedtke, former managing director of Robert Bosch UK made this revealing statement in 1995, 'What I've always admired in Britain is the excellent education of the elites. But for those lower down the scale it is different. I have the feeling that the government ignores the significance of the basic education of the masses' (*ibid.*). While these observations imply a neglect of Britain's state education system which is both economically absurd and morally repugnant, as I've tried to demonstrate in this chapter, in terms of the form of accumulation (the AGS) hegemonic in Britain, it is perfectly rational.

Essentially then, however impossible it may be in the long-run for capital as a whole to go straight from M to M', bypassing C, it is a perfectly rational course of action for individual owners of capital to take, if they can and are allowed to do so. In fact, it is illogical to invest in building a factory, buying equipment and hiring labour to procure a surplus in the relative long-term, if it can be procured tangentially through a shorter, more liquid, less risky investment. If, however, accumulation is predominantly derived nationally, the owners of money capital become much more dependent on successful industrial development. This reality determines a requirement, not only for long-term capital funding but also for labour, which only an accommodation with all sections of society could harmoniously supply. This, in turn, determines the need for education and healthcare, pensions etc. The question considered in the following section then is to what extent are changes presently taking place in Germany's financial sector leading to a restructuring of the governance of accumulation, one which is essentially independent of the long-term development of Germany's 'national' industrial base.

Restructuring the governance of German accumulation

In October 2000, the *Financial Times*, in a survey on German banking and finance, seemed rather delighted to announce that the German government's abolition of capital gains tax would 'accelerate' the transformation of business culture in Germany based on 'shareholder value', a transformation which over the previous four years had been 'so profound that it is now irreversible' (Barber, 2000a). Looking at the situation from the perspective of March 2001 (with global equity markets in disarray and the structural imbalances in the US economy of a burgeoning trade deficit and negative private savings becoming suddenly more visible) I wonder if the Anglo-Saxon modellers can still be so optimistic. Whether we get some respite or if this is the beginning of a global recession, I would expect that Germany's honeymoon with equity culture is over, although the collapse of the *Neuer Markt* has had *Bild* talking more in terms of a 'first-class funeral'.[20] What is clear is that the purer the Anglo-Saxon model, dominated as it is by the power of global financial capital largely divorced from the productive economy and by the market control of credit, the more likely it is to be prone to both inflationary and deflationary pressures and systemic crisis. Clearly, in an interdependent global trading market, especially given Germany's dependence on exports, a fall in US consumer spending will be quickly translated into a decline in German industrial growth. Nothing new there. However, the more that Germany's stock market is intertwined in its financial system, the more German households will be exposed to risk. The more that German capital is rooted in a set of interconnected national equity markets with the US at its hub, the more susceptible will be the German economy to an international capital crisis triggered by a dramatic fall in equity prices. For if this were to lead to the wholesale destruction of credit in the US, it will spread like a computer virus throughout the whole system.

However, as I explained in the introduction to this chapter, there is very little agreement as to how pure an Anglo-Saxon economy Germany can expect to become, if at all. Yet, if a form of accumulation based on the logic of money capital can become dominant in Germany, as it is in Britain, then we can anticipate the evolution of an institutional structure necessary for that particular form of accumulation to take place. I therefore return to the question: 'To what extent can internationalism become hegemonic in Germany?' I left off discussion of the German banking system by explaining that while the big commercial banks had evolved into global players, which the abolition of capital gains tax could only but reinforce, the existence of Germany's public and cooperative banks had ensured a level of domestic competition that precluded the Anglo-Saxon 'cult of equity' from being simply transferred to the *Mittelstand*. Yet, now these banks are themselves coming under threat of institutional change, both endogenously and exogenously, as the domestic unravelling of cross-shareholdings between Germany's big commercial banks and insurers following the reform of capital gains tax, interact with intensifying international competition and US- and EU-sponsored homogenisation of banking and accounting regulation around the Anglo-Saxon model, to drive a process of organisational convergence among the three German banking sectors and between them and their European and foreign competitors. Six distinct developments in this process can be identified.

First, the inability of the small under-capitalised cooperative and public savings banks to compete effectively in the provision of financial services in a European-wide integrated financial market is prompting intersector mergers to take place which can only but undermine their presence at local level, their very *raison d'être*. The network of *Landesbanken*, where profitability is traditionally low, is also facing mounting pressure to restructure and deregulate. While, up until now, these have been largely resisted by the *Länder* (federal state) governments, eager to retain control of such important economic policy tools, they have been unable to prevent a movement towards greater centralisation from taking place. This process was given impetus, initially after German reunification, when the eastern *Landesbanken* began to merge with their western counterparts, and more recently, following European monetary union and the move towards creating an integrated financial market in the EU. In addition, the *Landesbanken* have lost out in eastern Germany vis-à-vis the big three commercial banks, which moved quickly after reunification to grab market share (Deeg, 1999).

Second, the public status of the *Sparkassen* and *Landesbanken* as bankers to the *Mittelstand* is under threat from EU anti-subsidy laws, which, in turn, is putting them, once more under threat from privatisation. In this the EU is responding to complaints from not only British and French private bank associations, but also Germany's own federal association of private banks, the *Bundesverband deutscher Banken* (*BdB*), who rightly claim that the savings banks possess an unfair advantage by having their liabilities publicly guaranteed (Lutz, 1999). As Guido Hoymann of Bankhaus Metzler, a private Frankfurt bank, peevishly points out, 'the public-sector banking system is a way of legitimising loss-making' (Harnischfeger, 2000). Yet, should this guarantee be revoked the *Landesbanken* will loose their AAA credit status, which is especially important in regard to long-term debt.[21] This, in turn will force them to reduce their capital-lending ratio, either by holding more capital or by reducing the extent of their loans.[22] Either way, funds available for lending to the *Mittelstand* will tend to fall while the cost of their borrowings will tend to rise.[23] As the public banks' reduced capital base impacts on their ability to compete with the commercial banks, they will then have to cut services and shed businesses becoming more vulnerable to the logic of both privatisation and merger as a way forward, despite their powerful political support (Mayor, 2000b). This explains why Frankfurter *Sparkasse* has already started making plans to convert itself into a listed company.[24] Then, without the *Landesbanken* to hold down the cost of finance, *Mittelstand* firms will be increasingly drawn to the external equity markets, as an alternative means of procuring funding, accelerating the move from a 'bank-based' towards a 'securities market-based' corporate culture centred around the short-term optimisation of share value. In addition, if the EU can stop the cooperative and public savings banks from subsidising the provision of finance to industry, it is only a matter of time before they begin taking an interest in the activities of state and federal development banks such as *Kreditanstalt für Wiederaufbau* (*KfW*) and the *Deutsche Ausgleichbank* (*DAB*), which provide the *Mittelstand* with subsidised long-term funding (Harm, 1992).

Third, the future of the *Mittelstand* is also being defined by the tax disadvantage private firms will face, vis-à-vis limited liability corporations, when the Schröder government's capital gains tax reforms are introduced, encouraging the former, who remain for the most part legally defined as sole-proprietors i.e. *Personenunternehmen*, to convert into the latter, GmbHs (*Gesellschaft mit beschrankter Haftung*). The family-based control of many privately owned *Middelstand* firms is, in any case, under threat, as generational differences and cultural changes make successful successional progression, from one generation to another, increasingly unlikely, leading them inevitably, via mergers and acquisitions, to the private equity market and publicly owned corporate sector. As a recent report in the *FT* made clear, bringing *Mittelstand* companies with succession problems to the market, is 'becoming the bread-and-butter of private equity and leveraged finance in Germany' (Grant, 2000). Together these changes will fundamentally restructure German industry. For as Max Graf Drechsel of HSBC Private Equity in Germany predicts, they will lead directly to the 'spinning-off of business through management buy-outs' out of which 'a whole new *Mittelstand* will grow up' (Atkins and Enzweiler, 2000).

Fourth, the German government, in a further step to realise its 'vision', as Barber and Simonian (2001) poetically explain, 'of Germany as the dynamic hub of Europe's financial world', is proposing to reorganise the Bundesbank so as to create a six-member executive board containing no representatives from Germany's federal states. Clearly, if this goes ahead it will give the Bundesbank more authority over the nine *Landesbanken*. Taken together, these moves towards a greater centralisation of the German banking system suggest a homogenisation of investment funding. The extent to which competition will be thereby reduced, will, I believe, result in a commensurate increase in the power of Germany's commercial banks and global capital over Germany's domestic economy. Already, Commerzbank has 'hinted' it would welcome selling 20–30 per cent of its stock to a US investment bank, such as J. P. Morgan. As the *Economist* explained, 'the idea, presumably, would be to trade access to Germany's *Mittelstand* firms, which increasingly look to raise capital in markets, for investment-banking clout and technology'.[25]

Fifth, alterations in the institutional structure that determine the character of investment is being matched by even more significant changes in those which determine savings. While three out of four Germans still continue to place a part of their savings in the *Sparkassen* and cooperative banks, providing them with a low-interest or interest-free capital base with which to service local industry, this habit is on the decline. During the 1990s, therefore, the total value of these savings fell by 26 per cent and is still falling (Sanderson, 2000). Not only did the Bundesbank's approval of domestic money market funds in 1994 and the introduction of telephone banking combine to woo away some of the savings banks retail customers, but Germany finally began to embrace shareholder culture (Gray, 1996). An increasing attraction to the easy money that a long bull market appeared to guarantee, coupled with the emergence of the so-called 'erbengeneration' (benefiting from the liquidity of inherited wealth) plus the growing perception of the necessity for investing in the nascent grey capital market as the German government looked down a retirement 'black hole' and began making noises that state pension levels could not be guaranteed indefinitely, combined together and began to turn Germany towards an appreciation of shareholder culture (Targett, 2000). And in the world of the smart investor it is neither sensible nor cool to let your savings idle for *groschen* in the local *Sparkasse*. Instead they are demanding higher returns on their savings and are moving into securities (Deeg, 1999). This, in turn, is precipitating a fundamental restructuring of Germany's financial services sector towards the creation of powerful *bancassurers*, as Germany's insurance companies attempt to establish an immediate presence in the private pension market by seeking access to a means of product distribution though mergers and takeovers of German banks. If Targett (2000) is correct, it seems Germany's 'sleeping giant' is finally waking up to the 'cult of the equity'. Beginning with the partial privatisation of Deutsche Telecom in 1996, share ownership expanded dramatically, especially in 2000, when online brokerage accounts alone rose from 1.4 million to 3.9 million in 2000 and the number of Germans investing in equity-based funds doubled to 8 million in the first half of the year (Barber, 2000c; Targett, 2000). It would seem then that the public savings banks' access to a cheap capital base is closing.

Finally, the advent of the euro is deepening and unifying capital markets and creating pressure for the establishment of a fully integrated European capital market based on common standards of regulation and corporate governance. However, this process will only further institutionalise an 'arms-length' relationship between banks and industry, especially as the European Commission is driving through standards based on US accounting and legal principles. For, as Lutz (1999) points out, the power of the US through its Securities and Exchange Commission (SEC) to block any attempt by other states or international regimes to apply capital market regulations which 'appear to threaten American interests' (p. 157), means international harmonisation, as such, can be more truthfully described as adapting to US regulations. US pressure is being matched by that from Germany's own global players, the big commercial banks and industrial corporations listed, or planning to list, on the US Stock Exchange, who must anyway conform with American standards such as the GAAP (General Accepted Accounting Principles).[26] This poses a major problem for the German model, as the principle of transparency which pervades this standard, in the name of protecting the investor and increasing corporate clarity, acts to further entrench the rationality of short-termist shareholder value and is antagonistic to bank dominated 'insider-systems' of corporate governance which apply in Germany and Continental Europe (Bebchuk, 1999, cited in Edwards and Nibler, 2000).

German accounting principles reflect the German model. Based on the lowest value principle, they legally bind German firms to value their assets historically. German 'book' values are therefore substantially undervalued in terms of their true present-day market price. This facilitates the building up of 'hidden reserves' and a little creative accounting or 'income smoothing', which further reinforces, as Edwards and Nibler make clear, a tendency 'to bias downwards the book value of equity as a measure of the true market value of equity capital, and bias upwards the market-to-book ratio as a measure of returns to minority shareholders' (2000, p. 254). Yet these principles can not surely endure. The 1999 law, *Kapitalaufnahmeerleichterunggesetz* (KapAEG), which reformed accounting standards in regard to the raising of capital and the sanctioning of consolidated balance sheets in line with IAS/GAAP standards have already moved Germany towards Anglo-Saxon-style accounting methods. The German government's failure to defend traditional Continental European accounting principles in the EU, together with its championing of *Finanzplatz Deutschland*, as described above, suggest that further progress is inevitable (Lutz, 2000). And all this, at a time when major revolution in the 'philosophy of accounting', known as *fair value* accounting, is being promoted through the IAS, which is the antithesis of German principles. Demanding yet greater transparency, and making firms ever more susceptible to the fluctuations in global equity markets and more responsive to the inexorable logic of shareholder value, they will tend to place a premium on assets which are easy to price i.e. that can be traded on deep and liquid markets (Peel, 2001). Long-term loans which cannot be easily securitised will, in response, become relatively more expensive and institutionally illogical.

Conclusion: what future for the German model

Clearly, the abolition of capital gains tax is pushing at an open door, and one through which this particular horse has already bolted. To the Schröder government, the unravelling of bank-industry cross-shareholdings is perfectly rational in terms of the inexorable logic that defined *Finanzplatz Deutschland* – to occupy what Story describes as the 'no-man's land between the cosmopolitan pull of London and the national pull of domestic institutions' (1997, p. 245). Yet, with this Trojan Horse in place it is going to be almost impossible to maintain an effective firewall between the national and the global dimensions, as Schröder himself has already discovered in his fight to withstand pressure from the EU for removal of state guarantees to the *Landesbanken*. Suzanne Lütz is optimistic, believing 'institutional structures' can continue to hold back 'externally induced processes of adaption' (2000, p. 167), especially those relating to German federalism. Not so the *FT* which recently announced, 'the icepack is starting to break up around Germany's public sector and mutual banks'.[27] They predict that without their AAA credit rating these banks will be forced into consolidation with the big commercial banks, leading to a high-return retail sector. This would suggest that the years of easy money and long-term stability for the *Mittelstand* are nearing an end. Before Lionel Jospin can say, 'yes to the market economy, no to the market society', the logic of accumulation will do the rest. Only at an EU level can this process be reversed, which given its acceptance of the US-UK capital adequacy accord and much else of the Anglo-Saxon model, looks highly unlikely this side of a major capitalist crisis along the lines of 1931 (Kapstein, 1994).

Notes

1. On 21 December 1999.
2. *The Economist*, 8 January 2000.
3. For discussion of organised capitalism see Winkler (1974) and Lash and Urry (1987).
4. Especially the big three: Deutsche Bank, Commerzbank and Dresdner Bank.
5. Deutscher Bundestages. Offentliche Anhorung, May 1990, Protokoll nr. 74, pp. 130–31. Cited in Story (1997, p. 256).
6. Ralph Atkins, *Financial Times*, 23 March 2001, p. 33.
7. See Albert (1993); Coates (1999) and Deeg (1999). For a comprehensive review of the 'models of capitalism' debate see Coates (2000).
8. A consensus that emerged in the late 1980s among the 'political' Washington of the US Congress, the Administration and the 'technocratic' Washington of the IMF, World Bank and think tanks, based on neoliberal principles of free trade, 'sound money' and the promotion of a minimalist, non-interventionist state.
9. See Schonfeld (1965).
10. Coates (2000, p. 3).
11. E.g. see Palan and Abbott, 1999.
12. Defined as firms with less than DM 100 million turnover and fewer than 500 employees (Deeg, 1999, p. 252).
13. Although the concept *Finanzplatz Deutschland* was not formally introduced by the Finance Ministry until 1992 (Deeg, 1999, p. 92).

14. This sector accounts for approximately 99 per cent of firms, 66 per cent of employment, 44 per cent of gross investment and just less than 50 per cent of GDP (Deeg, 1999, p. 252).
15. Public savings banks provide 37 per cent of total credit business and 41 per cent of all depository business; cooperative banks 14.4 per cent and 19.6 per cent;, and the large commercial banks 24 per cent and 26 per cent respectively (Sanderson, 2000, p. 54). Together they make up 47 per cent of total German bank assets (Deutscher Bundesbank, September 2000).
16. Including the freedom of regional offices to set their own interest rates on saving deposit accounts (Deeg, 1999, p. 67).
17. Public liability is enshrined in two guarantees extended to the banks creditors: *Anstaltslast* and *Gewährträgerhaftung*.
18. *Financial Times*, 30 March 2001, p. 22.
19. OECD, 2000.
20. *The Economist*, 28 October 2000, p. 132.
21. *Ibid.*, 9 December 2000, p. 129.
22. In fact, in December 1999 this situation provoked Standard & Poor to cut the credit rating of some of the *Landesbanken* from AAA to A (Murray, 2000).
23. This tendency will be further enhanced when, if as predicted, revision of the Basel Committee's 1988 Capital Accord in 2004 alters the rules governing capital-lending ratios in accordance with level of risk, as measured by private credit agencies such as Moody's (Dwight, 2001, p. 44).
24. FT. Com, 16 January 2001, Lex Column.
25. *The Economist*, 27 May 2000, p. 117.
26. Daimler Chrysler, VEBA, Deutsche Telecom, SGL Carbon AG and Hoechst have already done so (Lutz, 2000, p. 163). As Loewendahl points out that even as Daimler-Benz, the company had altered 'bureaucratic control systems' so as to move them nearer 'globalised "Anglo-Saxon" profit and loss cost control mechanisms' (1999, p. 89). Siemens had done the same.
27. Lex Column, *Financial Times*, 26 November 2000.

5
Rethinking Resistance: Contesting Neoliberal Globalisation and the Zapatistas as a Critical Social Movement

Iain Watson

Social unrest with globalisation is gathering pace. The Zapatistas in Chiapas, the 1995 revolts in France, the battles in Seattle, Davos, Prague and the annual May day protests in London all indicate growing concern with the social vicissitudes of the ideas and institutions of the free global market (Amoore, 2000a; Escobar and Alvarez, 1992; Haynes, 1997; Krishnan, 1995). Moreover the linking of local concerns to global structures is an intriguing paradox of a globalisation process causing discontent whilst simultaneously forging solidarities that may cut across traditional class, age, gender and ethnic differences. The globalisation of capital may be proving a prophetic Marx correct (Fukuyama, 1991) as protest groups coin phrases such as 'we have to be as transnational as capital' to indicate that if capitalism has entered a new global era, then counterforces to it must similarly adopt such strategic coordination (Sklair, 1998).[1]

Critical IPE responses have tended to be understood and practised through the theory and practice of neo-Gramscian readings of social movements. Such readings argue that a transnational class is cultivating and orchestrating a project of interlocking ideas and institutions to generate a climate for accumulation in the present *and future* direction of the global political economy. In turn this has precipitated 'post-modern' responses to the 'metanarrative' of global struggle, which celebrate alternative localised and context-specific struggles. This chapter will challenge the conceptual and strategic rudiments of this debate by re-examining what it means to engage with and confront a politics of resistance to globalisation.[2] However, the chapter calls for an alternative politics of resistance *beyond* neo-Gramscian critical IPE that challenges the perceived understanding of post-modern resistance by focusing upon the activity of *critical* social movements which *rethink* and *re-orientate* the central themes of the Enlightenment. In elucidating their grievances, objectives and strategies these social movements refuse, through their actions, any kind of ideological/conceptual imposition of intellectual boundaries and activate within and across different political spaces and different political times. Such movements are *critical* in the sense that they not only challenge the authoritarian state 'out there' but they challenge the conceptual and strategic routines of what it means to confront power and to confront the political 'in here' (Walker, 1988).

The chapter shows how the Ejército Zapatista de Liberación Nacional (EZLN) (Zapatista National Liberation Army) that mobilised in Mexico in 1994, responding to the vicissitudes of neoliberal modernisation, has articulated a distinctive form of political struggle that is not based upon near-utopian visions of a future. Instead the EZLN has cultivated an encouraging *rethinking* of the site and practices of Mexican sovereignty, the site and nature of Mexican modernisation, and the institutions and practices of democracy. The EZLN also cultivates a distinctive political resistance that problematises the site and meaning of 'being political'. Using the work of Michel Foucault the chapter shows how critical social movements critically explore and redefine the meaning and nature of political protest, political community and political power (Rabinow, 1991; Patton, 1997). Such an input into critical IPE and a revisiting of 'post-structuralism' offers important conceptual and strategic insights for galvanising a truly *critical* IPE.

Reconnoitring post-modernism: themes and approaches

Neoliberalism and its maxim 'there is no alternative', coupled with the end of real existing socialism in 1989, seemed to have finished Marxism in theory and practice. Marxist revolutionary theories of development/ underdevelopment were radical alternatives to the liberal 'theories of growth model' promoted by Western liberal capitalism. Marxist and neo-Marxist theory heralded a distinctive understanding of the relationship between theory and practice where *organic* intellectuals sought to advise and guide revolution. However, Marxist development theory was rooted in the very Enlightenment project inhabited by its main liberal adversaries. Leys notes:

> the theory of social and economic development, in the original and most useful meaning of the term, is not in crisis. On the contrary the legacy of thinkers from Condorcet through Hegel and Marx,

to Francis Fukuyama who have speculated about the dynamics and directions of the evolution of human society, has never seemed more valuable, as the pace of technological change accelerates and the perils of a self regulating global market become rapidly clearer.

(1996, p. 41)

Yet the global expansion of capitalism indicates that Marx was right. Whilst labour resistance to global capital on a global scale is still pretty unlikely, resistances to neoliberal restructuring are occurring at an accelerated pace. However the old model of state-socialism, and the reclaiming of economic and political sovereignty in the face of global structures, also seems unlikely. Continuing this theme Leys writes:

> What is in crisis or more accurately what is no longer possible thanks to that same global market is development conceived as a project for change undertaken collectively by the population of a single, medium sized country, acting through the state.
>
> (*Ibid.*)

The crisis in radical development theory based on the actions of the state and the apparent outdated theories of dependency led some to look for alternative paths to (and interpretations of) development. Responses have varied; from establishing 'better' scientific theories of explanation to the development of *subaltern* studies characterised by a rejection of grand programmatic alternatives by focusing upon the reflexivity of concrete agents and institutions (Mallon, 1994). Intellectual energy is directed to the concrete/specific development *studies* galvanised by new social movements activating in civil society and reacting to diverse issues such as protecting ethnic rights, the plight of the homeless, empowering democracy and social justice and protecting the environment. Such a politics operates at a community/grassroots level and outside conventional political institutions. Throughout the 1990s this intellectual effort became known as 'post-modernism' and it precipitated methodological and political controversy.[3]

Neo-Gramscian responses to neoliberal globalisation

For conventional IR/IPE the theory and practice of social movements was initially seen to be ontologically and epistemologically peripheral (Mittelman, 1996; Murphy and Tooze, 1996; Pasha, 1996). For critical writers the actions of these individuals and groups at the margin of modernist/state-centric thinking and practice represented forces for exploration in a world of exclusions and exploitations (Ashley and Walker, 1990). Yet the questions remain. Are they conceptually (and politically) significant? Where does their actual power reside? Scepticism is understandable as social movements and the 'high' actors of international relations contained by the boundaries of state sovereignty seem to operate in ontologically different realms unable to conceptually and strategically impinge on each other (Walker, 1991, 1993, 1994, 1999). Despite this, critical academic analysis has rejected the teleological and deterministic assumptions of globalisation and instead focused upon the likely agents of change which have aimed to 'bring politics back in'. Underpinning much of this analysis has been a renewed interest in the ideas of Antonio Gramsci.

In contrast to a deterministic/structural Marxism, Gramsci sought to inject an anti-deterministic richness into the Marxist tradition and to understand how a specific capitalist mode of production was able to maintain and legitimate itself in the face of crisis tendencies. Gramsci argued that the dominant classes of capitalism maintained their leadership (or hegemony) through a conducive and coordinated (yet specifically situated) myriad of interlinkages of ideas, institutions and social forces. Class leadership was not only maintained through the coercive powers of the bestial state but it was simultaneously (and more importantly perhaps) maintained by consent located in, and transmitted through, the institutions of civil society and the realm of common sense. Gramsci was interested in the way the dominant institutions of capitalism related to and reinforced such narrow and false conceptions of the world. Gramsci sought to *historicise* and unpack what were traditionally believed to be 'natural' social, economic and political institutions. For Gramsci history was undecided and social change was a cumulative yet a non-repetitive processes. By elucidating a complex account of ideology Gramsci sought to deliver a politics of resistance to the hegemonic power of the ruling class blocs of capital accumulation. His concepts were markedly based upon the conflicts of ideas and contests *within* the emerging nation-state.

Gramsci's ideas have attracted considerable attention in disciplines such as IPE and have been significant in the discussion of cultivating alternative *world* orders. Gramsci's ideas on hegemony are transposed to an understanding of how states maintain their power and influence in the international system as well as focusing upon the shifts in forms of neoliberal economic accumulation on a global scale, the emergence of new class relations and how they are legitimised. This induced the fit between the ideas and institutions of transnational class blocs, international organisations, the role of the state and the emergence of new relationships forged between a variety of global social forces.[4] Here it is felt that local resistance becomes parochial and fragmented. As suggested by Amoore *et al.* (1997), the

> future success of resistance movements to neoliberal globalisation may be brought a step closer if resistance organisations themselves highlight the close relationship between the state and globalisation . . . to be successful resistance to neoliberalisation must be conducted in a coordinated manner on a local, national, regional and global level.
>
> (p.195)

Movements such as the EZLN are identified as part of an embryonic counter-hegemonic bloc to the ideas and institutions of neoliberal globalisation. As Cox argues, they are

> indicative of something moving in different societies across the globe towards a new vitality of a bottom up movement in civil society as a counterweight to the hegemonic power structure and ideology. This movement is however relatively weak and uncoordinated. It may contain some of the elements but has certainly not attained the status of a counterhegemonic alliance of forces on a world scale.
>
> (1999, p. 12)

For some (e.g. Burbach, 1992) the acceptance of neoliberal globalisation began when Nixon took the US off the gold standard in 1971 and after the Cancun Summit in Mexico in 1982 when the US and the Imperial Powers formally launched the era of global neoliberalism and began imposing structural adjustment programmes (*ibid.*). The welfare cuts and wage freezes that accompanied these programmes throughout the 1980s and 1990s crystallised socio-economic and political discontent within Mexico. As Burbach notes:

> the IMF in many cases agreed to help the countries restructure their debt loads but only if they carried out neoliberal economic programmes . . . these policies have failed. They have not induced growth in Latin America only more suffering and economic deprivation.
>
> (*Ibid.*, p. 245)

Among the results of such deprivation and widespread discontent was the birth of the Zapatista National Liberation Army.

On New Year's Day 1994 Subcommandante Marcos, the leading representative of the EZLN, stood on the balcony of the municipal presidency building in the Zocalo of San Cristobel de Las Casas in the highlands of Chiapas, Southern Mexico, and declared war on the government. Marcos read out the following statement:

> Today the North American Free Trade Agreement begins, which is nothing more than a death certificate for the indigenous ethnicities of Mexico, who are perfectly dispensable in the modernisation programs of Salinas de Gortari. Thus the *campeneros* decided to rise up on this same day to respond to the decree of death that the Free Trade Agreement gives them.
>
> (1994)

American journalists saw the EZLN as a Marxist revolutionary movement as the leading participants had once been schooled in the socialist tradition. During the 1960s and 1970s many peasants and Indians left to work in the more lucrative oil regions in Chiapas. They returned in the early 1980s having experienced wage labour, bringing back with them a tide of accentuated class differences and a new capitalist penetration through the introduction of new intensive agricultural technologies. Many returning workers of this ilk now had the capital to purchase modern machinery and were able to hire additional labour. These migrants became the local enforcers or so-called 'caciques' by controlling agricultural production in the highlands through money lending, land rental and sharecropping. Subsistence farmers and Indians in the east and in the Lacandon region were increasingly worse off because they had no access to the new technology which was now being used for intensive agricultural production on the plateaus and to the west.[5]

The end of the so-called 'Mexican economic miracle' after 1965 precipitated the bedrock for a mass mobilisation of radical peasant, worker and Indian groups. The autonomous campesino organisation, the Ejido Union United, was set up in the Chiapas town of Ocosingo around the mid-1970s. The Ejido Union Land and Liberty (Tierra y libertad) was set up in Las Margaritas with the Ejido Union of Peasant Struggle, all coming together under the Union of Unions (UU) or the Ejido Union and Solidarity of Peasant Groups in 1980 (Stephen, 1996). With a raised consciousness in the rural areas, the urban and Marxist-influenced Proletariat Line sent organisers to each of these groups. Campesino movements tied together the fight for land and work with the question of appropriating the means of production. In the rural areas, there were those who encouraged the formation of resistance organisations and the promotion of peasant self-government, while others argued that only armed struggle could provide a real solution. The first vision gave rise to organisations such as the UU and the second to what today has become the EZLN.

The EZLN. Post-modern (not robust globalist): moving to the critical social movements

In contrast to the 'robust globalist' perspectives, post-modernists challenged revolutionary Enlightenment themes because the EZLN seemed to represent a distinctively *novel* politics of resistance *exactly because* it came in the wake of the collapse of the modern bipolar world of the post-Second World War and the ideological exhaustion of most of the national liberation movements (Spegele, 1997). As Burbach claims, the

> Indian rebellion that burst upon the world scene in January is a post-modern political movement. The rebellion is an attempt to move beyond the politics of modernity, whether it be the modernisation of the Salinas de Gortari government or of past national liberation movements.
>
> (Burbach, 1994, p. 113)

Couched in these terms the Indian culture was a reminder of Mexico's unprogressive past. President Salinas (1988–94), in contrast, had stated that Mexicans were living 'in a moment of history' that meant 'looking for new terms of reference' (quoted in Hilbert, 1997). Salinas had emphasised that Mexico must not be construed as a relic and must tune into the progressive beat of neoliberalism which was *the only* (and perhaps paradoxical) way of ensuring Mexican sovereignty/Mexican development. This economic and political programme was a 'new realism' based on a 'unified' and culturally homogenised modern state/political community of territorial integrity. Moreover, the post-modern account was contested with the challenge that the EZLN was

> aware of itself as the product of five hundred years of struggle, that quotes from the Mexican constitution to legitimate its demand that the President of Mexico leaves office, that additionally demands work, land, housing, food, health, education, independence, liberty,

democracy, justice and peace for the people of Mexico, can be called a post-modern political movement when its language is so patently modernist.

(Nugent, 1995, p. 135)

Post-modernism has been rejected for its methodological/philosophical critiques (e.g. see Rosenau, 1990, 1992; Wickham, 1990), but this chapter shows how the EZLN as a *critical* social movement instead seeks to rethink and radicalise the project of the Enlightenment. This alternative reading of the EZLN is characteristic of those writings dedicated to challenging the staid nature of the 'Marxist/post-modern debate' (Foucault, 1991). Interest with critical social movements does not engender a 'better' conceptual understanding of collective action. On the contrary such a one-sided methodology (as much as is reasonably possible) is rejected. Instead an interpretive account of such movements that can reasonably be termed as *critical* is advanced. It is my intention to show how the EZLN rethinks the site and nature of Mexican modernisation and the Enlightenment to develop a modern politics based on an *inclusivity* of the communities of 'many worlds' and through direct political participation. Moreover I argue that the EZLN approaches the nature and meaning of political resistance and political power in ways that resemble the kind of political resistance envisaged by Michel Foucault.

Indeed it might be surprising that such interest would be shown in a resistance from a relatively remote corner of Latin America. I argue that the key to this ambiguity lies in the very nature of the Zapatista struggle itself. I argue that as a *critical* social movement the EZLN has, since 1994, engaged in an exploration of *connections* made by people in terms of their economic, political, social and cultural sites of struggle. Consequently, the EZLN forces a rethinking as to the meaning of *the political* and of the intellectual routines that keep us as we are.

According to Walker there are 'serious limits to the extent to which it is possible to categorise and analyse movements' (1988, p. 62). This should not be construed as a problem as there is always a danger of imposing premature classification onto political processes that have not run their course. Indeed this is an empowering intellectual exercise and politics that recognises that categories like 'revolutionary', 'reformist' or 'counter-revolutionary' are slippery and 'the difficulty of theorising about social movements in general gives an indication why they have become so interesting to people seeking to find some way through the conventional horizons of contemporary political debate' (*ibid.*, p. 7). Ostensibly this introduces a critical enquiry given that, 'it has become necessary to refuse received conceptual boundaries, to search for new forms of under-standing, and to develop a clearer sense of the complex relationship between theory and practice, knowing and being' (*ibid.*, p. 3).

Undoubtedly this ambiguous quality of the struggles in a troubled world of global structures is also of course a notorious weakness. Never-theless Walker suggests that

> although difficult to define, critical social movements are distin-guishable in part by their capacity to recognise and act creatively upon connections among structures, processes and peoples that do not enter significantly into the calculations of conventional political actors.
>
> (*Ibid.*, p. 140).

Foucault, for instance, engaged in a specific intellectual position that was 'different from technocratic or progressive uses of history for insti-tutional reform and from Marxist uses of history for ideological criticism or some global alternative' (Hindess, 1998, p. 80). Foucault's work on the site and nature of power links into the concerns that engender critical social movements. The movements have a concern with a Weberian and authoritarian power, or the authoritarian state out there *to be sure*: but they are also concerned with the rituals, the norms and values of what it means to engage politically 'in here'. Foucault rejected the repression/emancipation dualism and he asked 'why do we think that when we say yes to liberation we say no to power'. Foucault sought

> to explain the consequences of power everywhere...which has in-vaded even those points to where resistance is grounded...the subtle ways in which a yearning to be outside power has been produced by a particular regime and whose operation is obscured as a result of that desire.
>
> (Foucault, in McGowan, 1993, p. 97)

Foucault suggested that the emancipatory/repression dualism is stra-tegically inadequate for capturing the site and nature of power and politics in a politics of resistance. Foucault argued, contrary to concomi-tant Marxist approaches, that

> If power were never anything but repressive: if it never did anything but to say no do you really think one could be brought to obey it? What makes power hold good, what makes it accepted is simply the

fact that it doesn't only weigh on us as a force that says no but that it traverses and produces things, induces pleasure, forms knowledge, produces discourse. It needs to be considered as a productive network which runs through the whole social body, much more than as a negative instance whose function is repression . . . I don't want to say that the state isn't important: what I want to say is that relations of power necessarily extend beyond the limits of state.

(Foucault, in Rabinow, 1991, p. 199)

For Foucault the practice of a concrete micropolitics presupposes that power is conceived not as a sovereign property *per se* but as a strategy of manoeuvres, tactics and techniques all functioning in a network of specific power relations. But then if 'power is everywhere' does not this mean the end of politics? Why fight if the practices and sites of power are so ubiquitous and so all consuming? If there can be no emancipatory practice and knowledge outside the matrix of power/ knowledge then why is apathy and submission not preferable to emancipation? Foucault's response was unequivocal when he stated that

in power relations there is necessarily the possibility of resistance because if there were no possibility of resistance (of violent resistance, flight deception, strategies capable of reversing the situation), there would be no power relations at all. This being the general form I refuse to reply to the question that I am sometimes asked: 'But if power is everywhere there is no freedom'. I answer that if there are relations of power in every social field, this is because there is freedom everywhere.

(*Ibid.*, p. 108)

These relations do not require a revolutionary form of resistance aiming to overthrow sovereign and repressive political power. This alternative form of struggle goes much further than this:

Perhaps too we should abandon a whole tradition that allows us to imagine that knowledge can exist only where the power relations are suspended and that knowledge can develop only outside its injunctions, its demands and its interests. We should admit rather that power produces knowledge that power and knowledge directly imply one another.

(*Ibid.*, p. 245)

As a political and strategic consequence Foucault points out in his later interview entitled 'Space, Knowledge and Power':

> there may, in fact always be a certain number of projects whose aim is to modify some constraints to loosen, or even to break them, but none of these projects can simply by its nature, assure that people will have liberty automatically; that it will be established by the project itself. The liberty of men is never assured by the institutions and laws that are intended to guarantee them.
>
> *(Ibid.)*

The rethinking of what is meant by 'being political' and by 'having political power' has sustained the biography and politics of the EZLN. However like Foucault such a caricature of post-modernism is rejected in favour of a 'different' and inclusive Enlightenment that allows for critical reflection and for the transgressing of limits and boundaries. Foucault wrote:

> This philosophical ethos may be characterised as a limit attitude. We are not talking about a gesture of rejection. we have to move beyond the inside/outside alternative. We have to be at the frontiers. Criticism indeed consists of analysing and reflecting upon limits.
>
> *(Ibid.*, p. 41)

One of the principal themes of the EZLN has been to engender debate on formulating a modern Mexico based upon a recognition of 'difference' that challenges the exclusionary practices of neoliberal state sovereignty. The EZLN has engaged with civil society on this very issue. Subcommandante Marcos stated:

> the official history is as far from reality as the indexes of economic growth and in a world which already suffers the financial terrors of globalisation these have the constancy of a weathervane in the middle of a storm . . . the modernity of the neoliberal rulers in Mexico reveals a dry and empty country.
>
> (NCDM, 1998)[6]

The EZLN has aimed to construct *the true* Mexican modernity and has designated no privileged actor. It invites *other* groups, the peasantry, the workers, the Indians, women, gays and the homeless to create a modernisation, not of suppression and exclusion but one that incorporates 'many worlds'. Consequently through the 1999 National Consultation the EZLN clearly recognised the articulation of capitalism and modernity as being manifested and experienced at concrete sites. This precludes any rash and dogmatic politics of rejection but places the EZLN loosely as a *critical* social movement. Consequently there is increasing importance given to exploring alternative 'development movements' on the basis that 'attempts to encourage development from the top down have often been disastrous' and debate now centres upon 'competing conceptions of what development ought to entail' (Walker, 1988, p. 132). Consequently there is a 'recognition that it is neither necessary nor desirable to confuse economic development with development as such' (*ibid.*, p. 70).

Essentially this all breaks down into three interconnected issues. First, a rethinking of what is meant by 'modernity'. Second a debate on what is the relationship between development, capitalism and state. Third, the strategic issue of how a reorganisation of development and its institutions is to be attempted without recourse to grand narratives of robust globalism. The EZLN engagement with a recognition of a plurality of groups and issues requires an exploration of the way 'alternative conceptions of development must involve the creation of new understandings of work, production and ownership that are more meaningful socially than just processes of individual or aggregate capital accumulation' (*ibid.*). The critical social movements are especially aware that the vagaries of neoliberal modernisation may turn 'into a romanticised idealisation of premodern life' (*ibid.*) and critical social movements problematise the 'notion of a deeply rooted contrast between tradition and modernity so essential to dominant economic and political categories' (*ibid.*, p. 128). Instead critical social movements look for and explore alternative and specific developments which generate dialogue on a development based on the theme of *inclusivity*. Walker argues that

> the concept of development has become problematic in an even more complex and far reaching way than that of security. It has long been subject to bitter theoretical and ideological dispute. As a synonym for progress it has been criticised for all the arrogance of a universalistic reading of History. As a synonym for economic growth, it has been embroiled in a century of debate about the character and consequences of capitalism, industrialism, imperialism and socialism. In some places it is still treated as short hand for the inevitable way forward. Elsewhere quotation marks around it symbolise increasing embarrassment and anger.
>
> (*Ibid.*)

The 1996 San Andres Accords on Indigenous Rights and Culture

The EZLN sought to make San Andres symbolic of a wider-ranging malaise in Mexico and called upon the peoples of Mexico in the 1999 Consultation of Direct Participation and Dialogue to link the struggle in Chiapas with other individuals and groups in different economic, political and cultural sites. The EZLN have recognised that, in cutting across former solidarities and conceptual schematics, all individuals, groups, institutions, classes, ethnic groups, ages and all sides of the political spectrum concerned with the future of Mexico have equally valid points to make if made sensibly and maturely. This is a wish not to specify a definitive grievance or a definitive *programme for change*. Ostensibly the San Andres Accords[7] between the Zapatistas and a governmental peace-making body called for the recognition and creation of autonomous indigenous communities for the 900,000 Indians of Chiapas. Such 'ethnicity' and plurality was to be fundamentally incorporated *within* an inclusive modern Mexico.

Throughout the months of 1995 and 1996 the EZLN had recognised that they could not speak for all Indian peoples. Therefore, a number of guests and advisors, representatives from various NGOs and social movements, intellectuals and anthropologists were invited to Chiapas during 1995 to discuss the Indian question. After November 1995 regional forums were held throughout Mexico to choose various representatives for the dialogues. By 9 January 1996 at San Cristobel, consultations were in full flow and the National Indigenous Forum presided.

In fact, thirty-two indigenous peoples groups and 178 indigenous organisations had gathered in San Cristobel de las Casas. There were various speeches and documents drawn up leading to the final writing of a thirty-nine-page document which was to be discussed with the PRI[8] at the small town of San Andres de Larrainzar. The Federal government allegedly came to San Andres with no actual proposals of their own. The San Andres Accords proposed a radical rethinking of the direction of Mexican economic, political, social and cultural development. San Andres was therefore conceived over a process of grassroots dialogue and discussion and incorporating the views and advice from many worlds, intellectual worlds, anthropological worlds and the Indians. The question of new institutions was discussed openly. But it was clear that this was not a *top down* political decision. The San Andres Agreements were originally drafted for the basis of a new relationship between the state and the indigenous peoples it is necessary to recognise, insure and guarantee rights within an emended federalist framework. Such an objective implies the promotion of reforms and addenda to the Federal Constitution and the laws emerging from it, as well as to State Constitutions and local Judicial Dispositions, to further, on the one hand the establishment of general foundations that may ensure unity and national objectives, and, at the same time, allow the federative entities the true power to legislate and act in accordance to the particularities of the indigenous issues coming before them.

(see EN 7, p. 3)

In order for this to happen these specific demands were made:

1. To urge a profound transformation of the State, as well as of the political, social, cultural and economic relationships with the indigenous peoples, which satisfies their demands for justice.
2. To urge the emplacement of an all inclusive new social agreement, based on the understanding of the fundamental plurality of Mexican society and on the contribution that the indigenous people can make to national unity, beginning with the constitutional acknowledgement of their rights, and in particular, to their right to self-determination and autonomy.
3. The legal reforms to be promoted must originate from the principle of the equality of all Mexicans before the law and judicial organs, and not by the creation of special codes of law that privilege particular people, respecting the principle that the Mexican nation is a pluricultural entity which is originally supported by its indigenous peoples.
4. The constitutional modifications represent one of the most important factors in the new relationship between the indigenous people and the State within the framework of reforming the State so that their demands many find support within the state legal system.

San Andres called for the redistribution of resources and for administrative, economic, social, cultural, educational and judicial resources for the management and protection of public resources responding to the opportunities, requirements and demands of the indigenous peoples. This was based on a supposition that the indigenous communities must be allowed to determine their own development projects and programmes so that the design of this participation may take into consideration the aspirations, needs and priorities of the indigenous peoples. And finally, allowing the indigenous people participation in national and state channels of representation would be part of a new federalism. The tailoring of development towards the indigenous communities also forged a new consensus that

> the Mexican judicial system, both at Federal and State levels must push for the recognition of the indigenous people's right to the sustainable use and the derived benefits of the use and development of the material resources of the territories they occupy or utilise in a form, so that, in a framework of global development the economic underdevelopment and isolation may be overcome. This action implies an increase in and reorientation of social spending.
>
> (*Ibid.*)

Here the EZLN called on the political institutions of Mexico to reflect this inclusivity and accountability to the different and the colourful worlds of Mexico (*ibid.*). Brothers points out that the San Andres Agreements were plagued by immense controversy as the

> talks broke down when the two sides could not agree on language that would enshrine the accords in law, while moves to give the Indians greater autonomy were seen as a sticking point. The rebels quit the negotiating table in September 1996 accusing the government of backtracking on its promises. Negotiations have been stalled ever since. In his statement Marcos insisted the government had to fulfill the San Andres Accords and said what the two parties had already agreed was not negotiable...the government assured that it wanted to find a legal form to express them.
>
> (Brothers, 1998)

The PRI and the EZLN had very different views on the meaning and nature of Mexican modernity. President Zedillo argued that the PRI had, in 1992, in accordance with Indian demands,

> amended Article 4 of the Constitution so as to guarantee the multicultural nature of the nation, based on the diversity of origin of the indigenous peoples, to guarantee them access under conditions of equality, to the jurisdiction of the state and to make additional effort for to promote their full development... the bill of reforms to Articles 4, 18, 26, 53, 73, 115 and 116 of the Political Constitution of the

United Mexican States to make effective the social, economic, cultural and political rights of Mexico's indigenous peoples.[9]

However it was argued that if the EZLN was really proposing an ethnic struggle then why had there been no declaration of *ethnic nationalism* such as Bosnia (Rosset and Cunningham, 1994)? Ethnic concerns for rights and self-determination have to be linked to ethnic ceding from the state. But the dichotomous presentation is limiting. Carrigan notes that in Marcos

> the Zapatistas had found a unique linguist whose mastery of the idioms of both Mexicos allowed him to interpret each to the other. Straddling the historic chasm between the two, Marcos showed there were bridges to build and maps to be drawn to make each accessible to the other.
>
> (1998)[10]

In order to allow for the conditions for the demands of San Andres to be implemented in the 'true' Mexico, the EZLN often playfully invoke the language and imagery of Shakespeare's *Hamlet* – the ghostly chimera that is neoliberalism obscures the real Mexico simmering with colour and fairness underneath. The PRI in turn have claimed that Marcos is betraying the legacy of the Mexican revolutionary Zapata by waking up his restful ghost by challenging the neoliberal project and therefore the future of the state (Long, 1999, pp. 2–3).

Since the breakdown of talks in 1996, riven by these different interpretations of the meaning and nature of modernity and Mexico as a secure and democratic nation-state, there has been an increased militarisation of Chiapas. However the accession of Vicente Fox to the Presidency in 2000 generated new possibilities for dialogue concerning San Andres and the Zapatistas. Such a reorientation of development strategy by the Fox administration is unlikely to be a shift from neoliberalism. However, given new initiatives such as the UN's Global Compact it does show a willingness to engage in a fairer development. Negotiations continue.

Radical democracy

The EZLN reworks the site, meaning and nature of modern ideals such as democracy by connecting indigenous interpretations of democracy with contemporary theories of radical democracy and radical citizenship. The

EZLN envisages a democratic revolution but challenges liberal *and* Marxist revolutionary democratic traditions to exact the recovery of *politics* in an age of global structures. This vision of democratisation is not constructed from *the top down* nor constrained within existing political institutions. Instead the new radical democracy is brought about through a concomitant empowering of citizens through direct political action. Walker has argued that

> democracy does not have a single defining characteristic. It is not to be equated with particular forms of government, with parliaments, representative institutions, party hierachies or national wills. Again the practice of movements are informed by a readiness to pursue different strategies of deepening democracy depending on circumstance.
>
> (1988, p. 133)

Such an alternative understanding of democracy can include both a reforming of existing political institutions and the development of a richer and direct participatory democracy. Thus Walker argues that

> the importance of enhancing democratic processes within economic systems ... leads to a recognition that democratisation is not the equivalent of voting in periodic elections. It requires an ongoing insinuation of people's participation into all aspects of public life ... constant vigilance about the preservation of substantial rights, about how the basic investment conditions of a society are made, about how production is organised and goods distributed, about how cultures, values and ideas are constructed.
>
> (*Ibid.*, p. 7)

Despite the *New World Order* (sic) there is a scepticism with democratic institutions that takes many forms. It takes the form of disengaged apathy cultivated and driven by an elite political rhetoric which stresses in a rather perfunctory manner 'health and education'. Moreover, it seems that all political parties within the established electoral structures tend to have accepted the same *general* kind of agenda, particularly shown by the acceptance of global structures under the axiom that 'there is no alternative' whilst electoral polling and political trends tell a crude tale of political 'winners' and 'losers'. In 1994 Conger wrote:

On January 11, 10 days after guerrillas calling themselves the Zapatista National Liberation (EZLN) launched bold attacks on five towns and an army barracks in the Southern state of Chiapas, television newscaster Jorge Ramos fired a pointed question at a Mexican official 'Senor Consul, is the government concerned that in this election year people might want to vote for an opposition party because it might bring peace instead of staying with the ruling PRI that has brought war to the country?' With that single question, Ramos put the PRI's much touted record of 65 years of social peace on the line.

(p. 270)[11]

However the EZLN's project is not based upon robust globalism for alternative world orders. The First Declaration of the Lacandon Jungle asked for the end to the Salinas dictatorship justified on the basis of the Mexican constitution Article 39 where Mexican national sovereignty 'lies in the people' and that all 'political power emanates from the people, and its purpose is to help the people who have at all times the inalienable right to alter or modify the form of government'.[12] Furthermore as Conger (1994) notes, the Zapatistas 'renounced the standard leftist goals of leading revolution and taking power' by declaring in a communiqué on 25 January 1994 that '[t]here are and there will be other revolutionary organizations. We do not intend to be the one, sole, and true historic vanguard' (*ibid.*).

The EZLN's Second Declaration stated:

> this party... a party that has kept the fruits of every Mexican labourer for itself... cannot be allowed to continue. Understand the corruption of the Presidential elections that sustain the party that impedes our freedom and should not be allowed to continue. We understand the callous fraud in the method with which this party imposes and impedes democracy.
>
> (*Ibid.*)

The EZLN insisted that

> the problem of power in Mexico isn't due just to a lacking of resources. Our fundamental understanding and position is that whatever efforts are made, will only postpone the problem if these efforts are not made within the context of new local, regional and national political relationships marked by democracy, freedom and justice.

The problem of power is not a question of the rules, but of who exercises power.

(*Ibid.*)

In explicitly rejecting protracted and violent revolution they stated:

We are not proposing a New World, but an antechamber looking into a new Mexico. In this sense, the revolution will not end in a new class, faction of a class or group in power. It will end in a form of democratic spaces for political struggle. These free and democratic spaces will be born on the federal cadaver of the state/party system and the traditions of fixed Presidential succession.

(*Ibid.*)

Consequently the EZLN hoped that a new political relationship would be born, a relationship not based in the confrontation of political organisations amongst themselves, but in the confrontation of their political proposals. This would mean that

political leadership will depend on the support of the social classes, and not on the mere exercise of power. In this new political relationship, different political proposals (socialism, capitalism, social democrats, liberalism, Christian Democrats, etc.) will have to convince a majority of the nation whether the proposal is best for the country.

(Salazar *et al.*, 1994)

The EZLN has given each particular political 'ideology' a credence based on the democratic condition that if each political ideology can democratically and without fear of contradiction or hypocrisy convince the majority of peoples of Mexico then it is legitimate. Consequently the EZLN stated that

groups in power will be watched by the people in such a way that they will be obligated to give a regular account of themselves and the people will be able to decide whether they remain in power or not. This plebiscite is a regulated form of consultation among the nation's political participants.

(*Ibid.*)

A few months before the Presidential elections of 1994 Cardenas, leader of the Party of the Democratic Revolution (PRD) had announced the creation of the National Democratic Alliance (ADN) a pluralistic coalition that included parties from across the political spectrum, a multitude of local civic and labour organisations and the Citizens Movement for Democracy. The latter itself was a national coalition of 150 urban community associations, peasant leagues and ecology and human rights groups. In its *Charter for Democratic Change* the ADN set as its goal an end to the 'corporatist and authoritarian system' and the election of a pluralistic Congress that would draft a new Constitution and promote an equitable social policy.

Through the use of consultations the aim was to generate a new form of direct participatory democracy on a national scale that went beyond the party political machine. By June 1994 plans had been set up by the EZLN for a National Democratic Convention (CND) which was to be held in Chiapas prior to the 1994 presidential elections. The NDC was convened between 6 and 9 August 1994 in Guadaloupe Tepeyae, and comprised 6 000 representatives of various interested peasant and Indian movements from all over Mexico. But despite the CND the 1994 (as were the 2000) presidential elections were treated with scepticism by most Mexicans used to the cycle of electoral unaccountability, the lack of representation and post-electoral violence. Nonetheless the fact that 6 000 delegates had made it to the CND indicated a tremor of support for a movement listening to civil society.

There were two facets to the radical democratic programme of the EZLN. First, a willingness to try to *legally* make the existing institutions accountable and transparent; second, to forge a new participatory direct democracy from the grassroots through new channels of decision-making so that people felt 'empowered' and that they could 'make a difference'. There is a radical EZLN commitment to the 'verguenza' as the impertinent asking of questions and the impolite seeking of answers. The model of the radical democratisation of Mexico demanded by the EZLN is based on the way the democratic process is organised in the Indian communities which is built upon direct consultation and direct participatory democracy. Marcos states:

> I can't say when – its not something that's planned – the moment arrived in which the EZLN had to consult the communities in order to make a decision... [A] moment arrives in which you can't do anything without the approval of the people.
>
> (*Ibid.*)

Indeed, the inherent democratic organisation of the EZLN has enraged traditional Marxists and the PRI who have wanted quick and decisive answers to their proposals. A Mexican NGO reported that the communities of an indigenous zone, or area, are the ones who decide at an assembly of all their members whether or not they will belong to the autonomous municipality (Flood, 1999). Moreover,

> It is the communities who elect their representatives for the Autonomous Municipal Council, which is the authority for the municipality. Each representative is chosen from one area of administration from within the autonomous municipality, and they may be removed if they do not comply with the communities mandates... [T]hose who hold a position on the municipal council do not receive a salary for it, although their expenses should be paid by the same communities who request their presence, through cooperation amongst their members.
>
> (Enlace, 1998)[13]

Within each Zapatista community this council meets once a week. Overarching this local community is the Autonomous Municipal Council. This is an autonomous organisation in the sense that it is surgically removed from any PRI-affiliated political organisations and the local government structure. The assembly in each community is integral to each Zapatista community and is based on the equal participation of both women and men. Each assembly within the Zapatista indigenous communities selects its own officers and they also select delegates to participate in one of the six Clandestine Revolutionary Committees. Marcos stated that this was deliberate, consciously immersing oneself and '[S]urrendering [to the communities]' (quoted in Blixen and Fazio, 1995[14]). The EZLN, Marcos argues, is only useful as long as the communities think it is useful to have the EZLN. The Indian organisation

> is another culture, another way of practicing politics. They are not politically illiterate. They have another way of conducting politics. And what those in power want to do now is to teach them political literacy, that is to say, corrupt them within the current political system.
>
> (*Ibid.*)

The question is whether this model of democratic consultation and participation can work at the national level. The EZLN recognises that changes have occurred in Mexico despite their sense of 'betrayal' during the 1994 presidential campaign. This is not simply a demand for peri-odic elections, political parties and more ballot slips. Democracy, Mar-cos explains, should not simply be *accepted* as a corporate machine:

> There are many kinds of democracy. That's what I tell them (the Indians). I try to explain to them. You can do that (to solve by consensus) because you have a communal life. When they arrive at an assembly they know each other, they come to solve a common problem. But in other places it isn't so. I tell them. People live separate lives and they use the assembly for other things.
>
> (*Ibid.*)

This direct democracy is the *empowering* concrete democracy envisaged by the EZLN on a national scale. As such, democracy is not to be equated with particular forms of government with parliaments, representative institutions, party hierachies or national wills.

The 2000 Presidential elections heralded a new era for Mexican polit-ics with the defeat of the PRI's candidate Labastida ending seventy years of PRI power. For many this was a real political and democratic change as it signalled the end of continuity and the PRI's legacy of electoral coercion, patronage and the emergence of true multiparty politics with the accession of Vicente Fox of the National Coalition. There was also a sceptical sense that this was not so much a positive endorsement of Fox but a political weariness with the PRI, a desire for change however limited. Fox's campaign was designed and aimed at the media and this is where scepticism has emerged. There is concern that Fox will not question the doctrine of globalisation, NAFTA, neoliberalism and the concrete problems in Chiapas thereof (Fuentes, 2000). There was also a sense that Fox's victory was based on a cynical strategical supposition that he was the only likely candidate to defeat the PRI. Indeed the once presidential candidate Cardenas of the Party of the Democratic Revolu-tion (PRD) had previously labelled Fox as 'fascist', representing a regres-sive national politics based on a dangerous petty bourgeois nationalism. The role of the PRD intensified in significance during the 1997 mid-term elections as it swept away the PRI's majority in Congress.

Carlos Fuentes[15] argues that there are five 'commandments' for real Mexican democracy. First, to prevent Mexico bleeding itself through post-electoral conflict there must be electoral reform, the consecration of alternation in power and independent electoral organism and clear rules to party access to funding. Second, the implementation of a further four 'articles' of democracy: a working federalism; a true division of powers; electoral statute for Mexico City; and rule of law through reform of corrupt judiciary. Third, reform of the media and its 'comedy of errors'. Fourth, respect for human rights and NGOs; and finally a market economy but with a social dimension and a balance between the public and private sectors. However the EZLN want more than simple reform of the *existing* political system.

What concerns the EZLN is that the euphoria surrounding the 1997 mid-term elections and concomitant academic and political commentary gives the impression that real democratisation is occurring in Mexico. One response would be that Chiapas is undergoing an ongoing campaign of militarisation. Mexico's political system has been based on centralism and corporatism with a definitive symbiosis of party and state.

The 1997 elections in Mexico were held to elect 500 seats in Congress; thirty-two senators and governorships around the country seemed to suggest that in contrast to a strong authoritarianism, Mexican democracy was finally occurring. In the Chamber of Deputies, although the largest party with 29 per cent and 239 seats, the PRI lost majority control. PAN secured 27 per cent gaining 121 seats, the PRD took 26 per cent of the votes with 125 seats, the Green Party 4 per cent for eight seats and finally the Mexican Labour Party (PT) with 3 per cent won seven seats. The PRI lost control of Mexico City's local government in the local elections of 1997 and the mayoral race to the PRD presidential candidate Cardenas. Furthermore, in 1997 Zedillo (then President) had allowed Mexican citizens to form part of the board that oversaw the elections process, the Federal Electoral Tribunal (IFE) and remained committed to changing the system of party funding.[16]

Lawson (1998) argues that the electoral shift in 1997 represented dissatisfaction with the PRI's economic record and its handling of the 1995 economic crisis. But was the democratic space these writers identify in 1997, representative of a profound shift or merely a lack of willingness by the PRI to use its patronage and co-optive powers? Was it merely party political language used as a marketing device to attract the undecided voter? Or could it be interpreted as a recognition by the PRI that it needed to take a competitive edge in a party political system of pluralism, the beginning of a more enriching democratic process? The transfer to democratic electoral politics is not, however, a transfer akin to situations in other authoritarian and military-ruled states and pressures were coming from elsewhere as well (Klesner, 1998). First, there is international pressure from an 'international community' that is less tolerant of electoral intimidation and vote rigging; while second there is domestic pressure from the rise of NGOs and other actors within Mexican civil society.

Within the Mexican political system itself there are anti-systemic elite groups headed by political parties such as the PRD; there are systemic progressives or the neoliberal technocrats; and finally there are the systemic conservatives such as the PRI dinosaurs. It is often remarked that the Mexican political system is not simply bedevilled by corruption but that corruption *is* the political system. However groups such as the Anti-Corruption League and the Public Accounts Commission have aimed to make the political system more accountable in recent years. Indeed, members of these groups feel that political accountability may be served up if the public begin sponsoring their own politicians to maintain political integrity and by keeping them away from the temptation of bribery and corruption. The EZLN recognise that all of these trends are important, and that they may be the start of further democratisation but the ironic problem is that tinkering with the existing political system, or making it better, means that the structural democratic deficiencies remain while more radical challenges to the political system become marginal. Certainly the PRD have now begun to keep a distance from the EZLN.

Subcommandante Marcos, far from applauding the move to multiparty democracy rejects the intensification of multiparty politics, which he regards as a partisan politics and merely the absurd market-place of political parties. He takes his cue again from the Indian communities, stating:

> Try to place yourself on this side of the ski mask. On this side there are people who have lived twelve years in the Indigenous communities. Who have lived with them. He is an Indian, as they say 'Marcos is an Indian like us'. And he thinks like them. For them, what do the political parties do? A political party arrives to divide a community. The party looks for the people to back them up, and those who don't follow another party. The strongest one wins. Political parties divide the communities and fracture everything ... [P]olitical parties prevent the community from agreeing, because a political party is out to win individuals, then it is necessary to build a political force which will not divide. Which will not confront.
>
> (Bellinghausen, 1999)

The consumerism of multiparty politics, with its emphasis on capturing the centre ground, rejecting 'real' alternatives and maintaining the economic/political 'common sense' through spending on media and advertisements is not the radical democracy wanted by the EZLN. To all intents and purposes such a political system merely adds to the sense of citizenship powerlessness as political decisions become part of an autonomous political game of abstract figures and exit polls which become technocratic, and an *instrumental* part of a huge bureaucratic machine that has no accountability to the direct fears and desires of people in their specific communities. The EZLN want a *different* form of democracy that cannot be restricted to conventional political terms. On 2 September 1997 the Zapatista Army of National Liberation mobilising against the militarisation of the indigenous region, and to fulfil the San Andres Accords, marched on Mexico City and inaugurated the FZLN (The Zapatista Front of National Liberation) on 17 September. The FZLN is based upon a programme of struggle for a new, just constitution, a horizontal direct democracy, defence of the environment, the rights of workers and campesinos as well as the creation of strategic alliances with other social and political organisations.

However, the relationship between the EZLN and political left is fraught and raises the issue of political strategy. The PRD is a centre-left party with a broad support base amongst workers, peasants and the petit bourgeoisie led by Cardenas. It formally split from the PRI in 1988 because it was concerned with the programme of neoliberalism and its devestating social effects. But the PRD is distancing itself by focusing on the conventional 'big politics' of Mexico City. As Marcos states:

> in the political arena, we have two great realities; one is the real reality where the people are greatly disenchanted with politicians. But the opposition forces have also had election victories. They are creating expectations in the people, sometimes justified, that things can change. That's good. But the economic problems are continuously overwhelming everything.
>
> (*Ibid.*)

To this end, the consolidation of a real political culture in civil society is an important part of the process of real change. The generation of a *civic culture* implies that citizens express support for particular issues and parties. Such a culture expresses the requirement for tolerance towards opponents and alternative political views. The EZLN expressed a willingness to listen, as best illustrated in the 1999 National Consultation (*Consulta Nacional*, see below). The EZLN claim that real democracy will only occur if national politics is no longer dictated exclusively by the Executive. This is democracy, government of the people, by the people and for the people...the struggle for democracy in Mexico is not only a struggle for fair, free and just elections, multiparty participation or a change in power.

(NCDM, 1998b)

The EZLN desired an inclusive democratic process built from the grass-roots. This is a different understanding of the democratic revolution which is constantly aware of the dangers of democratic totalitarianism. The EZLN reacted to executive (but not simply PRI) dominance over the Mexican Congress noting that

the democratisation of the country has been set aside...there is no widespread democracy...we must salute the struggle for the autonomy and independence of some Parliamentarians in the legislative branch. The country needs a congress, which is truly independent as well as representative of the interests of all Mexicans. The struggle for the independence of the powers should continue to its ultimate consequences. In a healthy republican regime the Executive obeys the legislative. The Presidentialism suffered by our political system should disappear completely...democracy by the people and for the people.

(NCDM, 1998a)

As an example of national civic participation at all levels of Mexican society, in 1999 the EZLN proposed a nationwide direct consultation for all Mexicans to have a say about the direction of Mexican development, neoliberalism and the fate of the Indian communities in Chiapas. The *Consulta Nacional* was a nationwide

Consultation for the Recognition of the Rights of Indian Peoples and the End to the War of Extermination...In it we will ask four questions to the people of Mexico in order to know their opinion on four essential points of the National Agenda, the recognition of indigenous rights, the fulfillment of the San Andres Accords, demilitarisation and the democratic transformation of Mexico... the EZLN has designated 5,000 of its members (2,500 men, 2,500 women) to visit the municipalities of the 32 states of the Mexican Republic.

(Marcos, 1999c)

Marcos concluded in an interview:

> [W]e can summarise our project in the same manner in which we end
> all our communiqués...that is a nation with democracy, freedom
> and justice. By democracy though, we do not simply mean elec-
> tions... we fight for a democracy that will create a new relationship
> between those who govern and those who are governed, what we
> have called 'command obeying'. Until now and in the best of cases
> representative democracy or electoral democracy has referred simply
> to the citizen participating in an electoral process, choosing a candi-
> date on the basis of programmes or policies... in the new relation-
> ship that we are proposing, representative democracy would be more
> balanced. It would enrich itself with direct democracy... not only as
> electors or consumers, but as political actors.
>
> (de Huerta and Higgins, 1999, p. 71)

To say that capitalism is in an irreversible crisis is perhaps premature and
an overstatement. However, as perhaps best epitomised by the frequency of anti-capitalist protests, pockets of resistance are occurring
and challenging the hegemony of global capital, its ideas and its institutions. What is clear is that such challenges to global capitalism are
rejecting the strategies and objectives of previous challenges to capitalism with the implication that for traditional sites of authority and
power, this is an unnerving and elusive development. Undoubtedly
the often elusive and ambiguous nature of critical social movements
and their 'anarchy' eludes the conventional strategies used by capitalism
and states to neutralise resistance through coercion, violence or consensual co-option. The challenge for critical IPE is to recognise that
the actors and groups within these movements are analytically
and politically significant due to the very fact that *they do* act at the
local level and on the margins whilst *simultaneously* impinging on the
larger-scale processes due to the paradoxical nature of the practices of
globalisation. Indeed through new technologies the EZLN problematises
the way the local and the global have been articulated through the
exclusions of the geopolitics of state-sovereignty. These agents and
actors are rejecting the 'teleological' globalisation by searching for
actual concrete alternatives to neoliberalism without a unified proto-
type.

The EZLN represent a force for cultivating dialogue and a willingness
to listen if such consultations are engaged with transparently. Indeed
the EZLN offered the following to President Fox:

you have inherited a war in the Mexican southeast... [d]uring these almost seven years, the zapatistas have insisted, time and again, on the path of dialogue. We have done so because we have a commitment with civil society, which demanded that we silence... [d]uring your campaign... you, Senor Fox, have said time and again that you are going to choose dialogue in order to confront our demands. Zedillo said the same during the months which preceded his inauguration, and, nonetheless, two months later he ordered a large military offensive against us. You can understand that distrust in all things having to do with government, regardless of which political party it belongs to, has indelibly marked our thoughts and actions... We are not inspired to trust someone who, with the short-sightedness of managerial logic, has a government plan to turn the indigenous into mini-micro businesspersons or into employees of this administration's businessperson... the indigenous self does not have to do only with blood and origin, but also with the vision of life, death, culture, land, history, the future.

(Marcos, 2000)[17]

But, as Marcos continued,

as for the zapatistas you are starting from scratch as far as credibility and trust are concerned... you won the election but you did not defeat the PRI. It was the citizens. And not just those who voted against the State party but also those from previous and current generations who, one way or another, resisted and fought the culture of authoritarianism, impunity and crime built by PRI governments throughout 71 years. Although there is a radical difference in the way you came to power, your political, social and economic program is the same we have been suffering under during the last administrations. A program for the country which means the destruction of Mexico as a nation and its transformation into a department store.

(*Ibid.*)

Conclusion

Critical social movements now empower new political spaces by directly appealing to those disenfranchised. The exploration of these political spaces means that the critical social movements will operate at the margins of conventional political institutions. This relationship requires a careful strategy for a greater *communication* and *autonomy* from the state and capital to reflect and act to critical social movements within the existing political institutions. This is based upon the gradual recovery of the project of the Enlightenment and to escape the familiar pitfalls of idealism by arguing that prospects for greater freedom are in fact immanent within the existing political structures. At the same time there is a distinctive recognition of the weaknesses inherent in Marxism while social movements are able to judge the existing social arrangements by their capacity to embrace open dialogue with others and envisage new forms of political community that break with unjustified exclusion. All communicating subjects will need to rationalise and to account for themselves in terms of what is intelligible to others to maintain their legitimacy. This is the EZLN's critically democratic project. It is a project which produces a distinctive reflection on the site and nature of the political in IPE which is not constrained by the theory and practice of Marxism, which is constrained by conventional way of expressing and confronting 'the political' in IPE.

The EZLN's interest in redefining the site and nature of development and democracy offers an exploratory resistance to neoliberalism. It offers a resistance that eschews the classic models of revolutionary theory and practice, principally by eschewing a specific utopia with its necessary teleology. Furthermore, the EZLN have connected with other specific struggles around the world, to create forums for direct and democratic discussion based on listening and inclusivity as shown through the *Consulta Nacional* and the 1996 Encounters for Humanity Against Neoliberalism. In addition the struggle of the EZLN has become a leitmotif for 'resistance' globally.[18] To categorise the radicalism or power of such an initiative is difficult and in any case undesirable. After all, this is the whole point of being *political* and *critical*.

Notes

1. 'The Voice of the Turtle', http://www.voiceofthe-turtle.org/salutes/pga.htm Sometimes resistance is based on frivolous humour, see http://www.chumba.-com/_gospel.html The Zapatista movement is also characterised by irony and humour in the stories of subcommandante Marcos see Subcommandante Marcos, 'Underground Culture to a Culture of Resistance', http://flag.black-ened.net/revolt/mexico/ezln/1999/marcos_under_culture.oct99.html
2. Globalisation here is understood a *specific* historical formation and legitimation of capital accumulation most commonly referred to as neoliberalism.
3. For example see, James Alexander, 'Mod, Anti, Post, Neo', *New Left Review*, 210 (1995), pp. 65–105; Thomas Docherty (ed.), *Postmodernism A Reader* (1993);

Nick Rengger, *Modernity, Postmodernity and Political Theory. Beyond Enlightenment and Critique* (1993); Barry Smart, *Postmodernity* (1992); Gary Wickham, 'The Political Possibilities of Postmodernism', *Economy and Society*, vol. 19, no. 1 (1990); Daniel Nugent 'Northern Intellectuals and the EZLN (or why the EZLN is not post-modern), http://flag.blackened.net/revolt/mexico/comment/north_intellect_ezln.html; Ellen Meiksins-Woods, 'What is the Postmodern Agenda?', *Monthly Review* vol. 47, no. 3 (1995), pp. 1–13; Ellen Meiksins-Woods and John Bellamy-Foster, 'Marxism and Postmodernism', *Monthly Review*, vol. 48, no. 2 (1996), pp. 42–52; Ellen Meiksins-Woods, 'A Reply to Sivanandan', *Monthly Review*, vol. 48, no. 9, pp. 21–31; Ellen Meiksins-Woods 'Modernity, Postmodernity and Capitalism', *Monthly Review*, vol. 48, no. 3 (1996), pp. 21–40.

4. A study by Wilkinson and Hughes (2000), for example, demonstrates the extent to which neoliberal globalisation has permeated international labour organisations and NGOs such as the International Labour Organisation (ILO). See also Worth's chapter in this collection with reference to the World Health Organisation.

5. Roger Burbach and Peter Rosset (1994) *Chiapas and the Crisis Of Mexican Agriculture*, Food First Policy Brief, Food First Institute for Food and Development Policy, Oakland.

6. National Commission for Democracy in Mexico (NCDM).

7. The Zapatista Army of National Liberation, 'The San Andres Accords', http://flag.blackened.net/revolt/mexico/ezln/san_andres.html, 1996

8. Partido Revolucionario Institucional, until the 2000 election the ruling party of Mexico.

9. Zedillo Prince de Leon, President of the Federal Republic of Mexico 'Initiatives for Constitutional Reform Regarding Indigenous Rights and Culture', http://precsidentia.gob.mx/chiapas/document/initiati/htm

10. Ann Carrigan, 'Why is the Zapatista Movement so Attractive to Mexican Civil Society?', *Civreports*, vol. 2, no. 2, March/April 1998. Also at http://www.civ-net.cvg/journal/issue6/repacatt.htm

11. See also, Jim George, *Discourses of Global Politics. A Critical (Re)introduction* (1994); Samuel Huntingdon, 'After 20 years The Future of the Third Wave', *Journal of Democracy*, no. 8 (1997), pp. 3–13; Barry Gills, Joel Rocamora and Richard Wilson (eds), *Low Intensity Democracy. Power in the New World Order* (1993); Chaffell Lawson, 'Mexico's New Politics. The Elections of 1997', *Journal of Democracy*, no. 8 (1998), pp. 3–28.

12. The Zapatista Army of National Liberation (EZLN) 'Second Declaration of the Lacandon Jungle', located at http://www.ezln.org/fzln/2nd-decl.html

13. A. C. Enlace Civil, *Autonomous Municipalities: The resistance of the indigenous communities in response to the war in Chiapas* (1998), http://flag.blackened.net/revolt/mexico/comment/auto_munc_nov98.html

14. Samuel Blixen and C. Fazio (1995) 'Interview with Marcos about Neoliberalism, the Nation State and Democracy', http://flag.blackened.net/revolt/mexico/ezln/inter_marcos_aut95.html

15. C. Fuentes (2000) 'Mexico's Financial Crisis is Political, and the Remedy is Democracy,' *Documents on Mexican Politics*, http://www.cs.unb.ca/~alopez/politics/fuentes.html

16. Previously, the board had consisted of magistrates appointed by the legislature on the recommendation of the President.
17. 'Letter to Senor Vicente Fox', see http://flag.blackened.net/revolt/mexico/ezln/2000/ccri_to_fox_dec.html
18. For example the 'Zapatista Challenge Conference' (London, March 1998) comprised activists from a plethora of groups ranging from anarchist movements to groups campaigning against the Multilateral Agreement on Investment. Similarly one of the more influential anti-globalisation groups has been the Italian-based 'Ya Basta' (No more) whose name was the cry of thousands of indigenous peasants that formed the EZLN in 1994.

6
Health for All? Towards a Neo-Gramscian Critique of the WHO[1]

Owen Worth

There has in recent years been a significant impact by both 'critical' and Gramscian-inspired theories within the study of International Political Economy (IPE). In particular such contributions have been applied to shed greater light upon the nature of neoliberalism and on the phenomenon of globalisation (Cox, 1987, 1992; Murphy and Tooze, 1991; Gill, 1993; Lee, 1995; Palan and Abbott, 1999 Rupert, 2000). The inclusion of such theories has contributed towards a greater 'critical' understanding of the processes and structures that shape both the ideology and the working practises of the current neoliberal global order. Many contributors have furthered this with studies of certain institutions/organisations that have either been recently created (in the case of the World Trade Organisation) or have adapted their general rhetorical outlook (in the case of development agendas linked to the UN, or other economic forums such as IMF, OECD etc.) in order to maintain, consolidate and strengthen the workings of the neoliberal order. This chapter aims to elaborate upon these studies by focusing upon the issue of health and in particular the World Health Organisation (WHO), to demonstrate that by applying a neo-Gramscian framework to such global organisations one can realise the extent to which neoliberal ideology asserts its hegemonic influence. Furthermore, it aims to demonstrate the impact and influence that neoliberal hegemony has on organisational bodies that at first glance appear outside or marginal to the current global order.

The failure of the post-war economic settlement, as set down at Bretton Woods, and the move towards market liberalisation, highlighted by policy shifts by Western governments in the 1980s, has set a new agenda within the international (global) political economy. This trend has been coupled with the process of 'globalisation'; which, aided by the growth of international financial transactions and multinational corporations, has created a new form of consciousness, which strives towards greater multilateral cooperation. Drawing from the work of Cox, this ideological consciousness is formed through material capability and superstructural institutions that interrelate to produce a hegemonic order (Cox, 1981). While studies of the super-structures of neoliberal hegemony have mainly concentrated upon major economic institutions, that set the precedent for global practises and transactions,[2] with special attention given to the creation of the World Trade Organisation in 1995 (Rupert, 2000), it is necessary to look at how other, less prominent, international organisations have been affected by this hegemonic shift. Increasingly, organisations focusing on development and societal issues, whose interests might appear to greatly conflict with the neoliberal economic ideology, have adapted or re-invented themselves to embrace the practises and policies that the economic institutions propagate. By doing this they appear as further jigsaw pieces in the neoliberal picture, furthering its hegemony and legitimacy.

The WHO, with its concern for global health issues, naturally falls into the second category of institution. Existing under the umbrella of the United Nations, its main (and continuing) slogan has been that of 'health for all'. By addressing a more detailed theoretical discussion of how the neo-Gramscian approach can be critically applied to such international organisations this chapter will present a critique into the current global health regime. Furthermore by focusing upon the changing objectives of the WHO and in particular how the 'health for all' agenda is being continually redefined, a further critique can be added to demonstrate the role the WHO plays within the confines of the hegemonic order. Finally, by using both the health issue and the failure of the WHO to deliver its primary objective, I will discuss ways in which external NGOs[3] could open up avenues for reform and alternative health agendas.

Gramsci and hegemony as a critical ontology of international organisations

By taking a Gramscian-inspired approach to a certain problematic within GPE, it is paramount to clarify exactly how the theoretical insights of the work of Gramsci can be applied, without falling into the category of over-generalisation. In particular, since the work of Cox adapted Gramsci's insights to the complex environment of the international arena (Cox, 1987, 1996), his interpretations have been critiqued from various quarters for over-simplifying the work of Gramsci, so that it fits comfortably into the confines of GPE (Bellamy, 1990; Germain and Kenny, 1998). What such critiques essentially ask is, what is the relevance of the work of a man writing upon both a different subject and within a different era (Bellamy, 1990). This scrutiny is perhaps best executed by Germain and Kenny, who have challenged neo-Gramscians to rethink their application of Gramsci, as Cox's own usage overlooks certain problems that have to be addressed. In particular they point to the ambiguities that exist when attempting to convert the concepts of hegemony and civil society from within the nation-state (as Gramsci originally constructed it) to global practices and norms. Doubts are thus raised as to whether these can be defined unproblematically at the global level, because according to the logic of Gramsci's work, a form of concrete international state, based upon the hierarchal formation of the nation-state, would have to exist to reflect Gramsci's equation of state = political + civil society. Thus the systematic existence of a global civil society and Cox's own model of global hegemonic order, are rejected as they lack both the governmental structure and the cultural identity that is found within the state (Germain and Kenny, 1998). How then can Gramsci's concepts be applied so that they provide the epistemological benefits that the model of hegemonic orders can give, while at the same time respecting that the confines and contradictions of global practices are far more complex than those within a nation-state? In addition how can such a reading benefit the study (within the precedent of the working of hegemony) of the workings of international organisations and more particular the WHO?

In order to achieve this is it necessary to use the main theoretical reasoning evident within Cox's work and then to turn towards the more sophisticated work of Rupert (1998) and Hall (1998). Responding to Germain and Kenny, Rupert illustrates several ways in which Gramsci's thought can be developed to the study of GPE. Borrowing from Marx's alienation theorem he suggests that because the modern state was made possible by capitalism's abstraction of the explicitly political out of economic life, then through the process of free trade and transnational capital, a similar process can be seen at the global level (Rupert, 1998). Hall's definitions of hegemony give us a further critical tool for application. He defines hegemonic processes as being the result of a combination of several cultural, social and economic agents that are often complex and contradictory in nature, which serve to construct certain positions and practises in order that they make consensual common sense of the ideological constraints which characterise the hegemonic order as a whole (Hall, 1988). These provide adequate responses, when converted to the notion of hegemony on the global arena. Viewed in such a manner the terms 'trade liberalisation' and 'globalisation' can be seen as an economic movement that has moved outwardly, gradually (or to use Gramsci's own terminology, through the process of *passive revolution*) gaining legitimacy, until being consensually and hegemonicly accepted as a normalised 'natural' process. Similarly Hall's emphasis on agents provides a further departure point, both for addressing the problems that are raised by Germain and Kenny, and for the study of international organisations. In order to view differing international organisations as forms of agents that contribute towards the shaping and reshaping of the dominant ideology upon which a hegemony is based, a deeper representation of the essence of global hegemony can be applied that both addresses the question involving the structural problems of converting Gramscian notions from the domestic to the global arena, and at the same time allows for a better understanding of the reasons why certain organisations adopt the policies and rhetoric that they do. In addition, it is my opinion that this interpretation of Gramsci does not stray from the core principles that Gramsci himself was constructing in the 1920s. Gramsci's theoretical usage of hegemony was not constructed *just* to investigate the development of Italy at that time as some have suggested (Bellamy, 1990), but also as a universal model, aimed to provide a critical understanding to the complex processes of power, consent and ideological consciousness. As Gramsci observes in the *Prison Notebooks*:

> Critical understanding of self takes place through a struggle of political 'hegemonies' and of opposing directions, first in the ethical field and then that of politics proper, in order to arrive at the working out at a higher level of one's own conception of reality. Consciousness of being part of a particular hegemonic force is the first stage towards a further progressive self-consciousness in which theory and practice will finally be on. Thus the unity of theory and practice is not just a matter of mechanical fact, but a part of the historical process, whose elementary and primitive phrase is to be found in the sense of being 'different' and 'apart', in an instinctive feeling of independence, and which progresses to the level of real possession of a single and coherent conception of the world.
>
> (Gramsci, 1971, p. 333)

Particularly prominent in analysing the extent to which 'secondary' international institutions, concerned with non-core policy areas – such as the WHO – have also adopted the neoliberal ideology, is the work of Kelley Lee.[4] By taking a broadly critical, neo-Gramscian stance to both the study of international organisations as a whole (Lee, 1995) and to the policies of global health (Lee, 1999a+b), she has greatly contributed towards the application of 'critical' IPE to an area that has to date been neglected by most academics including the neo-Gramscians. Although her theoretical approach does have certain problems, in the sense that she does not expand sufficiently on her production of it,[5] her work provides us with a detailed analysis of how UN-led institutions have moved, after previous periods of struggle, to accept the processes of globalisation as an inevitable condition which has to be worked within. It also provides a useful critique of liberal institutionalists and regime theorists, such as Keohane, Krasner etc., who argue from a positivist position that international organisations act as forums in which rational choices can be made (Keohane and Nye, 1977). Drawing on the belief that human behaviour is rational, rules and norms are obtained within these forums that can provide an objective reality that adequately reflects the true nature of the world (Krasner, 1983). Thus, in light of the end of bipolarity and the Cold War, a New World Order has emerged, in which the focus has shifted within these forums from conflict prevention to a higher concentration of economic and political cooperation. Both globalisation and the processes of free trade and multinational activity are symptoms of this (Krasner, 1983; Keohane, 1984; critique by Lee, 1995). Lee critiques this by locating the historical role and development of international organisations, and demonstrating that the roles they play merely reflect the overarching ideology of the hegemonic order (Lee, 1995).

Lee shows that the activities and creations within the UN after the Second World War followed amid a broad sense of consensus. With the ideological conflict of the Cold War in its full swing, the agenda within the UN focused upon factors such as population issues, urban development and the creation of both human and women's rights. In terms of development, the UN became overwhelmingly influenced by Rostow's model of development (1960) – which determined that development was a normative programme for the transformation of societies from 'backward', 'rural', predominantly authoritarian societies, into 'modern', urban, democratic ones.[6] Thus financial aid was given to developing nations so that they could achieve the 'preconditions for growth' and development and so avoid the alternative developmental model presented by Marxist-Leninism.[7] By championing these policies the UN, continues Lee, developed within the ideological parameters of the Pax Americana, epitomised by the Bretton Woods system, the support for a mixed economy, *national* welfare provision and the productive appliance of Fordism – which in turn became the hegemonic project of the time (Cox, 1987; Lee, 1995; Rupert, 1995). Consequently in terms of health development, the welfare provisions that were being constructed in the developed world were intended as models, which the developing world should strive for (WHO, 1950).

In tandem with her critical analysis of international organisations, Lee aims to show that a historical struggle emerged in the early 1970s over the direction the UN should take. As the crisis of the post-war hegemonic order became evident, representatives from developing countries within the UN attempted to form a type of 'progressive counter-hegemonic movement' by reforming certain UN institutions. This is best illustrated by attempts to place development issues on a more substantial platform as epitomised by the 1974 United Nations General Assembly resolution approving a 'Declaration on the Establishment of a New International Economic Order' (NIEO) and a 'Charter of Economic Rights and Duties of States.'[8] Principal among the aims of the developing countries were to shift responsibility for economic development away from the Western-dominated 'specialised' (economic) agencies such as the IMF and World Bank so that more scope was given to social and developmental forums that reflected the needs of developing nations (Lee, 1995).[9] In terms of world health, this period of a new progressive vision was reflected in the concrete construction of the 'health for all' programme; which set out in documented footage a clear target that illustrated how, through an extensive programme of socio-economic reform, healthcare should be universally provided by the year 2000 in order to 'permit all people to lead a socially and economically productive life' (WHO, 1977, 2001).

However, while the developing countries pushed for reform they were becoming more and more marginalised by the core industrial states that dominate the economic management of the world order, and which were strengthening their hold on the workings of the global political economy. In addition, and perhaps more substantially, the end of the 1970s saw Western governments (in particular and perhaps most notoriously, the UK and the USA) begin to adopt strategies in response to the Keynesian economic crisis, that heralded a new age of Smithian-inspired liberalism. Not only did the neoliberal revolution that subsequently arrived in the 1980s provide a perfect environment for private multi national investment, which had become prominent a decade earlier, but the economic direction which was set made it increasingly difficult for the developing nations to attempt to push for reform from within the UN.

The shift in the character of the global economy also made it difficult for developing countries to resist the subsequent rhetoric and practises of neoliberalism and globalisation. As such, by the 1990s, the neoliberal model was being sold to developing countries as a framework that could work for development. Simply by adopting free-market principles and integrating more into the global economy, developing countries could 'help themselves' to achieve development and economic growth. Furthermore, both economists and political practitioners, from the West have increasingly devised various models and theories that demonstrate a strong conviction that free-market practices provide the only mechanism for poverty alleviation (Krugman and Obstfeld, 2000; Friedman, 1982). One particularly poignant example of this is seen in the recent comments and views expressed by the UK Oversees Development Minister, Claire Short. Short, a long-time *left-wing* member of the Labour Party and *critic* of Thatcherism has, since taking up her post, affirmed the opinion that poverty can be best tackled within the hegemonic confines of neoliberal institutions and practices.[10]

The concentration of market ideology within the structural confines of the global political economy, coupled with its near-universal acceptance by political parties in the developed world, almost regardless of where such parties are located on the ideological spectrum,[11] has created a number of knock-on effects, both theoretical and political, that have served to strengthen the hegemonic order. First, by consolidating such a consensus within Western nations, a clear message has been sent to developing nations – that by accepting globalisation and by participating within the global political economy, socio-economic conditions will be improved. Second, by realising that the ideological changes, evident from the 1980s onwards, made it impossible to carry out the development reforms originally proposed under the very different economic conditions of the 1970s, developing countries have adapted the proposals to reform the effectiveness of development agencies within the UN, so that they are constructed within a neoliberal framework. Third, by accepting the ideological 'norms' of neoliberalism, economic institutions that work as a mechanism for the global economy are strengthened, as a wider number of actors participate and comply with its rhetoric. Finally, by committing to give other agencies (for example, development and health) a larger role, the hegemonic order is strengthened further, as these agencies become increasingly interlinked and barracked under the aims set by the larger economic institutions. This series of consequences and steps are what Gramsci observed as a process of *passive revolution* (Gramsci, 1971; van der Pijl, 1993). They fit within a form of historical transformation, where the dominant class inspires towards a new revolutionary position, before making certain concessions with the subaltern so that the position is more consensual – which leads to a greater ideological saturation.

Indeed, in recent years economic institutions – particularly the World Bank – have spent a great deal of effort on their 'Development Reports' providing various prescriptions on how globalisation can lead not just to economic but human and social development too (World Bank, 2000). In this vein the WHO have collaborated with the World Bank in providing strategies for, and evaluations of, health development in such reports,[12] underlining the need for governments to create a more decentralised environment for health by redirecting state funds towards 'cost-effective' activities and allowing the private sector and the market to be competitively applied (World Bank, 1993). 'Globalisation' has also entered the vocabulary of the WHO, with the aim to use the greater mobility of materials as an aid towards greater health improvement. This has been reflected by the current Director-General, Gro Harlem Brundtland, who has commented that globalisation can be used as a 'force for better health' (Brundtland, 2001b). As such, by working in relation with the economic structures defined by the IMF, World Bank and more crucially the WTO, the WHO has moved towards a role as a metaphoric agent for neoliberal hegemony.

The WHO in historical context

Viewed from within its historical development, the formation and relevance of the WHO has tended to reflect both the degree of multilateral cooperation at a particular time and, more relevant to this enquiry, the ideological bent of the world order at a particular time. The first international health convention, The International Sanitary Conference of 1851, was held, not for the purpose of better health provision, but because continuous epidemics and quarantine regulations were mainly seen as obstacles to commerce (World Health Forum, WHO, 1995a+b). By the end of the nineteenth century health agencies had emerged across Europe and by 1907 the first recognised health forum to contain official members from different countries, the OIHP (Office International d'Hygiene Publique) was set up. However, it wasn't until the creation of the League of Nations, in the aftermath of the First World War, that a comprehensive international health organisation was finally created. Constructed within the idealistic setting of the League itself, this organisation, simply named the 'League's Health Organisation', was constructed to amalgamate the OIHP and other supporting agencies that had emerged. However, like the League itself, its impact was extremely minimal. Its chief purpose was in the provision of factual material on epidemics to the *national* health authorities of its member states. This in itself was problematic for as the inter-war years continued, certain states restricted revealing data to the organisation, either for the possibility of seeking political and economic gain, or for security reasons (World Health Forum, 1995). Due to the less than comprehensive membership of the League[13] as a whole, its health organisation never had enough global authority or influence to provide any purpose for serious action. Indeed the origins of the WHO lie perhaps more in the International Sanitary Convention, which was still in prominence during the inter-war years.

Further foundations for the WHO itself can be traced back to 1943, when the United Nations Relief and Rehabilitation Administration (UNRRA) was established. Among the functions of the UNRRA was support for national health services after liberation. While these measures were arrived at *ad hoc*, they represented a larger purpose. In conjunction with other draft documents and visions at the time (such as the Beveridge report etc.), the relief administration drew up health 'welfare' plans for after the war that were to run in parallel with the creation of a new ideological world order as characterised by the creation of the United Nations and the Bretton Woods system.

The WHO as it was officially constructed was proposed not by the West, but by delegates at the 1945 United Nations Conference on International Organisation from Brazil and China (WHO, 2001). The WHO presented itself, at least on paper, as the first comprehensive multilateral health organisation, democratically structured around a one-member one-vote, two-thirds majority system. Members in turn were expected to comply with the recommendations put forward by the organisation and prepare annual reports, which demonstrated the progress of health systems within their respective countries. The constitution, which member states used as a normative guideline until the 1970s, was framed under the objective of the 'obtainment by all peoples of the highest possible level of health' (WHO constitution, 1946) and concentrated primarily on strengthening national health services within member states. Thus recommendations were offered and assistance provided on request (WHO constitution, 1946). In historical relevance this first period since the official declaration proclaimed it as an international body (from 1946 to around 1974), systematically intertwined with the post-war economic order. Based on both Rostow's model of take-off development and the consensual mixed-economy model that formalised the uneasy compromise between capitalist development and welfare provision, the first years of the agency's life can be viewed as an attempt to promote economic development, while constructing some framework to assist the building of health services at a national governmental level. Thus the post-war health-building plan facilitated both a top-down and a bottom-up purpose of action that was in keeping with the mixed-economic form of 'capitalism with a human face' that the participants of Bretton Woods were aiming to apply. By this I refer to a process that on the one hand is seen to externally promote a form of capitalist development in the Third World that mimics similar industrial and developmental processes undertaken in the West (Rostow, 1960, 2nd ed.), while at the same time encouraging domestic governments to build health and welfare programmes within their respective countries. In cooperation with the other agencies within the United Nations (including economic bodies, such as the World Bank), the workings and directions of the WHO largely became consolidated, with few contestations being made to its objectives until the 1970s.

As the WHO reflected both the ideological and political realities of the post-war hegemonic order, then its attempt to redefine itself in the 1970s was similarly a reflection of the changed realities of the international political economy during that decade. As the post-war settlement fell into a 'legitimation' crisis, in which both the embedded liberal compromise of a mixed economy and the Rostowian prescription for development were being contested, then one area where such contestation occurred was within the international institutions upon which the post-war settlement had been founded. The World Health Organisation thus became a forum in which policy-makers from developing nations could challenge the dominance of the West, by drafting alternative health agendas to those that had predominated the post-war era until that point. The first signs of dissatisfaction with the efficacy of the WHO appeared in the early 1970s, concluding with a report, issued by the organisation's executive board, which demonstrated that little progress towards adequate global health provision had been made during the post-war years. In particular the report revealed that national healthcare systems in the developing world were being neglected, and that certain radical changes were needed. The *WHO Executive report* was backed by developing countries at the 26th World Health Assembly in 1973, which voted to turn the report into a plan of action. This became a landmark in the WHO's overall development, as for the first significant time since its creation the working framework of its constitution was challenged.

In addition, it became clear to the developing nations that, as they held the majority of the votes,[14] they had the capability to push for reform. In real terms, the directives reached at the 26th assembly were not as radical as they could have been, but a clear precedent was set to enable the WHO to *collaborate*, rather than just assist with developing practical guidelines for national healthcare systems (WHO, 2001).

The 1973 assembly provided a platform for negotiators to focus on more radical plans that would provide a greater challenge to the post-war order. This became evident four years later with the formulation of the 'health for all' programme. Initially set as a target – that the level of health to be attained by the year 2000 should be that which will permit all people to lead a socially and economically productive life – the 'health for all' agenda was regarded within UN circles as symbolic of the call for progressive change to combat inequality. Thus, different agencies were to combine to aid the WHO in the ensuing years to attempt to ensure a working framework for the agenda.[15] This was recognised most noticeably in 1981, when 'health for all' was endorsed by the United Nations General Assembly, alongside a directive devised to ensure that other key bodies within the UN would cooperate with the WHO towards the implementation of the programme (WHO, 2001). What is of interest here is that the endorsement of 'health for all' coincided with the World Bank's reconsideration of their own policy agenda towards poverty. Despite the fact that no radical alteration was actually undertaken, there was a movement, under McNamara's leadership in the late 1970s and early 1980s to rethink the Bank's own agenda that had been set within the post-war settlement, towards one which reflected the concerns being put forward by the developing nations (McNamara, 1981; Lee, 1995).

While these movements in the 1970s provided a new clear direction for global health, the challenge to the overall economic management of its implementation was reversed in the mid-1980s, with the growing acceptance of neoliberal marketisation. The WHO were, only years after the radical formulation of 'health for all', to adopt a stance that placed greater relevance upon the use of multinationals and the private sector to enable them to reach their goal. While progressive moves were being made to create a more democratic and equitable international system that could challenge the actions of the core states, the Thatcher–Reagan doctrine of the 1980s was to provide a new direction for the global economy which agencies within the UN felt inclined to accept.

This acceptance became even more relevant with the end of the Cold War and the promotion by core states that the emerging global neoliberal order required universal acceptance, so that both trading benefits and private-sector-transnational development could be 'enjoyed by all'. Thus, developing nations have moved to embrace neoliberalism by accepting a framework of action for healthcare that places reliance upon private global financial investment and the workings of the market. Recent moves within the WHO reflect this overall acceptance, as globalisation and neoliberalism have been regarded as important tools for 'health for all' to be worked within. This has been reflected in the 1990s with increasing collaborations with World Bank-orchestrated programmes, which have been quick to underline the necessity of working within the norms and conditions of the global economic order (World Bank Report, 1993, 2000). This newfound partnership with the World Bank (which I will investigate in more detail below) had resulted in a redefinition of the 'health for all' programme. For in 1995, the 'health for all renewal process' was launched which placed the WHO in direct partnership with the private sector, the UN, Bretton Woods bodies and the WTO. The programme was successfully endorsed at the 1998 World Health Assembly session, thus formally demonstrating that the WHO had become another agent contributing to the hegemony of neoliberalism.

As these movements have shown, the alternative strategies placed by developing nations in the 1970s have subsequently been revised and immersed into a new redefined form of hegemonic order, in which the policies and decision-making have been shaped and moulded around its dominant economic ideology. The revision to the 'health for all' strategy and the influence from the World Bank suggests that the formulation of a new consensus towards health development appears to have been consolidated within the WHO. Disillusioned by the failure of Rostowian developmental plans, the neoliberal action plan for development, as outlined by the World Bank, seems to have attracted genuine support among intellectuals and governmental policy officials. To quote from Lee again, 'since the early 1980s, the failure of import substitution and planned economic models to redress persistent inequalities between rich and poor has created an intellectual void in development theory. Neoliberalism has stepped in to fill the gap' (Lee, 1995, p. 158).

Globalisation and 'health for all'

The recent use of the term 'globalisation' within world health circles demonstrates the acceptance by policy-makers to work within a framework that engages with the workings of the global political economy. Furthermore, the leadership of the WHO itself seems increasingly intent both to defend the characteristics of globalisation and to use it as a platform for 'progressive' action. This is perhaps reflected best by some of the direct statements released recently by the WHO hierarchy. In particular the Director-General, Gro Harlem Brundtland, emphasises the importance of globalisation in the promotion of healthcare, by focusing on how technological revolutions and the removal of domestic tariffs will allow developing countries to have easier access to essential drugs and medical equipment (Brundtland, 2001b). Brundtland's reasoning follows those of the World Bank development programmes, by confirming that globalisation does not have to lead to inequality, but can instead work towards creating a more just and inclusive global society (Brundtland; 2001a; 2001b; World Bank, 2000). On the one hand Brundtland recognises that globalisation can have negative societal effects including adverse impacts in health systems. These include: the widening of inequalities in health well-being; the reduction of national public funding of health systems; the increase in global problems such as epidemics; and the negative impact of the growth in production, consumption and marketing of food and beverage products that are harmful (for example, tobacco consumption). On the other hand, however, Brundtland also states that globalisation itself can provide solutions to these problems. This is not to say that she separates globalisation from neoliberalism, but rather that the neoliberal global economy itself can be directed towards a condition that helps relieve, rather than exacerbate such concerns. Indeed, in order to achieve this end Brundtland stresses the need for an engaging 'partnership' between national governments, the private sector and civil society, to provide the best possible solutions for all sides, e.g. both the provision of adequate health services on one side, and increased profit margins on the other. For this partnership to work progressively, she continues, this WHO must forge strong consensual links with all leading economic and governmental bodies (such as the EU, WTO, G8, etc.) (Brundtland, 2001a).

Aided, by the revisions to the 'health for all' strategy, the WHO, under Brundtland's leadership, has moved towards 'modernising' the programme of global health by continually building upon the new framework of 'progressive institutional partnership'. In April 2001 the WHO and WTO collaborated for a 'landmark meeting', to discuss how health could benefit from the trading directives and practices that the WTO presides over. Brundtland concluded that the 'international trade agreement' and the 'protection of intellectual property' (creations of the WTO) provided a suitable structural environment for the promotion of global health (Brundtland, 2001c).

To a certain extent the position adopted by Brundtland, runs parallel with the centre-left formulation of the 'third way' philosophy that first gained popularity with the Clinton administration and the Democratic Party in the US, but has since become synonymous with the reformist Left in Western Europe.[16] This political standpoint confirms the necessity of the global market, but stresses that the application of the free-market principles of the 1980s disregarded the problems that can occur with deregulation and privatisation (Giddens, 1998). Instead it favours the 'marriage' of the private and public sectors towards a common goal that both contributes towards the stability of the global economy and to the establishment of effective and attainable societal needs and provisions. While 'third way' apostles would suggest that their own 'way forward' differs markedly from the neoliberal approach, its rhetorical ontology, as framed by those who use it in the West, is still contained very much within the parameters of the neoliberal hegemonic order (Hall, 1998; Worth, 2001)

The emergence of this so-called 'third way' has added more legitimacy to both the World Bank's and the WHO's plans for global health. By collaborating with major private sector enterprises operating within the global market (such as pharmaceutical firms), nation-states and health workers alike can, provide a viable partnership, aimed at fulfilling the goals that are outlined in the 'health for all' directive. In conjunction with this process, institutional officials are increasingly advising upon several moves. First, that the decentralisation of government health services is necessary in order to cut both bureaucratic costs and to invite more competitive procurement practices within national systems. Second, that this be followed up by the privatisation of certain sections within national health services, enabling both non-governmental organisations and private firms to introduce market principles allowing increased opportunities to attain high-quality drugs and medical technology. Third, that government spending should be directed away from specialised healthcare in developing countries, towards low-cost, but highly effective activities that would create a more suitable environment for a 'basic-needs'[17] approach towards poverty alleviation. These proposals are coupled with the affirmation that an extensive collaboration with the global economy itself will provide a nation with a competitive and economic environment that will give its citizens the opportunity to improve upon their own health themselves (World Bank, 1993).

Common with social democratic parties in Europe, the WHO under Brundtland has been directed to 'modernise' its attitude towards the private sector and to market reform. Commonly regarded by the neo-liberal press as a 'gentleman's club' (Abbasi, 1999a), that 'regard government as ultimately good, profit ultimately bad and intellectual property as theft',[18] the WHO is coming to terms with the Brundtland regime, conceding (albeit lukewarmly) without much of a struggle the need for a revised 'health for all' programme and the influence of the World Bank. Although Brundtland can be seen as the 'Tony Blair of the WHO', especially in her vocal enthusiasm to the aims of the WTO, the lack of funds and capital for more autonomous enterprises has left the WHO with little incentive to resist the financial advancements of the World Bank (Godlee, 2001).[19] For the World Bank's involvement in health as been such in recent years, that some within the WHO feel that they have to cooperate with their overall agenda (Abbasi, 1999a, 1999b).[20]

Despite the optimisms of Brundtland, the marketisation commitment taken by the WHO appears both contradictory and ineffective as a basis to enact the programme of 'health for all' as it was envisaged in the 1970s (its goals have, after all, remained the same, despite the revisions). For the adoption of these policies merely serves to enhance the negative effects of globalisation and further marginalise those who benefit from such new developments, fuelling greater inequalities not just on a global scale, but perhaps more relevantly *within* nation-states themselves. These examples are probably best demonstrated within developed countries (and in particular the United States) where, for example, increased competition between/with pharmaceutical and insurance firms, has led to a growing polarisation between different social classes. By following similar patterns and models, the WHO seem intent on over-looking the inequalities that arise *within* national services, focusing upon a more external project, intent on improving an individual nation's aggregate health provision. Similarly, while health politics scholars within the WHO and economists within the World Bank point to how privatisation can be applied within a public/private framework towards a feasible outcome (Muschell, 1996; Abbasi interview with Feacham, 1999c), its practice still results in societal problems. The pharmaceutical industry provides a case in point here. While the global market has allowed the industry to venture into areas more freely than they have before, the developing world remains largely unprofitable for such companies. As a result the new technological advancements made in medical healthcare has become more fragmented in terms of access, due largely to the working essence of the private sector. Arguments made to the contrary (notable by economic institutions), suggest that it is partly the responsibility of governments to provide an attractive economic environment for companies and to adopt regulatory facilities that encourage firms to practice (World Bank, 1993; Kanavos, Mrazek and Mossialos, 1999). This fine, yet contradictory balance has only led to further problems. In countries where certain private practices have been set up (such as certain regions in the northern African state of Mali), the charges placed serve to alienate those who cannot afford them, while in states where multinational firms have been successful, they have been able to manipulate the market to negative effects (such as in India, reported by the People's Health Assembly PHA, 2000).[21]

The processes of globalisation have also led to several knock-on effects concerning health that have accompanied the new developments in technology. For example there is increasing evidence to suggest that epidemics and diseases are being spread more rapidly, due to an increase of global mobility. This has not just become noticeable with the spread of the HIV/AIDS virus, but with more treatable outbreaks such as cholera, dysentery, influenza, tuberculosis, etc., that only create serious problems in the developing world. New health risks have also arisen due to trade liberalisation and the increased export of foodstuffs, such as a global increase in poisons-related illnesses (e-coli, salmonella etc.), while continued ecological concerns have had a derogatory effect upon ecosystems that indirectly effects health due to food shortages caused by sudden climatic changes (Lee, 1999; PHA, 2000).[22] Globalisation has also brought an expansion in the export and promotion of foodstuffs, beverages and narcotics that can have an adverse impact on health (such as the growth of 'junk food' industries, and increased tobacco and alcohol consumption). In addition the creation of a global underclass has led to a marked increase in the consumption of illegal narcotics for recreational use. Such trends have had a particularly negative impact not just on developing nations, but on former socialist countries now characterised as 'in transition'. Russia, for example, has suffered serious health problems since the collapse of the communist system, with average male life expectancy falling by ten years, and alcohol abuse being pinpointed as one of the main reasons for this.

Despite these obvious obstacles, the Brundtland-led WHO remains firmly committed to achieving the targets put down in the 1970s in the original 'health for all' programme, through neoliberal practices. While the original goal of the programme has clearly already been missed – the provision of universal access to basic healthcare by the year 2000 – the main goals still remain for the twenty-first century (World Health Forum, 1995); only reshaped and repackaged, through the legitimation of the 'health for all *renewal* programme' (sic). This programme, seen through the lens of a 'critical eye', has resulted in a global health policy that both contributes to and aids the consolidation of the neoliberal hegemonic order.

Conclusion: towards a fresh challenge for world health

This chapter has illustrated that, by taking both a critical and neo-Gramscian stance towards global health policy, a greater epistemological enquiry can be applied in understanding the workings of both the neoliberal hegemonic order and the impact that this order is having on the framing of health policy nationally, internationally and globally. By locating health policy in terms of its position within a historical structure shaped by a material capability, health planning is falling into the trap of limiting the consciousness of its own potential. Any form of ontological challenge to this must be capable of recognising the barriers that can be opened and explored to create possible transformations and alternatives.

How can valid forms of contestation provide a sustained and viable influence that will be enough to alter the direction currently taken by the WHO. This appears quite problematic. As long as the WTO and key UN institutions like the World Bank remain upon the firm course of neoliberalism, any alternative towards the policies of health are likely to fall upon deaf ears. In addition with key economic institutions working in close proximity with health bodies, it remains financially beneficial in terms of funding programmes for the WHO to adopt to the ideological consensus. Any challenge from inside the WHO therefore has to be placed alongside a greater challenge for reform within the United Nations and neoliberal economic system itself. The challenges presented in the 1970s gave some indication as to how this is possible, although as I have outlined in this chapter, this arose more from a crisis within a particular hegemonic order, than from a concentrated drive towards bridging the inequality gap. United Nations representatives need to identify that problem-solving agendas should not necessarily be dominated by the dominant principles of the global political economy. This again contains problems, as core states and private actors, intent upon protecting their own interests and influence within the global political economy, would move to consolidate their authority.

However, outside governmental, international institutions and UN circles, social forces do exist, in different organisational appearances that do challenge the current practices of the WHO. Several NGO pressure groups, consisting of health professionals and development workers, have been set up to both educate the public upon the state of the global health regime, draft alternative policies and pinpoint areas of reform that the UN should be looking into. Perhaps this is illustrated best by the People's Health Assembly (PHA), a forum set up to highlight the needs and problems associated with healthcare and the impact that globalisation is having upon it. The PHA is an international movement, aimed at uniting the loose collection of individuals, NGOs, networks and movements towards a common alternative strategy for global health. Rooted in the original strategies of 'health for all', the origins of the PHA date back some fifteen years, arising from a growing disillusionment with the failure to address any of the concerns that the original document laid out (PHA, 2000). In addition the PHA feels that an alternative global health organisation is required, as the WHO has 'weakened over the past two decades', allowing the World Bank to 'take the lead in formulating international health policy' (Chowdhury and Rowson, 2000), thus relegating the WHO to the consensual junior partner. The PHA aims to take the lobbying role that the WHO has slowly vacated since the 1970s, by building upon a network of lobbyists at the local, national and international level; their aim being to allow the public citizen a voice in expressing health concerns (PHA, 2000).[23] The aims of the PHA are shared by collaborating international bodies such as the International People's Health Council, a coalition of grassroots health programmes, movements and networks, and Health Action International, concerned primarily with the practices of transnational pharmaceutical companies and the WTO's ruling on Intellectual Property Rights.

While obviously lacking funds and solid financial backing, non-governmental organisations such as these can at least attempt to gain public support, illustrate different problems with the present healthcare system and place certain pressure upon government insiders. At least with the development of communications, which globalisation has provided, such counter-arguments have the potential of attracting a wider audience.

Notes

1. A word of thanks must go to Jason Abbott for his comments, insight and suggested revisions to an earlier version of this chapter.
2. For example the World Bank, IMF, G7, etc.
3. That is NGOs which operate outside the overall umbrella and influence of the United Nations.
4. Kelley Lee is Senior Lecturer in the Health Policy Unit of the London School of Hygiene and Tropical Medicine and Honorary Lecturer, Division of International Health, School of Medicine, Yale University.

5. She fails, for example, to address some of the problems that certain Grams-cian's are faced with, to which Germain and Kenny refer.

6. Not only did the developed states provide a model for the future develop-ment of the Third World, but explicit in this viewpoint was both an empirical relationship and positive correlation between economic development and political development. The more developed a society was economically the more democratic it would be politically. As well as Rostow see also, Almond and Coleman, 1960; Almond and Powell, 1966.

7. We should not underestimate the political significance of Rostow's work. His landmark text *The Stages of Economic Growth* was subtitled *A non-communist manifesto*.

8. The NIEO also called for greater self-sufficiency, an increased share of world trade and level of industrialisation, protection of their resources through international codes governing the conduct of transnational corporations, and a gradual shifting of the pattern of exchange to reflect more fully the interdependence of nations.

9. Although both the IMF and World Bank are specialised agencies of the UN, unlike the majority of organs of the UN system which operate on a one member one vote system (OMOV), the IMF and World Bank are based on a weighted vote commensurate with the size of the members' financial contri-butions. Consequently within the UN system developing world countries enjoy a majority whereas in the IMF and World Bank Western states and specifically the US are dominant.

10. In a recent interview to *New Internationalist*, Short explains her 'modernising' vision : 'We want sensible use of markets and an efficient state that sets the economic conditions that allow economies to prosper; that regulates markets, banks and commerce so that they're not corrupt, so that there's a change to get sustainable economic growth and deliver the essentials of human developments': www.oneworld.org/ni/issue296/short/html

11. Neoliberal economic policies have been adopted by former communist parties (e.g. in many of the 'new democracies' of Eastern Europe and in Italy by the Olive Tree coalition dominated by the Social-democratic Party of the Democratic Left – formerly the PCI), by centre-left parties (e.g. the Labour Party in Britain and the SPD in Germany), to the more 'natural' support of the centre-right and right (e.g. the British Conservative party, Berlusconi's *Forza Italia*, the US Republican Party etc.).

12. The most notable of these was the 1993 16th World Development Report (World Bank, 1993).

13. There were originally only forty-two members of the League which in 1920, significantly, did not include the United States (who remained outside the League), Germany and the Soviet Union. Between 1920 and 1925 another thirteen states joined the League before Costa Rica became the first among several states to withdraw from the organisation. Over the next fifteen years the most prominent states to withdraw were Germany and Japan (1933), Italy (1937), Hungary and Spain (1940). Furthermore, in 1939 the Soviet Union was expelled from the League following the invasion of Finland. 'The World at War', League of Nations timetable, http://worldatwar.net/time-line/other/league18–46.html, accessed 22 June 2001.

14. See note 9 above.

15. The 'health for all' plan was endorsed in collaboration with UNICEF at the joint WHO/UNICEF Conference in Alma-Ata, in the USSR, in 1978.

16. Particularly the 'New' Labour Party of Prime Minister Tony Blair and the SPD under the leadership of Gerhard Schröder. At one point between 1997 and 1999 it looked as if this 'third way' might become the new consensus among centre-left and leftist political parties and movements across Europe. However growing disillusionment with the approach has weakened the German government's commitment to such policies while the French Socialist Party under Lionel Jospin was always more lukewarm in its enthusiasm for the Blair-Giddens vision.

17. A 'basic-needs' approach to health refers to the process of minimising bureaucratic costs within national health services, so that national governments can concentrate their funding towards essential medicines and treatments. During the 1970s, many WHO members were becomingly increasingly concerned about the way in which developmental national health services were being constructed. The post-war era favoured a 'vertical approach' to development. That is, it focused primarily upon developing health welfare programmes, rather than focusing upon a more horizontal goal. 'Health for all' was established as a more fundamental aim (Siddiqi, 1995).

18. Quote from an economist at the World Bank cited in Abbasi, 1999b.

19. The WHO has currently got a biennial income deficit of $51 million, partly due to unpaid contributions of member nations. The former Soviet Union and the USA are amongst those countries who have failed to 'pay their dues'.

20. One senior representative of the WHO described the World Bank as the 'new 800 lb gorilla in world healthcare'. Although playing a minimum role in terms of funding since the end of the 1970s, the main crux of its contribution has been since the publication of the World Bank report in 1993, and with the revamping of the 'health for all' programme (Abbasi, 1999a). Figures from the World Bank show that by the late 1990s, lending had increased to $12 billion and $225 billion had been spent on projects.

21. The project in Mali has been welcomed by the World Bank. In India, it is reported by the PHA that up to 95 per cent of the population cannot adequately afford the drug prescription charges that have been placed on new, essential drugs, marketed by transnational pharmaceutical firms.

22. www.Nation-Online.com, an online newspaper focusing on issues in Bangledsdesh, reports that in 1998, 2.2 million died from e-coli-related diseases, with a significant minority being from developed countries.

23. The increase of local concern groups have become particularly relevant in both the developing and the developed world, with the establishment of groups such as the Gonoshaasthaya Kendra in Bangladesh, in which village women have become community health workers and agents of change; the Centre for Information and Advice in Health in Nicaragua, that provides education and communication services; and the Telemanita in Mexico. In the UK general election of 2001 a local GP, Dr Richard Taylor, was returned as an independent MP for Kiddiminster because of the downgrading of the local hospital's services and the closure of its Accident and Emergency department.

7
The Internet and the Digital Divide: Representational Space or Representation of Space?

Jason P. Abbott

Libertarian and technologically determinist accounts of the growth of the Internet (e.g. Dyson *et al.*, 1994; Friedman, 2000; Negroponte, 1996; Toffler, 1991; Wriston, 1992) argue that the medium is a universal space allowing faccess to unfiltered flows of information, that it lacks established hierarchies of power and is 'a raucous and highly democratic world with no overlords or gatekeepers' (Warf and Grimes, 1997, p. 261). For many cyberspace presents a social utopia in which class, ethnicity, gender, race and status are rendered invisible. In part such characteristics derive from messages and adverts from the mainstream media[1] but also from the nature of computer-mediated communication. The anarchical and bottom-up structure of the Internet is regarded by some as both giving a voice to those who would not otherwise be heard[2] and of being a more expressive medium, largely because the principal form of communication is text based. As a consequence the age, economic class, race or sex of the user cannot be easily identified (Everard, 2000; Sproul and Kiesler, 1991).

However, how 'real' are such depictions of this 'virtual' reality? To what extent does the Internet live up to such hype? This chapter argues that such questions *must* be posed within the overall context of the political economy of the Internet. In particular the chapter suggests that social scientists should be wary of accepting a social and technological utopian vision of the Internet for two principal reasons. First, drawing from the work of the French philosopher Henri Lefebvre the chapter argues that in order to understand the Internet more thoroughly we need to explore the political economy of spatiality, to recognise that the Internet is *both* a representational space and a *representation* of space (Lefebvre, 1991). In terms of accessibility and usage it is patently clear that vast discrepancies exist in terms of gender, education and wealth and between a *wired* core and a *less wired* periphery. Second, that the Internet has become increasingly commercialised and privatised, transforming the universality of the medium (Sassen, 1998). As a consequence we are presented with a contradictory space, a space where on the one hand 'technology and technicity tend to . . . reinforce domination' (Lefebvre, 1991, p. 392), but on the other a 'space which the imagination seeks to change and appropriate' (*ibid.*, p. 39).

The need for a reconceptualisation of spatiality

IR continues to have a limited conception of spatiality, with the dominant discourse being one that reifies the historically specific spatiality of the territorial nation-state (Walker, 1991, 1993). Consequently it is easy to see why this limited conception of space is inadequate for examining the impact of the Internet. The anarchic nature of the system designed to overcome the problem of how to maintain land-line telephone communication in the United States in the event of a small nuclear exchange has effectively ensured that traditional state-centred forms of communication, control and even propaganda have been undermined. From individual use of the Net to find alternative social, economic and political information to the activities of NGOs increasingly coordinating action via e-mail and websites, the efficacy of government control over information is increasingly laid bare.

However, there is an ever-increasing body of academics and literature that challenge this limited conception of spatiality. From the impact of 'global', 'new' or 'critical' perspectives of International Political Economy,[3] to the influential works of Linklater (1990, 1998), Rosenau (1997) and Walker (1993), the geographical writings of Agnew and Corbridge (1995) and the work of many feminist theorists, there is a growing discourse that challenges this limited conceptualisation of space.[4] What such new approaches challenge is the 'discursive closure' of mainstream IR and IPE. In terms of spatiality this necessitates breaking open the fallacy of a neatly divided conceptualisation of space. Reconceptualising an international system characterised by internal politics within discrete territorial units (states) on the one hand and relations between these units on the other. However while much of this work issues a clarion call for de-emphasising the state (usually in favour of a new plurality of actors), few theorists in IR or IPE have sought to explicitly look to spatial theory for alternative conceptualisations. Without doing so how can we adequately frame the 'borderless world' (Ohmae, 1990) of the Internet? Furthermore if pre-existing conceptualisations of spatiality in IR are not useful as tools for understanding the function, impact and potential of the Internet, how then might we conceive of spatiality in a way that does not simply introduce new discrete units (the global or international, the regional, the local)?

Henri Lefebvre and *The Production of Space*

Arguably one of the most influential philosophers of 'space' was Henri Lefebvre. Throughout a career that spanned sixty years Lefebvre's life and work thrust him into the intellectual torrents of the twentieth century. Beginning his career as one of the *jeune philosophes* of the 1920s Lefebvre associated himself with the avant-garde and surrealists before joining the French Communist Party in 1928 where he produced an acclaimed exposition on dialectical materialism (1939). Eventually excluded from the Communist Party in 1958 for his opposition to its Stalinism, Lefebvre turned to exploring the history and sociology of everyday life critiquing the structuralism of Althusser, Foucault's 'detachment from everyday life' (Harvey, in Lefebvre, 1991, p. 429) and the hegemony of historicism and positivism. Against Althusser, Lefebvre refused to accept the division between the so-called young 'Hegelian' Marx and the later more structurally deterministic Marx, because, as Harvey comments,

> Life is lived as a project ... and Marx's life had to be seen as a totality of interests, flowing concurrently rather than as fragmented pieces. From this stance he [Lefebvre] fought to rescue dialectical materialism from the Marxists, history from the historians, the capacity for revolutionary action from the structuralists and the social from the sociologists.
>
> (*Ibid.*)

It was the events of 1968 and their aftermath that led Lefebvre to enquire into the nature of urbanisation and the production of space. In particular he was to argue that 'a process of urbanisation or more generally of the production of space ... was binding together the global and the local, the city and the country, the centre and the periphery, in new and quite unfamiliar ways' (*ibid.*, p. 431).

Lefebvre argues that traditional conceptions of space are largely mathematical, grounded in a 'strictly geometrical, meaning' (1991, p. 1) that consequently ensured that spaces were empty, measurable and finite until they were mapped, measured and quantified. In this light, talk of space as a social entity was a controversial and strange concept.

However this traditional notion of space was challenged by the notion that spaces are socially constructed. While often associated with the post-positivist turn in philosophy and the works of post-modernists (or more accurately, post-structuralists such as Derrida, Foucault, Deleuze and Gutarri) there is a long tradition of examining the social construction of space. From the works of the French *annales* school exemplified in the work of Fernand Braudel to the increasingly influential and often cited works of Karl Polanyi (1944) and Thorstein Veblen (1899).

However, Lefebvre argues that while the post-structural turn has resulted in a greater realisation of the extent to which spaces are socially constructed they nonetheless continue to privilege time over space. In other words a 'space' is defined and then considered historically. Indeed this concern for *historicism* has been one of the growth areas of more critical research in IR and IPE in recent years.[5] For Lefebvre and other spatial theorists their principal concern is to arrest this balance, to reveal the dynamism of space. In other words space should not be regarded as a static arena but instead an arena of flux. Spaces are socially constructed but they often have a multiplicity of meanings, with different actors conceiving of them in different ways. In other words space is relational, adaptive and contested.

The multiple characterisations of the 'virtual' world of the Internet reveal this perhaps more evidently than most of the spaces of everyday life. We are presented with contradictory claims and evidence for this new frontier. On the one hand authoritarian regimes struggle to control the access to 'alternative', often Western media by their civilians, yet conversely Infomation Communication Technologies (ICTs) and the Internet are also presented as realising the possibility of permanent surveillance, a Big Brother world perhaps best illustrated in science fiction movies like *Enemy of the State* and *The Net*. It is a world that presents the possibility of a social utopia, a world free of the social divisions of age, ethnicity, gender, race and sexual preference, but it is also a world that has led to the proliferation of pornography and given 'oxygen' to polit-ical extremism. Consequently a conceptualisation of space that allows for fluidity, flux and contestation provides a particularly salient theoret-ical background for problematising the impact of the Net.

One way of conceptualising this 'space' is to use the conceptual triad that Lefebvre derives from the reproduction of the social relations of production, the reproduction of labour power and biological reproduc-tion and first introduces in his seminal work, *The Production of Space*

(1991 [1974]). This conceptual triad comprises: *spatial practice, represen-tations of space* and *representational spaces*. First published in French in 1974, Lefebvre foresaw the likely impact that technological changes would have upon the existing conceptualisations of space within our lived experiences, 'the forces of production and technology now permit of intervention at every level, local, regional, national, worldwide' (*ibid.*, p. 90). However, rather than annihilate existing social relations, rather than result in the emergence of an unmapped arena or frontier, this 'new reality' would not abolish the underpinnings of the international system 'those initial points, those first foci, or nexuses, those 'places' (localities, regions, countries) lying at different levels of a social space in which nature's space has been replaced by a space-qua-product' (*ibid.*).

Spatial practice is defined as constituting production and reproduction in particular locations and spatial sets. *Representations of space* are tied to relations of production and the 'order' which those relations impose, while *representational spaces* are the spaces 'directly lived . . . the space which imagination seeks to change and appropriate' (*ibid.*, p. 39). For the purposes of this chapter Lefebvre's second and third categories are more salient, since the central question this chapter seeks to address the extent to which the Internet is a representational space or a representation of space.

As will be demonstrated later in this chapter there exist clear digital divides on the Internet and in the use of ICTs. To a certain extent this is the clearest example of the *spatial practice* of the Internet, if by this we are referring to the access or lack of access of particular groups, individuals and indeed states to ICTs, the availability of technolo-gies and so forth. Furthermore, the *spatial practice* of the Internet would examine the impact, the extent to which actors and action in cyberspace are able to affect the material conditions of production and the social and political environment. While this theme will be returned to in more detail later the central concern of this chapter is to examine to what extent the Internet is a space in which the dominant discourses of contemporary society are being imposed against the unfet-tered claims that it represents a social utopia, an emancipatory environ-ment.

Whether the Internet is a representation of space or a representational space is much more than philosophical play on words. For Lefebvre *representations of space* are the dominant spaces in society. Its is through the representation of space that dominant discourses are articulated; 'they are part of the history of ideologies' (*ibid.*, p. 116), forming tools in the exercise of control and authority, in the exercise of discipline and punishment. It is the world of maps and plans, communication systems, information conveyed by images and signs, imbued in epistemologies and in dominant discourses.

Conversely *representational spaces* are the *lived* spaces of 'inhabitants' and 'users' (*ibid.*, p. 39); it is the realm of everyday life albeit constrained by representations of space. Because for Lefebvre space is fluid and dynamic, it is the representational spaces where we will find the 'clandestine or underground' (*ibid.*, p. 33), where we will find dominant values challenged, resisted, where we will find struggle be it in art, architecture, philosophy, poetry or politics. It is the space, 'which the imagination seeks to change and appropriate' (*ibid.*, p. 39), 'Representational space is alive: it speaks . . . It embraces the loci of passion, of action and of lived situations' (*ibid.*, p. 42).

Relations between Lefebvre's conceptual triad are not fixed and it would certainly be incorrect to view the latter two, representations of space and representational space, as binary oppositions, '[r]elations between the three moments of the perceived, the conceived and the lived are neither simple or stable' (*ibid.*, p. 46). Indeed Lefebvre argues that every society produces its own space (*ibid.*, p. 53), but that such spaces are a product of the mode of production with its variants and local peculiarities. Furthermore, residual elements of previous 'spaces' continue to exist; for example, despite the urbanisation of much of the developed world, and despite the dominance of *neo*capitalism with its space 'founded on the vast networks of banks, business centres . . . major productive entities . . . motorways, airports and information lattices' (*ibid.*), '[t]he fact remains, however, that communal or shared spaces, the possession or consumption of which cannot be entirely privatised, continue to exist' (*ibid.*, p. 57). The relationship between these two spaces is at once oppositional and dynamic, it is one that is informed by dialectical materialism but not slavishly tied to it. Having outlined an imperfect and over-simplified summary of Lefebvre's conceptualisation of space how might we take these concepts and apply them to the study of the Internet?

This chapter will proceed to illustrate three things: first, that the introduction, development and appearance of marked digital divides on the Internet in part informs the spatial practice of 'cyberspace'; second, that the digital divides reveal or uncover the dominant discourses on it; and finally that the envisioning of 'social utopia', 'unfettered individualism' and new *online* communities reveal the representational space of the Internet.

The commercialisation of the Internet and the digital divide(s)

> The Net can empower, as well as disempower, but to read the hype over the advantages of the Net, there seems to be little space to render visible the Other of the wired society.
>
> (Everard, 2000, p. 66)

Commercial interests have always played a role in the development of the Net. In its early beginnings the commercialisation of the Internet principally involved both the development of competitive, private network services, and the development of commercial products implementing the Internet technology. However, with the establishment of the World Wide Web in 1992 we have witnessed a new phase of commercialisation (Sassen, 1998, p. 548). The creation of a user-friendly graphic-dominated environment allowed commercial use to really take off and by 1994 commercial use of the Internet had surpassed academic usage for the first time. This steady encroachment of the Net commercial purposes, primarily technical support and shopping (Cronin, 1996) has continued unabated arguably to the the point where this is fast becoming the dominant usage of the Internet.

Originally, commercial efforts mainly comprised vendors providing the basic networking products, and service providers offering connection and basic Internet services such as e-mail and browser software. However, the Internet is fast becoming a 'commodity' service, with the global information infrastructure increasingly utilised to support other commercial services from Internet bookshops to home-delivery grocery services. In 1999 for example e-commerce transactions in the United States amounted to $8 billion and are forecast to grow to $108 billion by 2003.

In recognition of the growing importance of e-commerce on 16 January 1999 leading transnational corporations from across the globe formed a lobby group to discourage governments from imposing Internet taxes and other measures that could hurt business over the Internet. The Global Business Dialogue on E-Commerce includes, among others, IBM, Time Warner, Bank of Tokyo-Mitsubishi, Fujitsu, NEC, Nokia, France Telecom, Bertelsmann and Marks & Spencer. The group, representing businesses in technology, media and finance, plans to present suggestions on policy to governments around the world as well as send a general message against government regulation of the exploding medium (Kalish, 1999).

There is no doubt that the main reason for corporate interest in the Internet lies in the fact that it is seen as opening up vast new markets. However many fear that, '[c]ommercialisation may well dampen the impact of the Internet in terms of political practices' (Sassen, 1998, p. 556). One immediate consequence of the growth of e-commerce is that counter-movements will find themselves unable to compete with private commerce for access to fast broad bandwidth;[6] another may be that information itself will increasingly become a commodity traded on the Internet. As Bill Gates himself comments:

> [t]here are those who think that the Internet has shown that information will be free ... [a]lthough a great deal of information, from NASA photos to bulletin board entries donated by users, will continue to be free, I believe the most attractive information ... will continue to be produced for profit.
>
> (Gates, 1995, p. 100)

Consequently as the Internet becomes more and more dominated by commercial activities we will see, '[t]he information superhighway grafted onto a capitalist system already characterised by inequality, economic stagnation, market saturation, financial instability, urban crisis, social polarisation, graded access to information and ecological degradation' (Dawson and Foster, 1996, p. 55). In other words market relations and the ideologies of neoliberalism and transnational corporate culture will increasingly dominate the representations of 'cyberspace'. The Internet will (indeed already does) reflect the hierarchies and divisions of the existing global capitalist system and those borne out of the new spatial practices of cyberspace (Sassen, 1998).

Digital divides in cyberspace

Given the military-academic origins of the Internet we should not be surprised that by the mid-1990s analysts and commentators began to notice and analyse digital divides among Internet users. Indeed several commentators maintain that the demography of the Net is clearly a result of the gender and racial inequalities that exist within the professions and industries producing the technologies of the Internet while the divide between the developed world and developing world is a product of where and how it evolved – namely the Anglo-American world. As Everard comments, 'it is clear that little about its development arose from female culture, or from a culture in which women participated to any great extent. Moreover little about its development came from or really addressed the needs of the poor within states or the poor states themselves' (2000, p. 21).

In terms of accessibility and usage it is patently clear that vast discrepancies do indeed exist in terms of wealth, gender and race. In the United States Internet users 'are overwhelmingly male, white and middle class, well educated and in professional occupations that demand college education. The average age of Net users in the US in 2000 is 41 years old, male,[7] college educated or higher and earns $65 000.'[8]

This is not a localised phenomenon since we find that the gender, education and income bias of Internet users is a pattern repeated globally. For example according to a survey by Nikkei Business Publications,[9] 49.9 per cent of Japanese with an annual income over 10 million yen (US$ 93 000) are online compared with only 11 per cent of those on 3.5 million yen or less (US$32 500). In addition there is a significant disparity by geographic location with over 30 per cent of Japan's urban population online contrasted to 18 per cent of those living in rural areas and small towns. Similarly in China, which has one of the fastest growing internet populations, 79 per cent of users are male, 75.6 per cent are under thirty and 85 per cent are, college educated or above and earn more than $121 per month,[10] with nearly half of all users living in the provinces of Beijing, Guandong or Shanghai.

While there is evidence to show that initiatives begun by the Clinton administration to reduce the digital divide in the United States is having an impact,[11] significant disparities continue to exist by income, race and disability.[12] For example, more than three-quarters (78 per cent) of households earning more than $75 000 have Internet access compared to only 31 per cent of those living on $31 000 or less. In addition, white Americans are more likely to be online than those in other racial groups; approximately 50 per cent compared to only 36 per cent of African-Americans and 44 per cent of Hispanics.[13] What is interesting here to note is that racial and ethnic variances are largely explained by income since the proportion of African-Americans and Hispanic families earning higher incomes that are online, are proportionally comparable to white households. For instance, while 78 per cent of white households earning $75 000 have internet access, 79 per cent of Hispanics in similar income brackets also have access and 69 per cent of blacks.[14]

Globally there is a marked gender gap between male and female users. Again while this has fallen significantly in the United States over the past three years, of the 94 million Americans who do not have access 55 per cent of them are women.[15] The gender gap is also evident across nearly all sub-groups (age, education, geography, income and race).[16]

Access and the developing world

The clearest digital divide is between the developed world and the developing world. Before the hype of broadband access, WAP phones and satellite modems carries us away, we need to remember that the world as a whole is *not* as wired as the proponents of technological utopianism would like us to think. According to Nua Internet Surveys approximately 407 million have access to the internet – or put more starkly, only 6.7 per cent of the world's population.[17] Of these users, 68.8 per cent are located in Europe and North America (excluding Mexico), with 41 per cent in Canada and the United States alone. While Internet access is growing, in 1998 approximately 40 per cent of the 200 countries recognised by the UN had no access at all. While 64 per cent had some form of basic e-mail access, a third had the most basic of Internet services and only 15 per cent had full open system architecture (Everard, 2000, p. 33).

Across the developing world the cost of access remains one of the biggest obstacles to greater use of the Internet. Although the cost of PCs continues to fall they remain beyond the reach of the majority of the world's population. As noted above the majority of China's Internet users earn 1000 RMB a month or more – approximately $120. While this is by no means an enormous amount of money, the United Nations estimates that 57.8 per cent of China's population live on less than $2 a day, with nearly a quarter on less than $1 (World Development Report, 1998/9).

Compounding the problem of poverty is the fact that in relative terms Internet costs in the developing world are greater than in the developed world and the United States in particular. A study by International Data Corporation found that the average monthly cost of using the web[18] in the US stood at $25.35 compared to an average of $31.26 in the Asia-Pacific region as a whole (excluding Japan).[19]

However, it is not only income differentials that are of concern here. Access to the skills, equipment and software necessary to gain entry to the electronic highway threatens to create a large minority that is substantially disenfranchised from the benefits of cyberspace in the developed world. Perhaps more significantly than income, access is limited by the level of literacy both in terms of general literacy and specific IT literacy. Furthermore, with female illiteracy more prevalent in developing-world countries the global gender gap on the Net is likely to remain.

One of the growing concerns among policy-makers in developed and developing countries alike is that existing digital divides could be exacerbated by a lack of IT literacy. A US survey conducted by the Gartner

Group [20] predicted that in the United States alone, 50 million Americans were in danger of becoming 'functionally illiterate'. The report characterised three distinct digital divides: the first based on access to the Net, the second an experience gap and the third based on speed of access. The 'experience' gap measures the degree of IT literacy, highlighting a divide between those that know how to benefit from the Internet and those that lack sufficient knowledge of its capabilities and possibilities. Increasingly the speed of access to the Net is opening new divisions among Internet users between those that have access to and can afford broadband (or 'always on') access lines (e.g. digital lines) and those without it. Again this 'emerging' division will not just create divisions within states but also *globally.*

In addition to basic literacy and some level of IT literacy, given that English is the principal language of use on the Net, access is further limited in the non-English-speaking world since at least some knowledge of English is almost a prerequisite for those who wish to fully access the World Wide Web. Although non-English language use has increased sharply it still accounts for less than a third of all web pages (31.5 per cent).[21] After English the most widely used language was Japanese (5.85 per cent) followed by German (3.87 per cent), French (2.96 per cent) and Spanish (2.42 per cent). However with the exception of French, Spanish and Portuguese (where a proportion of the Internet users will be of non-European origin) the growth of non-English languages currently reflects the growth of Internet use in other parts of the developed world. For example, excluding English, twenty-three of the top thirty languages for Web pages are European. There are, for instance, more web pages in Icelandic than in Arabic.

This should not come as a surprise since the Net was devised principally for Anglo-European use by the military and government so no thought was given in its design as to how to ensure access for a range of alphabetic and non-alphabetic scripts. For example non-phonetic languages (such as Mandarin and Japanese) have to be transmitted as images rather than text.[22] This can cause problems with bandwidth since old slower land-line telecommunication networks are less able to handle higher bandwidth than fibre-optic cable and satellite networks; furthermore, traditional land-line networks are affected by greater noise levels, which also adversely affects download times. As Sassen notes this creates an unequal geography of access where '[t]hose who can pay for it will have fast speed servicing, and those who cannot will increasingly find themselves in very slow lanes' (1998, p. 552).

In many developing-world countries the former colonial telecommunication structures hinder further expansion of the Net and access to it. For example, there are more telephone lines on Manhattan island than in sub-Saharan Africa (excluding South Africa) as a whole (Doole, 2000). Furthermore, in Africa, as a direct result of the legacy of colonial rule, incompatibilities exist between national telephone systems that mean that, 'a call placed from Dakar in Senegal to Lusaka in Zambia has to be routed from Dakar to Banjul in Gambia, from Banjul to London, then London to Lusaka' (Everard, 2000, p. 34). Such problems inevitably increase the cost and speed of access.

Additionally the age and reliability of these systems creates further problems, since increasingly the developing world has also become the 'dumping ground' for the West's obsolete communications and computing technologies (Castells, 1996, p. 133). Companies finding their existing systems rendered obsolete by newer ones are faced with the choice of either simply throwing them away or selling them to countries for whom the technology would still represent an upgrade, often at inflated 'real worth' prices (Everard, 2000, p. 35). Recently NGO groups have also joined the act collecting 'obsolete' technologies to 'donate' to the developing world. While arguably some technology is better than no technology, such 'obsolete' systems still maintain a significant technological gap since the systems are often no longer compatible with newer machines, allow limited access (e.g. to graphics and video-loaded websites) or at best ensure longer download times and hence higher telephone costs. Clearly the newest computer equipment is the fastest and most versatile and although much of this equipment can be found in some developing countries, where it is available the average disposable income ensures that such systems are beyond the reach of all but a small proportion of the country's population.

It is the contention of this chapter that the existence of such digital divides are a manifestation that the dominant discourses of power and domination in the international system continue to exist in this new space, in cyberspace. The discourses of sexuality, ethnicity, inequality and the domination of the developing world by the developed are representations of space, a tool in the exercise of hegemony and the structuring codes of social, economic and political activity.

The 'enclosure' of representational spaces?

As alluded to earlier, for many, cyberspace is a space in which the inequalities borne out of differences in age, ethnicity, gender, race and sexual orientation are effectively eliminated. As Frederick points out, '[U]sers of the Internet are stripped of voice inflections, body language, and other common cues of conversation . . . the . . . lack of these cues and the lack of hierarchy in the structure of the Internet provide the potential for equality in cyberspace' (1999, p. 187). Within cyberspace virtual communities have consequently arisen, communities that transcend the existing divisions of the 'real' world. One measure of this is the growth in the number of lesbian and gay users of the Internet. A survey by *Computer Economics*, predicts that based on current growth rates there will be 13.5 million gay and lesbian Internet users by 2001 and 22.4 million by 2005. It also concludes that the online gay and lesbian community is growing at a much higher rate than the overall Internet population due to the privacy, relevant information and virtual communities that are available online. The largest concentration of this group is currently in North America but although populations in other areas will be smaller, they are predicted to grow rapidly with the fastest growing regional gay and lesbian Internet population in the Middle East.

However other research reveals that computer-mediated communication 'has many of the same power issues found in other communities' (*ibid.*). Frederick's survey revealed that 'women tend to use language that is attenuated, apologetic, and personally oriented in computer conversations' (*ibid.*, p. 188). Indeed, in her revealing study, Frederick argues that the *ethos* of virtual spaces can have an important effects on social inclusion and exclusion. The use of sarcasm, *flaming* (accusations against a user that are designed to exclude), sexist language and strong and attenuated assertions, she argues, can and does create an ethos. The manner of participation of members of the group define the *ethos* of the group, and this *ethos*'. Her conclusion suggests that we should be cautious in depicting the Internet as a space free from inequalities since 'though CMC [computer mediated communication] is a non-hierarchical and expressive medium, it does not guarantee a feminist manner in how people communicate with others – even on newsgroups dedicated to feminism' (*ibid.*, p. 196).[23] In other words the representational space of the Internet is encroached by the representations of space. The relationship is fluid, dynamic and contradictory.

Everard (2000) reveals a similar paradox in multiuser domains (MUDs) and in particular in multiuser-domain-object orientated (MOOs), where users can describe themselves textually to be graphically represented by *avatars*. Turkle (1996) maintains that this allows users to express important aspects of their individual identity and indeed to express a multiplicity of identities that collectively constitute the individual. Given the textual and increasingly graphical nature of the Internet, users can experience other points of view, try out other identities, in Everard's words, 'the use of multiple identities in cyberspace merely extends the range of selves available, thus making the individual in a sense more complete' (*ibid.*, p. 125)!

However, in one infamous incident – 'the rape in cyberspace' – a user in a MUD known as Lambada MOO, was able to gain sufficient access to the system to manipulate avatars operated by other users. Having done so the person was able to force these avatars to engage in unwanted sexual activity with other avatars (*ibid.*, p. 130). The issue of how the online community dealt with this user is irrelevant here, rather the example highlights the extent to which the Internet cannot guarantee a space devoid of the worst kind of prejudices and chauvinism that exist in the 'real world'. The vast number of pornographic sites that exist on the Web best illustrates this further. Indeed the nature of the Internet means that despite restrictions on content that might be imposed within a national regulatory environment, users are able to access images with ease that they would be unable to in traditional media unless they were particularly determined to scour the black market. The proliferation of such sites, some depicting extreme images of violence and abuse, clearly does little to advance the cause of feminism and sexual equality since invariably the majority of sites have women as the subservient party to the act. Indeed, given the dominance of the pornographic industry by men, Internet pornography is largely targeted at a male audience, appealing to traditional male fantasies and masculine-dominated depictions of compliant females. In this way the worst kinds of representations of space pervade the representational space of the Net.

Sadly it is not just attitudes to women where the claims for a social utopia are undermined by the proliferation of sites of intolerance. According to the Simon Wiesenthal Center there are currently 2,800 Web hate sites on the Internet, compared to 1,426 in 1998, 600 hate sites at the end of 1997, and just one hate site in 1995. The list includes sites that are anti-Semitic, anti-Catholic, anti-Moslem, anti-gay, anti-abortion, as well as sites that promote racism, hate music, neo-Nazism and bomb-making. According to Rabbi Abraham Cooper, Associate Dean of the Weisenthal Center, the Net has given these groups a sense of empowerment, and it has also provided them with an unprecedented opportunity to market themselves, unencumbered, twenty-four hours a day.[24] Indeed a number of academics are increasingly turning their attention to examining the role, impact and significance of anti-progressive groups in analyses of counter-hegemonic movements in the global political economy (see Rupert, 1995, 1997;[25] Worth, 2000).

Voices of the developing world

Although the use of visual and aural channels of communication through RealAudio and similar narrow-cast technologies is changing the way information is provided over the Net, the dilemma for developing countries as a whole is that the debates over the Net by weight of numbers is overwhelmingly being generated in relation to Western values, Western culture and Western economic agendas. Furthermore, there is also the danger of a new kind of Orientalism[26] since, as Everard comments, 'wherever there is communication, cultural domination and the exercise of power there is always an *Other* who is the recipient, the dominated, the disempowered' (Everard, 2000, p. 66).

Indeed, given the predominance of Western voices on the Net, much of what is published on the Net about developing-world countries is written 'on behalf' of the developing world. Information about the developing world is primarily written from information and research produced in the developed world. In such circumstances there is a very real danger that rather than encouraging the opening of discursive spaces existing stereotypes and identities will simply be reinforced. Indeed, concerned that too much of the information on the Net about Asia was sourced from the West, Malaysian Prime Minister Mahathir called on ASEAN members to become more assertive about their presence on the Net and to produce more content from an Asian perspective.

While the Internet may be growing rapidly in the developing world, and in particular in countries such as China and Malaysia, current trends suggest that we are witnessing the creation of *wired* core and a *less wired* periphery. In this context while the Internet may provide a new medium for activists in the developing world (Abbott, 2001), their voice may be drowned both by the sheer weight of voices emanating from the developed world and by the commercialisation of the Internet. This new international division of information technologies is more dynamic than a simple division of cyberspace into core and periphery since divisions exist and will continue to exist within states and societies as well as between them.

Indeed, in many ways the 'international' divisions in cyberspace resemble much more the 'chain of exploitation' portrayed by Andre Gunder Frank in his seminal work *Capitalism and Underdevelopment in Latin America* (1967). Frank's division of the international economic system depicted a complex spatial relationship of urban-rural divisions from the hacienda and landless peasantry of Latin America to the divisions between the core industrialised world and its 'agents' in the developing world, the 'comprador class'. In cyberspace the Web is still dominated by the core industrialised 'nodes', but these are linked increasingly to concentrations of online peoples in the developing world. Invariably the 'nodes' are concentrated in the core urban spaces of the developing world as the data presented earlier in the chapter clearly reveals. And while the online communities in the developing world continue to grow rapidly, this growth is clearly an uneven growth, dominated by particular classes, communities and spaces.

Conclusion

Perhaps the best analogy for cyberspace is presented in the cult science fiction movie *The Matrix*. *The Matrix* presents a dystopian vision of the future, a future dominated by cyborgs and the technological production of space. But the world of *The Matrix* is one in which there is no clear division between the 'virtual' and the 'desert of the real', both are lived spaces, both are contingent, both are interconnected, impacting upon each other. Indeed, while the world of *The Matrix* might be one in which 'technology and technicity... reinforce domination' (Lefebvre, 1991, p. 392), it is nonetheless a space in which there is room, albeit limited, for subaltern groups to manipulate the same technologies to contest the spatial arena. Representational space may be dominated, indeed may be enclosed but it is not absorbed. So, ultimately, to answer to the question posed in the title of this chapter: to what extent is the Internet a representational space or a representation of space? The answer, perhaps unsurprisingly, is that the Internet is both simultaneously a representation of space and a representational space.

To conclude with although '*The Production of Space*' was written before the Internet became a widely known and accessible space, Lefebvre's comments on the deterritorialisation of capital nonetheless provide an apt description of this complex and contradictory space:

> The realisation of surplus value has... been 'deterritorialised'. Urban space though it has thus lost its former role in this process, nevertheless continues to ensure that links are properly maintained between the various flows involved: flows of energy and labour, of commodities and capital. The economy may be defined... as the linkage between flows and networks, a linkage guaranteed in a more rational

way by institutions and programmed to work within the spatial framework where these institutions exercise operational influence. Each
flow is of course defined by its origin, its endpoint, and its path ... But,
while it may thus be defined separately, a flow is only effective to the
extent that it enters into relationship with others; the use of the
energy flow, for instance is meaningless without a corresponding
flow of raw materials. The coordination of such flows occurs within
a space. As for the distribution of surplus value, this too is achieved
spatially – territorially – as a function of the forces in play (countries,
economic sectors) and as a function of the strategies of the managers.

(*Ibid.*, p. 347)

For many the territorial trap of the nation-state has hindered the study
of IR as an academic discourse. The development of the Internet
challenges both the practical and theoretical foundations of a territorially defined system arguably more so than ever before. Moreover
it also challenges our conceptions of time and space, of the real
and virtual, of the self and other. Lefebvre's conceptualisation of space
provides an alternative conception that by (re)introducing space as a
dynamic and fluid concept offers a unique way of examining cyberspace, a space that is and will continue to be both contested and contradictory.

Notes

An earlier version of this chapter was presented at the British International
Studies Association Annual Conference, Bradford, December 2000.

1. This recent blurb from a survey published by the market leaders on Internet
   research, Nua captures the mood of the mainstream media towards the Net,

   Key characteristics of the Web and indeed the PC itself are the decentralisation
   of power and the subsequent empowerment of the individual. The ability
   to self-publish marked the Internet as a medium which supported self-
   expression, creativity and communication – fundamental hallmarks of
   human freedom evident in the cave paintings of Neanderthal man. 'Political
   Economy of the Search Engine', 22 March 1999, http://www.nua.net/surveys

2. Increasingly easy access to e-mail and the World Wide Web globally allows
   politically disenfranchised groups to communicate with like-minded or sympathetic audiences (see Abbott, 2001).

3. Although a growing 'school' of thought this 'turn' is associated with the works
   of the neo-Gramscian or 'Italian school' of IPE (e.g. Cox, 1986; Gill, 1988,
   1992, 1993; Murphy, 1988, 1991; Rupert, 1992, etc.).

4. Much of this challenge is associated with the so-called post-positivist turn in
   International Relations.

5. Largely though not exclusively due to the influence of historical sociologists such as Michael Mann (1978, 1992), McNeil (1976) and Tilly (1990) and the influence of the neo-Gramscian or 'Italian school' of IPE, see note 3 above.

6. As Sassen notes while these technologies may not be that expensive they still involve costs that cannot be afforded by the generally underfunded sectors of civil society (Sassen, 1998, 557).

7. Although the average user is likely to be male the gender gap between users in the United States at least has narrowed considerably. Today the gap is less than 7 per cent (56 per cent– 49 per cent). Pew Internet and American Life Project, http://pewinternet.org/reports

8. 'Average US Internet user over 40', Gartner Group, 2 November 2000, cited at Nua Internet Surveys, http://www.nua.net/surveys, accessed 12 December 2000.

9. Cited at Nua Internet Surveys, 10 November 2000, http://www.nua.net/surveys, accessed 12 December 2000.

10. The World Development Report estimates that 57.8 per cent of China's population live on less than $61 a month (1998/9).

11. US Department of Commerce, 18 November 2000, cited at Nua Internet Surveys, http://www.nua.net/surveys, accessed 12 December 2000.

12. A survey by the US Department of Commerce revealed that only 28 per cent of disabled people have access to the Internet, 'US Digital Divide Narrows', 18 November 2000, cited at Nua Internet Surveys, http://www.nua.net/surveys, accessed 12 December 2000.

13. 'Internet Naysayers', 26 September 2000, Pew Internet and American Life Project, http://pewinternet.org/reports

14. *Ibid.*

15. *Ibid.*

16. *Ibid.*

17. http://www.nua.ie/surveys/how_many_online/index.html.

18. Expenditures based on ISP, telephone and phone line fees.

19. http://www.idcresearch.com/

20. 'Survey finds "illiteracy" problem in the US', reported by Reuters, 3 November 2000, cited at Nua Internet Surveys, http://www.nua.net/surveys, accessed 12 December 2000.

21. For data on the language of Internet users see 'The Global Reach Express', http://glreach.com/eng/ed/gre/230400.php3, accessed 2 August 2000. For a table of web pages by language see 'CyberAtlas' http://cyberatlas.internet.com/big_picture/demographics/article/0,,5901_408521,00.html, accessed 14 February 2001.

22. This is a particular problem for e-mail use.

23. Everard takes this further suggesting that we should not consider online communities to be any different from 'real' communities to the extent that they 'engage in cultural practices of exclusion and inclusion' (2000, p. 78).

24. See The Digital Hate 2000 report, http://www.wiesenthal.com/feature/digitalhatecd.html, accessed 14 December 2000.

25. See also Mark Rupert's *Virtual Guided Tour of Far-Right Anti-Globalist Ideology*, http://www.maxwell.syr.edu/maxpages/faculty/merupert/Research/far-right/far_right.htm

26. Orientalism here is understood as both a condition of relations between two cultures and a habit of mind in the study of their relations such that a hegemonic culture simplifies, exoticises and stereotypes the dominated culture and its representative forms, ideas and images. The main characteristic of Orientalism is a tendency to reductionism (see Said, 1978; Bhabha, 1994).

8
Conclusions: Explaining a Thriving Heterodoxy[1]

Craig N. Murphy and Douglas R. Nelson

Today's field of International Political Economy (IPE) can be traced back to 1971 when Susan Strange, then at the Royal Institute of International Affairs at Chatham House, founded the International Political Economy Group (IPEG). In its early days, this company of scholars, journalists and policy-makers focused on issues like how to resuscitate the fixed exchange rate system and on the thesis of another early IPEG convener, Fred Hirsch, that comfortable middle-class people in the industrialised world would come to doubt the utility of further economic growth (Hirsch, 1976).

These were not to be the subjects that would lead to the institutionalisation of IPE by attracting funders, shifting the research agendas of active scholars, initiating graduate programmes and creating the ubiquitous undergraduate courses in the field that every credible department of political science or international relations now must have. Rather, the key was the 1973 October War in the Middle East, with its first deployment of the oil weapon, and the long recession that followed. Courses sprang up on campuses throughout the English-speaking world. Within three years two competing textbooks were bestsellers (Blake and Walters, 1976; Spero, 1977). IPEG became a research group of the British International Studies Association (BISA) and a similar IPE section was established within the largely North American International Studies Association (ISA). For the most part, the field has continued to prosper ever since.

Two characteristics of the field are striking. First, it is deeply divided between a critical school, often described as a 'British' school (whose leading proponents are often US citizens or resident in Canada) and what might be called the American school or the *International Organization (IO)* school of IPE, after the US journal that has been the primary site of its development. Second, perhaps paradoxically, even though both schools are successful – as measured by their ability to attract students, publishers, and funders – both are somewhat heterodox when compared to either the norms of political science (the field in which they are most often enmeshed), economics (the field to which they wish to make bridges), or even mainstream IR, at least as it was constituted at the moment of IPE's origin.

Our aim in this concluding chapter is to shed light on this paradox with reference to the critical school, but to do so we need first to say something about IPE's division into two schools, especially because scholars in the American or *IO* school are apt to charge critical scholars with heterodoxy and a lack of attention to the scientific norms that the *IO* scholars see themselves as sharing with mainstream political science, economics, and the behaviourist tradition in IR. We do not believe this distinction is valid. Neither school of IPE conforms to norms of 'science' in these terms. Rather, each has become a site of thoughtful commentary on questions of the relations between politics and economics globally. The American school has been characterised more by reflection on recent events in the world, mid-level 'debates' among proponents of different conceptual lenses and a regular shifting of emphasis, the British by a critical attitude towards contemporary American-led projects of international economic integration, a greater tendency to make links to other disciplines and an interest in an ever-greater inclusiveness of issues under consideration.

Critical IPE and the two schools

Scholars who work on both sides of the Atlantic, members, for example of both IPEG and the IPE section of the ISA, readily recognise the distinction between the two schools. The critical school has its major journals, *Review of International Political Economy* (*RIPE*) and *New Political Economy* (begun in 1996). In contrast, the leaders of the *IO* school argue that that IPE has been 'centered in [the journal] *IO* since 1971' (Katzenstein, Keohane and Krasner, 1999, p. 645) when Robert Keohane, his mentor and collaborator, Joseph Nye and a number of scholars of Keohane's generation of men who had been graduate students at Harvard, took control of that journal.

In the 1999 celebration of the role of *IO* in fostering the field of IPE, Keohane and his colleagues note the important roles that Susan Strange and Robert W. Cox played in the early development of IPE within the journal *IO* (*ibid.*, pp. 651, 657), and the issue itself is dedicated to

Strange. Yet, neither Cox nor Strange is widely cited in the 415-page issue that aims to present the development and the state of the art in IPE. As a rough measure of citations, a count of the number of separate references to specific authors in the volume's reference list identifies the scholars in the first column of the table below as those who are the most important to the *IO*. All are Americans whose careers have been inter-connected at a relatively small number of elite, mostly private, colleges and universities: Harvard, Stanford, Columbia, the University of California at Berkeley, Cornell, Yale, Duke and Swarthmore College.

The second column provides a contrasting list for the critical school taken from the number of separate citations in the 'suggested readings' sections of the 422-page 2000 edition of Richard Stubbs and Geoffrey D. Underhill's *Political Economy and the Changing Global Order*, also dedicated to Susan Strange. Here the group is more international and con-nected with fewer specific institutions (LSE, linked to both Strange and Tsoukalis, and York in Ontario, linked to Cox and Gill). Unlike the *IO* group, these are not people who went to school with each other or were each other's teachers and students. Cornell University's Peter J. Katzen-stein provides the only overlap between the two lists.

Substantively, the two volumes also contrast. Almost a third of the chapters in Stubbs and Underhill are concerned with globalisation and another quarter with prospects for regional integration in the global south as well as the north. Other topics, in order of the number of chapters devoted to each include: changing structures of production and the relationship between labour and capital; questions of power and knowledge; gender; the environment; international finance; and the role of non-state actors and global networks of political communi-cation. In the *IO* issue at least half of the articles are concerned with

International Organization at Fifty	Political Economy and the Changing Global Order
27 R. O. Keohane	33 S. Strange
16 J. G. Ruggie	7 R. W. Cox
15 S. D. Krasner	6 S. Gill
15 J. G. March	3 F. Block
12 E. B. Haas	3 P. G. Cerny
11 G. Garrett	3 W. D. Coleman
11 S. Hoffmann	3 E. Helleiner
11 K. N. Waltz	3 P. J. Katzenstein
10 R. Jervis	3 K. Polanyi
10 P. J. Katzenstein	3 L. Tsoukalis

contrasting different approaches to the study of IPE – liberal, realist, rationalist and constructivist. The chapters devoted to specific topics focus on connections between domestic and international politics (including questions of globalisation understood in that context), between American security policy and American economic policy, and the dynamics of changes in the normative bases of world affairs.

Arguably, the *IO* volume's purpose of assessing the state of the field is not Stubbs and Underhill's concern with providing a collection of essays that can serve as an introductory IPE text. Gill and Mittelman's (1997) *Innovation and Transformation in International Studies* may provide a better critical school comparison. In it, five of the sixteen chapters are dedicated to discussions of social theory, with three substantive chapters on globalisation and two each on issues of the environment, labour and capital, race and gender, and civil society movements of the disadvantaged. In Frieden and Lake's (2000) *IO* school textbook collection four of thirty-one chapters are devoted to contrasting approaches, four to historical studies, six to money, six to trade, four to questions of development and so-called economies in transition, four to multinational corporations and the state, two to globalisation and one to the environment.

However one looks at it, the *IO* school is more concerned with set debates about ways to study IR. The critical school is more focused on questions of globalisation and possible alternatives as well as on the contentious politics of gender, class, race and the environment. This volume is no different. Amoore and Langley, Burn and Watson all contribute new understandings of globalisation, the limited resistance that can be mounted by even one of the most powerful states (Germany), and the surprising potential of social movements that are able to refuse to adopt the logic of globalisation (the Zapatistas).

What internal unity and distinctiveness there is to the critical school developed slowly. No doubt, this is, in part, because its leading figures, Susan Strange and Robert Cox, have deliberately eschewed any temptation to found a school or to be identified as the centre of one. Strange argued that IPE should not be a field of study but, 'an open range, like the old Wild West, accessible...to liberate people of all walks of life, from all professions, and all political proclivities' (1991, p. 33). Cox dismisses the importance of disciplinarity and the ontological perspective underlying most current studies of international politics, arguing that what we can really know is a set of moral and political imperatives for civil society from which we can begin, 'working out an ontology that focuses on the key elements in this struggle', that will challenge, according to Cox, 'biospheric collapse, extreme social polarization, [and] exclusionary politics' (2001, p. 59).

Cox's current agenda is far wider than the concerns about the breakdown of the Bretton Woods system of fixed exchange rates or the social psychological limits to consumerism that troubled Susan Strange and Fred Hirsch in the early 1970s. Nonetheless, there is a connection between the two agendas. Strange's and Hirsch's critiques of the breakdown of the Bretton Woods monetary system were, in large part, critiques of US leadership, in particular, critiques of the shift from a period of relatively benign supremacy in the three decades after the US entered the Second World War, to one characterised by a more self-interested, even venal, form of leadership. Richard Nixon's unilateral decisions of August 1971 removing the underpinnings of the fixed-exchange rate system served as a marker of this change. What bothered many of the early critical school scholars was their sense that this shift was in no way necessary. Not only could the US have served its interests equally well by taking into account those of other nations, what seemed to be the ultimate goal of US policy – maintaining an ever-expanding consumer society – seemed pointless in light of the social limits that Hirsch had identified.

The appeal of Hirsch's thesis waned in the long recession that followed the first oil crisis, but critical school questions about US leadership remained. By the early 1980s many of the scholars who would come to cluster around Strange's and Cox's work had come to see themselves as working to articulate visions of the global political economy that would provide alternatives to what Cox called the 'hyperliberalism' promoted by the United States, and, of course, by the Thatcher government. Before 1980 much of Cox's own work had concentrated on the issues of interest to one of the social forces most excluded from global decision-making – labour in all parts of the world. His widely cited 1981 article, 'Social Forces, States, and World Orders: Beyond International Relations Theory', laid down the gauntlet in its claim that social theorising was always '*for* someone and *for* some purpose'. Critical school scholars made a point of demonstrating that their work was 'for' those excluded from decision-making about the global economy, whether they were unpaid women labouring on African farms, or relatively privileged northern supporters of the marginalised Canadian New Democrats or Britain's (old) Labour Party. When *RIPE* was founded in the early 1990s there was a deliberate attempt to cross all the schools of thought that challenged the hegemony of hyperliberalism: eclectic admirers of Susan Strange, those who had joined Cox in finding insight into the contemporary global political economy from the work of Antonio Gramsci and Karl Polanyi, Latin American *Dependentistas* and representatives of various schools of Third World-orientated world-system's theory, the tradition dominated by Immanuel Wallerstein.

The intent of the critical school fuelled its tendency to expand its agenda both of topics under consideration and of approaches to them. Murphy and Tooze's 1991 textbook-style collection included both a Foucauldian genealogy of the construction of the 'Third World' (Johnston, 1991) as well as one of the first feminist analyses of IPE (Tickner, 1991). By the late 1990s feminist contributions were standard fare in any critical school collection, as were articles about environmental issues. Characteristically, it was Eric Helleiner, arguably the scholar with the most perceptive analysis of the consequences of the end of the fixed-exchange rate system (Helleiner, 1993), who published the first major article on 'green' IPE in the inaugural issue of *New Political Economy* (Helleiner, 1996). One strand of Helleiner's work explained how political leadership, in particular, that of the United States, had led to the creation of unprecedented global markets (in this case, the uncontrolled international financial markets of the late twentieth century), an example of the critical school preoccupation with the ways in which decisions of identifiable powerful actors have created contemporary globalisation. The second strand of his work concentrates on the political economic visions of one set of social movements that believe that the problems on which they focus – environmental issues – have been exacerbated by that globalisation.

This present volume continues the trend. Worth's critical political economy of global health governance further expands the agenda of the critical school, and builds upon important work by a growing community of critical scholars concerned with international health issues. Abbott's analysis of the Internet is part of a rapidly expanding research programme on the political economy of communication and information technology, much of it initiated by students of Strange and Cox, a research programme that has already created one of the largest and most rapidly growing sections within the International Studies Association. Both Abbott's and Worth's work retain the characteristic critical school focus on the interests and aspirations of the least-advantaged in these issue areas, the concerns of those who do not have access to the global information system and those for whom the WHO's abandonment of a concern with 'health for all' would truly be tragic.

Chris Brown (2001), in summing up the current situation in critical international relations scholarship – critical security studies as well as critical IPE – quotes William Morris writing to a close friend and comrade in the 1880s, 'You ought to read Marx, he is the only completely scientific economist on our side' (p. 191). No matter whether or not it is 'completely scientific', critical IPE is very much about being 'on our side'.

The norms of science and IPE

In fact, neither school of IPE can claim to be 'completely scientific' even as compared to their most obvious cognate fields – IR, international economics and national and comparative political economy. IPE's weaker attachment to the norms of social science current in those other fields is an underlying continuity between the British and American schools and a source of certain ironic differences.

To avoid getting bogged down in details of the debates about the exact characterisation of science and its norms, we will focus on two elements that are central to virtually all attempts to describe the theory and practice of science: *systematic collection and analysis of data* and *systematic theory building*. It is not necessary to assert the priority of one or the other of these in describing practice, or in constructing narratives of progress, since neither of these is particularly central to the discourse of either school of IPE. We also leave open the normative issue with respect to the norms of science. That is, it may be a good thing that neither school of IPE is attracted to the norms of scientific practice. We simply proceed from the fact that, unlike cognate sub-fields and the broader fields within which it is institutionally embedded, IPE is distinctive in its limited application of these norms.

Consider first, systematic collection and analysis of data. It is probably unnecessary to stress the centrality of empirical research to the development of economics, especially macroeconomics, but it interesting that systematic collection, essentially independent of the state's need for fiscal data, is relatively recent: we think of individuals like Simon Kuznets, James Meade and Colin Clarke; and institutions like the League of Nations and the National Bureau of Economic Research as pioneers in this regard. Contemporary data collection efforts are simply to numerous to cite. Developing in tandem, with exemplars like Ragnar Frisch, H. O. A. Wold, Jan Tinbergen and Trygve Haavelmo in Europe and Irving Fisher, Jacob Marschak and Tjalling Koopmans in the US, was the field of econometrics, the systematic analysis of economic data (see Hendry and Morgan, 1995). One only need consult undergraduate and graduate curricula in economics for evidence of the centrality of econometrics.[2]

While somewhat later in political science, the behavioural revolution fully established the central role of data collection and analysis by the mid-1960s. In domestic and comparative politics, much of the data collection effort focused on voting and survey data, with the manifest successes of *The American Voter* (Campbell *et al.*, 1960) creating fundamental momentum. Perhaps more strikingly from the perspective of an analysis of IPE, IR and comparative foreign policy, as fields, were early converts to the behavioural revolution, with major research programmes focused on the correlates of war, and peace, and variation in foreign policies. Early leaders in these areas included Lewis Fry Richardson, Quincy Wright, J. David Singer and Edward E. Azar. With accumulating data, these fields were increasingly concerned with statistical analysis and self-conscious evaluation of cumulation, with leaders like Robert North, Nazli Choucri and Bruce Russett. It is here, by the way, that the *IO* school makes its one systematic contact with data. Growing out of the fundamental empirical work of Karl Deutsch and Ernst Haas on integration, and Simon Kuznets' work on economic growth, a number of scholars began to focus on measuring interdependence and, in the mid-1970s, this work began to appear in *IO*. Finally, contemporary research on national and comparative political economy, in political science, economics and sociology, retains a strong systematic empirical orientation in work on political business cycles, fiscal consequences of globalisation and the role of domestic political economic institutions in responding to international economic shocks.

The second key norm of social science is an orientation to systematic theory building. At its most basic level, this norm is about clarity of communication and cumulation. That is, the more explicit we are about the assumptions that underlie our analysis and the logical processes by which we get from assumptions to conclusions, the more easily is empirical work linked to the theoretical and, perhaps more importantly, the more easily can critics identify entry points to the analysis. As a purely practical matter, mathematical formalism is an exceptionally useful tool in achieving this clarity.

The formalisation of economics, for better or worse, is an accomplished fact. As an example of the value of such formalisation in disciplining arguments, consider the recent boom in research on globalisation and labour markets. There are pointed arguments between trade and labour economists over issues of modelling, as well as within the community of trade economists over the interpretation of econometric work. What is striking, especially by comparison to similar disputes in related areas, is the extent to which the use of common formalisms has aided understanding and allowed for advance in the development of more inclusive formalisms and more systematic empirical work (see Gaston and Nelson, forthcoming). IR, and particularly strategic studies, has long benefited from an extensive use of formal theory. From early work by Richardson and Thomas Schelling, formal modelling of international conflict has developed into an increasingly sophisticated body of theory, and made systematic contributions to methodology in this area.[3]

Perhaps the easiest way to gauge the centrality of the norms of systematic collection and analysis of data and systematic theory building in political science or economics, at least in North America, is simply to open any issue of the major *general* journals such as the *American Political Science Review* or the *American Economic Review*. Sub-field journals show a similar pattern. In North America a notable exception, abstracting from sub-fields with an essentially philosophical orientation (and here only in political science), is the field of IPE where *International Organization* has a substantially lower frequency of quantitative and formal articles than the leading general IR journal, *International Studies Quarterly* (Waever, 1999, p. 702).

Of course, systematic data analysis and formal theory do appear in *IO*, *RIPE* and *New Political Economy*. What is particularly striking is not just that the relative emphasis on social scientific analysis is smaller, but that, even when such analysis is presented, it generally appears not as part of a programme of such analysis but, rather, as part of a broader rhetorical strategy, especially in the *IO* school. The characteristic mode of research in the *IO* school focuses on what the proponents see and characterise as 'great debates': realism, idealism, complex interdependence; liberalism, Marxism, statism; neorealism, neoliberal institutionalism, constructivism, etc. Consistent with their status as participants in great debates, these are grand theories, not conveniently reducible to formalisation for empirical or formal theoretical analysis. These debates are about how we (academics) should view the international political economy. The debates are essentially internal to the community of *IO* scholars, the contenders are all prima facie plausible, and, given the nature of the question, systematic theoretical and empirical frameworks can only be a subordinate part of the discourse.

Interestingly, this way of organising the work of an intellectual community is usually associated with heterodox research programmes that view themselves in conscious opposition to some orthodoxy. Within economics it is Marxist, post-Keynesian and Austrian economists that engage in this sort of analysis, not mainstream neoclassical economists.

In economics and political science, when reporting results from within mainstream/orthodox research programmes, literature reviews seek to identify points of continuity and distinction with respect to clearly, and fairly narrowly, posed research questions. The main point in such work is the empirical or theoretical result, not the broader argument. In the characteristic *IO* paper, the reverse is the case.

Characterising the rest of the field of IPE, when faced with a heterodox orthodoxy, is difficult. This is rendered more difficult by the *IO* school's rhetorical, attachment to the language of science. Thus, the language of theory, data and testing are deployed throughout the journal, even in the context of work which is essentially discursive. The critical school is clearly heterodox relative to American social science in general and the *IO* school in particular. Ironically, given the conscious and programmatic rejection of the norms of science which play a fundamental role in the constitution of American political science, the critical school spends a larger part of its published output on direct analysis of issues in the world as they appear. Thus, it is quite striking that *IO* has, for better or worse, been considerably less interested in globalisation *per se*, and the trailing issues of international finance, poverty, national sovereignty, gender, etc, than *RIPE* or *New Political Economy*, even though many of these were central to the *IO* problematic in the early years of its development.

Within the critical school, adherence to the norms of orthodox social science is less widespread for at least three reasons. First, as Chris Brown (2001, p. 192) suggests, as a part of critical international relations, critical school IPE has a tendency to become a 'catchall of the disaffected', an 'oppositional frame of mind [that] is not, in and of itself, sufficient to delineate an approach', whether scientific, historical, hermeneutic, or anything else. Second, the commitment to addressing the largest possible audience bequeathed to the critical school by Susan Strange runs counter to the tendency towards some kind of formalisation that marks all sciences. Third, and perhaps most significantly, Cox's (1981) admonition to see IPE as the study of how social structures, especially structures of inequality, come into being and are transformed, leads critical school scholars towards the epistemological foundations of history and to concern with reflectivist questions about the ways that a social science observer can shape history through her own work and the entire problem of effective persuasive communication that cannot be formalised easily.

Nonetheless, it is important to recognise that the difference between historical and social scientific norms is far from clear, as E. H. Carr

(1967) emphasised in *What is History?*, one of the epistemological touch-stones of the critical school. When Randall Germain (2000) outlines a systematic historical approach to globalisation, it is difficult to distin-guish from a comparative, hypothesis-driven, empirical social science approach aimed systematic theory building. Significantly, despite their character as a broad, oppositional church, British IPE's major institu-tions – IPEG, *RIPE*, *New Political Economy*, texts such as Stubbs and Underhill, and major summaries of theory such as Gill and Mittelman or Germain – rarely invite in the strong (and equally oppositional) post-structuralists and post-modernists who deny the possibility of the scien-tific project. As Alex Wendt (2001, p. 221) argues, the champions of critical international relations may be slowly coming to recognise that positivism could actually be a foundation for critical theory rather than always its other, a possibility arguably manifested in the fact that a realist view of science is implicit in Marxism, the origin of contemporary critical theory.

Explaining a heterodox field

One part of the success of critical school IPE is relatively easy to explain. American hegemony, and the hegemony of *IO* school IPE, created op-portunities for those who opposed either or both projects. Leading scholars such as Strange and Cox who found themselves increasingly distant from the *IO* orthodoxy, and a diverse generation of younger scholars, had institutional resources in Britain, Canada and elsewhere that allowed them to establish and maintain programmes intellectually separate from the orthodoxy. Finally, and perhaps most significantly, the critical school produces works that are popular, as a quick search by 'bestselling' on the amazon.co(m) sites in both the Britain and the US will verify. Three years after her death, Susan Strange's books sell much better on both sides of the Atlantic than works by any of the *IO* scholars, and even in the United States, Robert W. Cox's bestselling work is just as popular as Robert O. Keohane's.

Yet, a question remains: why did the more scientific students of IR fail to take on the new agenda of topics that were addressed by nascent IPE on both sides of the Atlantic? The complete answer is perhaps less clear, but a partial answer is certainly the incredible investment that had, by the 1970s, already been made in creating data sets and developing tools to analyse the topics that initially engaged scientific IR: questions of war and peace, of arms races and arms control, of conflict escalation and abatement. The modal response to the new agenda was often for scholars deeply involved in the developing and use of conflict events data to cooperate with international economists, deeply conversant with economic data, in studies that explored their linkage (see e.g. Gasiorowski and Polachek, 1982).

At the same time, there were other scientifically trained scholars in North America whose own research led them to epistemological conundra that could not be resolved within the simple versions of positivism that they had embraced in their earlier work; Richard Ashley, Michael Schapiro, Hayward Alker, James Rosenau and others (Murphy, 1998). Some of these scholars became significant contributors to critical school IPE. Alker was one of the early major backers of *RIPE*; Rosenau a contributor to the Gill and Mittelman volume. Similarly, a number of North American feminists whose work is now considered part of critical IPE, including Cynthia Enloe and J. Ann Tickner, made similar epistemological moves. Significantly, though, many of these scholars – e.g. Alker, Rosenau, Tickner – did not abandon an explicit preference for the most basic goals of a scientific approach: systematic data collection and some degree of rigorous formalisation of propositions even if in common language. Others, such as Enloe, followed a pattern similar to that of Strange of writing for a large audience and claiming a degree of epistemological eclecticism, yet tending to honour conventional scientific principles in practice. Significantly, this group of critics among the rigorously scientifically trained scholars did not come to embrace the *IO* school as *the only* or even sometimes as *a* legitimate contributor of knowledge of the global political economy.

Why the broader field of more scientific political science in the US – in comparative politics and American politics – accepted the relatively heterodox *IO* school work as a reasonable addition or substitute for more scientific IR in increasingly orthodox departments may require a very specific explanation. Part of the story is surely the rhetorical attachment to the norms of social science by the leading figures of the *IO* school. Thus, in the waning years of the wars over the behavioural revolution, many of the then young leaders of what was to become American IPE were strong supporters of the introducing of a more social scientific approach in both graduate education and in research. A number of the central figures in the *IO* school, especially Keohane, became major advocates of the scientific approach. Keohane played a central role in bringing a major cohort of scholars doing formal and empirical work to Harvard, an institution whose Government Department remains the most prestigious in the US, and Keohane worked with two of his Harvard colleagues to write what has become one of the standard scientific methodological texts in the field (King, Keohane and Verba, 1994). *IO* itself also looked, in these early years, more committed to social science than it would – with scholars like Oran Young working on systematic theory building and others, like Peter Katzenstein and Richard Rosecrance, attempting to measure interdependence in ways that were fully consistent with the sort of work being done in other branches of political science. The kind of scholastic exercises of 'great debates' that filled the pages of *IO* may have looked heterodox to many political scientists, but for those committed to science, the *IO* school often both looked like it was on the same side and, perhaps, was more in touch with issues that interested students and funders than many of the scientists of international conflict.

Prospects

Ole Waever predicts that US-based IPE, centred on the journal *International Organization*, will become both less heterodox and less relevant to scholars in other parts of the world. In fact, 'The best hope for a more global, less asymmetrical discipline lies in the American turn to rational choice, which is not going to be copied in Europe' (1999, p. 726). We believe that Waever is correct, at least to the extent that it is a basis for a continuing differentiation between the *IO* school and critical school IPE. Critical school IPE will survive and thrive in the social contexts of professional communities that need not respond to the fashions of American foreign policy or of American social science. We question, though, whether the continued embrace of a strictly heterodox attitude towards social science methodology will be that helpful to the emancipatory project of critical IPE.

Significantly, the empirical chapters within this volume embrace (mostly implicitly) a realist view of science that is not that far afield from the epistemology underlying much of mainstream economics and political science, even if, clearly, the emancipatory goals differ. Similarly, the scholarly exemplars proposed by Chris White (Mark Rupert) and Chris Farrands (Pierre Bourdieu) are not that distant from the standard model of social science. Bourdieu is a systematic collector of data, ready to make statistical arguments (when appropriate) as well as a self-conscious and reflexive concept-builder and developer of precise ways of formulating research expectations and reporting on their confirmation or refutation. While not as much an inventor of new formalisms as (say) Karl Marx was, Bourdieu is, certainly, just as fundamentally a social scientist. Rupert is a self-conscious scientific realist, a master of empirical archival research, and one of the IPE Gramscians who most explicitly and most accurately embraces the methodology reflected in the work of the Italian theorist whose touchstones were the evolutionary ('Darwinian') Marxist, Labriola and the idealist historian, Croce. Of course, Rupert seeks insights from as broad a range of social theory as possible, as did Gramsci, as did Marx, as did Thorstein Veblen (the academic social scientist whose theory of society some claim most resembled Gramsci's), as, for that matter, did Adam Smith.

There are, of course, real epistemological conundra that have to be confronted by all social scientists. Sandra Harding's (1992) or Robert Cox's understanding of 'objectivity' is certainly more accurate than the simplistic notion that there can be a social science beholden only to an abstract idea of truth. Moreover, the central point of Robert O. Keohane's (2001, pp. 10–11; cf. Murphy, 1998) recent American Political Science Association presidential address is one that critical IR scholars like Hayward Alker (following Anatol Rapoport) have been trying to make for decades: we understand very little about the processes of persuasive communication and, in the ideal case of unconstrained communication under perfectly democratic institutions, we *cannot* expect to find covering laws to explain the result of attempts at persuasion. Nonetheless, as Wendt (2001) has argued, the scope for liberating knowledge production under the relatively simple norms of social science remains large.

Notes

1. This chapter is largely based on Craig N. Murphy and Douglas R. Nelson (2001) 'International Political Economy: A Tale of Two Heterodoxies', *British Journal of Politics and International Relations*, vol. 3, no. 3. We are grateful to the journal and the publisher.
2. In addition to the four (soon to be five) volumes of Elsevier's *Handbook of Econometrics*, and with the exceptions of the *Handbooks of Mathematical Economics*, *Game Theory with Economic Applications* and *Social Choice and Welfare*, all the other handbooks feature econometric research prominently.
3. Bueno de Mesquita (2000) provides an excellent bibliography.

Bibliography

Abbasi, K. (1999a) 'The World Bank and world health: changing sides', *British Medical Journal*, vol. 318, pp. 865–8

Abbasi, K. (1999b) 'The World Bank and world health: healthcare strategy', *British Medical Journal*, vol. 318, pp. 933–6

Abbasi, K. (1999c) 'The World Bank and world health: interview with Richard Feachem', *British Medical Journal*, vol. 318, pp. 1206–8

Abbott, J. (2001) 'Democracy@internet.asia? The challenges to the emancipatory potential of the net: lessons from China and Malaysia', *Third World Quarterly*, vol. 22, no. 1, pp. 99–114

Adorno, T. and Horkheimer, J. (1986) *Dialectics of Enlightenment* (Verso, London)

Aglietta, M. (2000) 'Shareholder value and corporate governance: a comment and some tricky questions', *Economy and Society*, vol. 29, no. 1, pp. 146–59

Agnew, J. and Corbridge, S. (1995) *Mastering Space: Hegemony, Territory and International Political Economy* (Routledge, London)

Albert, M. (1993) *Capitalism Against Capitalism* (Whurr Publishers, London)

Alexander, J. (1995) 'Mod, Anti, Post, Neo', *New Left Review*, 210, pp. 65–105

Allen, F. and Gale, D. (2000) *Comparing Financial Systems* (MIT Press, London)

Allen, R. E. (1994) *Financial Crises and Recession in the Global Economy* (Elgar, Aldershot)

Almond, G., and Coleman, J. (eds) (1960) *The Politics of the Developing Areas* (Princeton University Press, Princeton).

Almond, G., and Powell, G. B. (1966) *Comparative Politics: A Developmental Approach*, (Little, Brown Boston).

Amin, A. and Palan, R. (1996) 'Editorial: the need to historicise IPE', *Review of International Political Economy*, vol. 3, no. 2, pp. 209–15

Amoore, L. (2000a) 'International Political Economy and the Contested Firm', *New Political Economy*, 5, pp. 183–204

Amoore, L., Dodgson, R., Gills, B. K., Langley, P., Marshall, D. and Watson, I. (1997) 'Overturning globalisation: resisting the teleological, reclaiming the political', *New Political Economy*, 2, pp. 179–95

Amoore, L., Dodgson, R., Gills, B., Marshall, D. Langley, P. and Watson, I. (2000b) 'Overturning globalisation: resisting the teleological, reclaiming the political', in B. K. Gills (ed.), *Globalisation and the Politics of Resistance* (Palgrave Macmillan, London)

Amoore, L., Dodgson, R., Germain, R., Gills, B., Langley, P. and Watson, I. (2000c), 'Paths to a historicised international political economy', *Review of International Political Economy*, vol. 7, no. 1, pp. 53–71

Anderson, B. (2000) *Doing the Dirty Work: The Global Politics of Domestic Labour* (Zed, London)

Archer, M. (ed.) (1998) Critical Realism: Essential readings (Routledge, London)

Arendt, H. (1993) 'Truth and politics', in *Between Past and Future* (Penguin Books, Harmondsworth), pp. 227–64

Arrow, K. J. K. J., Sen, A. K., and Suzumura, K., (1992) *Handbook of Social Choice and Welfare* (1992) (Amsterdam: Elsevier Science)

Ashley, R. and Walker, R. B. J. (1990) 'Reading dissidence/writing the discipline. crisis and the question of sovereignty in international studies', *International Studies Quarterly*, vol. 34, no. 3, pp. 367–416

Ashley, R. and Walker, R. B. J. (1990) 'Reading dissidence/writing the discipline. Crisis and the question of sovereignty in international studies', *International Studies Quarterly* vol. 34, no. 3, pp. 367–416

Atkins, R. and Enzweiler, T. (2000) 'German fiscal reform may "weaken corporate culture"', *Financial Times*, 14 August

Aumann, R. J. and Hart, S. (1994–2002) *Handbook of Game Theory with Economic Applications* (Elsevier Science, Amsterdam)

Baker, A. (1999) 'Nebuleuse and the "internationalization of the state" in the UK? The Case of HM Treasury and the Bank of England', *Review of International Political Economy*, vol. 6, no. 1 (spring), pp. 79–100

Bales, K. (1999) *Disposable People: New Slavery in the Global Economy*, (University of California Press, Berkeley)

Ball, D. and Macgregor, D. (1999) 'A net gain for Africa?', *BBC News Online Network* 10 September, http://news.bbc.co.uk

Barber, T. (2000a) 'Business landscape takes on a new shape', *Financial Times*, 23 October, p. i

Barber, T. (2000b) 'A cure for the German disease', *Financial Times*, 23 October, p. ii

Barber, T. (2000c) 'The biggest winners in the new equity culture', *Financial Times*, 23 October, p. iv

Barber, T. and Simonian, H. (2001) 'Germany's financial vision', *Financial Times*, 12 February

Bauman, Z. (1998) *Globalization: The Human Consequences* (Polity, Cambridge)

BBC, *Panorama*, 'Gap and Nike: no sweat', 15 November 2000

Bebchuk, L. (1999) 'A rent-protection theory of corporate ownership and control', *Harvard Law School Working Paper*, no. 260

Beck, U. (2000a) *What is Globalization?* (Polity, Cambridge)

Beck, U. (2000b) *The Brave New World of Work* (Polity, Cambridge)

Bellamy, R. (1990) 'Gramsci, Croce and the Italian tradition', *History of Political Thought*, vol. XI, no. 2

Bellinghausen, H. (1999) 'Bellinghausen interviews Marcos about Consulta', *La Jornada*, 11 and 12 March. Also at: http://flag.blackened.net/revolt/mexico/ezln/1999/inter_marcos_consul_mar.html

Bhabha, H. K. (1994) *The Location of Culture* (Routledge, London)

Bhaskar, R. (1991) *Philosophy and the Idea of Freedom* (Blackwell, Oxford).

Bimber, B. (2000) 'Measuring the gender gap on the Internet', *Social Science Quarterly*, vol. 81, no. 3, pp. 868–76

Birchfield, V. (1999) 'Contesting the hegemony of market ideology: Gramsci's "good sense" and Polanyi's "double movement"', *Review of International Political Economy*, vol. 6, no. 1, pp. 27–54

Blake, D. H. and Walters, R. S. (1976) *The Politics of Global Economic Relations* (Prentice-Hall, Englewood Cliffs, NJ)

Blixen, S and Fazio, C. (1995) 'Interview with Marcos about neoliberalism, the nation-state and democracy', http://flag.blackened.net/revolt/mexico/ezln/inter_marcos_aut95.html

Booth, K. (1997) 'Discussion: a reply to Wallace', *Review of International Studies*, vol. 23, no. 3, pp. 371–7

Born, K. (1983) *International Banking in the 19th and 20th Centuries* (Berg Publishers, Leamington Spa)

Bourdieu, P. (1977) *Outline of a Theory of Practice* (Cambridge University Press, Cambridge)

Bourdieu, P. (1982) *Ce Que Parler Veut Dire* (Fayard, Paris)

Bourdieu, P. (1984) *Homo Academicus* (Éditions de Minuit, Paris)

Bourdieu, P. (1991) *Language and Symbollic Power* (Harvard University Press, Cambridge, Mass).

Bourdieu, P. (1993) *The Field of Cultural Production*, ed. and trans. R. Johnson (Polity, Cambridge)

Bourdieu, P. (1999) 'Scattered remarks', *European Journal of Social Theory*, vol. 2, no. 3, pp. 334–40

Bourdieu, P. and Wacquant, L. (1992) *Invitation to Reflexive Sociology* (Chicago University Press, Chicago)

Boyer, R. (2000) 'Is a finance-led growth regime a viable alternative to Fordism? A preliminary analysis', *Economy and Society*, vol. 29, no. 1, pp. 111–45

Braudel, F. (1973) *The Mediterranean and the Mediterranean world in the age of Philip II*, (Collins, London)

Braudel, F. (1984) *Civilization and Capitalism, 15th–18th Centuries*, vols I–III (University of California Press, Berkeley)

Brothers, C. (1998) 'Mexico denies Zapatista claims for clandestine talks', *National Commission for Democracy in Mexico* (NCDM) 3 February

Brown, C. (2001) 'Our side? Critical theory and international relations', in R. Wyn Jones (ed.), *Critical Theory and World Politics* (Lynne Rienner, Boulder, CO)

Brundtland, G. H. (2001a) 'Health policies in the global economy', Speech to the Energy Policy Foundation of norway Conference, 10 February

Brundtland, G. H. (2001b) 'Globalization as a force for better health', Lecture at the London School of Economics, 16 March

Brundtland, G. H. (2001c) 'Closing speech', WHO/WTO Workshop on Differential Pricing and Financing of Essential Drugs, 11 April

Bueno de Mesquita, B. (2000) *Principles of International Politics: People's Power, Preferences and Perceptions* (CQ Press, Washington, DC)

Burbach, R. (1992) 'Ruptured frontiers: the transformation of the US/Latin American System', *Socialist Register*, pp. 239–50

Burbach, R. (1994) 'The roots of the post-modern rebellion in Chiapas', *New Left Review*, 205, May/June, pp. 113–24

Burbach, R. and Rosset, P. (1994) *Chiapas and the Crisis Of Mexican Agriculture*, Food First Policy Brief, Food First Institute for Food and Development Policy, Oakland. Also at: http://www.cs.unb.ca/~alopez/politics/chiapasagri.html.

Burch, K. and Denemark, R. (eds) (1997) *Constituting International Political Economy* (Lynne Rienner, Boulder)

Burn, G. (2000) *The Role of the British State in the Re-emergence of Global Capital*, PhD dissertation (unpublished) University of Sussex

Callinicos, A. (1995) *Theories and Narratives: Reflections on the Philosophy of History* (Polity, Cambridge)

Campbell, A., Converse, P., Miller, W. and Stokes D. (1960) *The American Voter* (Wiley, New York)

Carr, E. H. (1967) *What is History?* (Knopf, New York)

Carrigan, A. (1998) 'Why is the Zapatista Movement so Attractive to Mexican Civil Society?', *Civreports*, vol. 2, no. 2, March/April. Also at http://www.civnet .cvg/journal/issue6/repacatt.htm

Castells, M. (1996) *The Information Age: Economy, Society and Culture. Vol. I: The Rise of the Network Society* (Oxford, UK: Blackwell, Cambridge, Mass)

Cerny, P. G. (1990) *The Changing Architecture of Politics: Structure, Agency and the Future of the State* (Sage, London)

Cerny, P. G. (ed.) (1993a) *Finance and World Politics: Markets, Regimes and States in the Post-Hegemonic Era* (Elgar, Aldershot)

Cerny, P. G. (1993b) 'American decline and embedded financial orthodoxy', in P. G. Cerny (ed.), *Finance and World Politics: Markets, Regimes, and States in the Post-hegemonic Era* (Ashgate, Aldershot)

Cerny, P. G. (1994) 'The dynamics of financial globalization: technology, market structure and policy response', *Policy Sciences*, vol. 27, no. 4, pp. 319–42

Cerny, P. G. (1995) 'Globalization and the changing logic of collective action', *International Organization*, vol. 49, no. 4, pp. 595ff

Cerny, P. G. (2000) 'Political agency in a globalizing world: toward a structurational approach', *European Journal of International Relations*, vol. 6, no. 4, pp. 435–63

Cheru, F. (1997) 'The silent revolution and the weapons of the weak: transformation and innovation from below', in S. Gill and J. Mittelman (eds), *Innovation and Transformation in International Studies* (Cambridge University Press, Cambridge), pp. 153–69

China Internet Network Information Centre (2000) 'Semi-annual Survey report on Internet Development in China (2000.1)', *CINIC*, January, at http://www.cnnic.net.cn/Develst_e/cnnic2000_e.htm

Chowdhury, Z. and Rowson, M. (2000) 'The People's Health Assembly: revitalising the promise of "Health for All"', *British Medical Journal*, vol. 321, 1361–2

Clark, G. L. (1999) 'The retreat of the state and the rise of pension fund capitalism', in R. Martin (ed.) *Money and the Space Economy* (John Wiley & Sons, Chichester), pp. 241–60

Coates, D. (1999) 'Models of capitalism in the new world order: the UK case', *Political Studies*, vol. 47, no. 4, pp. 643–60

Coates, D. (2000) *Models of Capitalism: Growth and Stagnation in the Modern Era* (Polity Press, Cambridge)

COM (1999) 134, *Commission Communication: Towards a Single Market for Supplementary Pensions*, 11 May

Computer Industry Almanac (1998) '15 leading countries in Internet users per capita', *Computer Industry Almanac Inc.*, 19 March, at http://www.c-i-a.com/19980319.htm

Computer Industry Almanac (1999) 'US tops 100 million Internet users according to computer industry almanac', *Computer Industry Almanac Inc.* 1 January at http://www.c-i-a.com/199911iu.htm

Conger, L. (1994) 'Zapatista Thunder', *Current History*, March at http://www.cs.unb.ca/~alopez-o/politics/zapatista.html

Connolly, W. E. (1995) *The Ethos of Pluralization (University of Minnesota, Minneapolis)*

Cox, A. (1986) 'The state, finance and industry relationship in comparative perspective', in A. Cox (ed.), *State, Finance and Industry* (Harvester Wheatsheaf, London)

Cox, R. W. (1981) 'Social forces, states, and world orders: beyond international relations theory', *Millennium Journal of International Studies*, vol. 10, no. 2

Cox, R., (1986) 'Social forces, states and world orders: beyond international relations theory', in R. O. Keohane and J. Nye (eds), *Neorealism and its Critics* (Columbia University Press, New York)

Cox, R. W. (1987) *Power, Production and World Order: Social Forces in the Making of History* (Columbia University Press, New York)

Cox, R. W. (1992) 'Globalization, multilateralism, and democracy', John Holmes Memorial Lecture to the 1992 conference of the Academic Council on the United Nations System, Washington, DC

Cox, R. W. (1996) 'Globalization, multilateralism, and democracy', in R. Cox, *Approaches to World Order* (Cambridge University Press, Cambridge)

Cox, R. W. (1996) *Approaches to World Order* (Cambridge University Press, Cambridge)

Cox, R. W. (ed.) (1998) *The New Realism* (Palgrave Macmillan, London and New York)

Cox, R. W. (1999) 'Civil Society at the turn of the Millennium; Prospects for an Alternative World Order', *Review of International Studies*, vol. 25, no. 1, pp. 5–29

Cox, R. W. (2001) 'The way ahead: toward a new ontology of world order', in R. Wyn Jones (ed.), *Critical Theory and World Politics* (Lynne Rienner, Boulder, CO)

Cox, R. W. and Jacobson, H. K. (1973) *The Anatomy of Influence: decision Making in International Organization (Yale University Press, London and New Haven)*

Cox R. W. (1983) 'Gramsci, Hegemony and international relations: an essay in method', *Millennium Journal of International Studies*, vol. 12, no. 2, pp. 162–75

Coyle, D. (1997) *Weightless World* (Capstone, Oxford)

Crafts, N. (1993) *Can De-Industrialisation Seriously Damage Your Health? A Review of Why Growth Rates Differ and How to Improve Economic Performance* (Institute of Economic Affairs, London)

Cronin, Mary J. (1996) *Global Advantage on the Internet: From Corporate Connectivity to International Competitiveness*, Van Nostrand Reinhold, New York

Crossley, Nick (2001) 'The phenomenological habitus and its construction', *Theory and Society*, 30, February, pp. 81–120

Crouch, C. (1997) 'Skills-based full employment: the latest philosopher's stone', *British Journal of Industrial Relations*, vol. 35, no. 3, pp. 367–91

Crouch, C. and Streeck, W. (eds.) (1997) *Political Economy of Modern Capitalism* (Sage, London)

Cully, M. (1999) *Britain at Work: As Depicted by 1998 Workplace Employee Relations Survey* (Routledge, New York)

Curley, M. (1999) *Participation, Empowerment and Microsecurity: Implications for the Security Debate in International Relations*, unpublished doctoral thesis

Danford, A. (1998) 'Work organisation inside Japanese firms in South Wales', in Thompson and Warhurst (eds), *Workplaces of the Future* (Palgrave Macmillan, Basingstoke)

Dawson, Michael and Foster, John Bellamy, (1996) 'Virtual Capitalism: The Political Economy of the Information Highway', *Monthly Review* 48

Davies, M. and Niemann, M. (2000) 'Henri Lefebvre and global politics: social spaces and everyday struggles', Paper presented to the Annual Convention of the International Studies Association, Los Angeles, 14–18 March

Deeg, R. (1993) 'The state, banks, and economic governance in Germany', *German Politics*, vol. 2, no. 2 (August), pp. 149–76

Deeg, R. (1999) *Finance Capitalism Unveiled: Banks and the German Political Economy* (University of Michigan Press, Michigan)

de Huerta, M. D. and Higgins, N. (1999) 'Interview with Zapatista Leader Subcommandante Marcos', *International Affairs*, 75, April, pp. 269–81

Der Derian, J. and Schapiro, M. (eds) (1989) *International/Intertextual Relations: Post-modern Readings of World Politics* (Lexington Books, Lexington, Mass)

Deutsche Bundesbank (1997) 'Shares as financing and investment instruments', *Monthly Report of the Deutsches Bundesbank*, vol. 49, no. 1, pp. 27–40

Docherty, T. (ed.) (1993) *Postmodernism A Reader* (Harvester Wheatsheaf, London)

Doole, C. (2000) 'Is the web widening the poverty gap?', *BBC News Online Network*, 29 January, at http://news.bbc.co.uk

Dore, R., Lazonick, W. and O'Sullivan, M. (1999) 'Varieties of capitalism in the twentieth century', *Oxford Review of Economic Policy*, vol. 15, no. 4 (winter), pp. 102–20

Dwight, R. (2001) 'The winners and losers as Basel rewrites the bank rules', *Evening Standard*, 18 January, p. 44

Dyson, E., Gilder, G., Keyworth, G., and Toffler, A., (1994) 'Cyberspace and the American Dream: A Magna Carta for the Knowledge Age', at http://www.pff.org/position.html, Washington: Progress and Freedom Foundation.

Eatwell, J. and Taylor, L. (2000) *Global Finance at Risk: The Case for International Regulation* (New York Press, New York)

Economist (1994) 'A survey of international Banking: recalled to life', 30 April

Economist (1995) 'The myth of the powerless state', 7 October

Edwards, J. and Fischer, K. (1996) *Banks, Finance and Investment in Germany* (Cambridge University Press, Cambridge)

Edwards, J. and Nibler, M. (2000) 'Corporate governance in Germany: the role of banks and ownership concentration', *Economic Policy*, 31, pp. 237–68

Edwards, J. and Ogilvie, S. (1996) 'Universal banks and German industrialization: a reappraisal', *Economic History Review*, vol. 49, no. 3, pp. 427–46

Ejército Zapatista de Liberación Nacional (1994) 'Second declaration of the Lacandon Jungle', http://www.ezln.org/fzln/2nd-decl.html

Ejército Zapatista de Liberación Nacional (1996) 'The San Andres Accords', http://flag.blackened.net/revolt/mexico/ezln/san_andres.html, 1996

Enlace Civil, A. C. (1988) *Autonomous Municipalities: The resistance of the indigenous communities in response to the war in Chiapas*, November, http://flag.blackened.net/revolt/mexico/comment/auto_munc_nov98.html

Enloe, C. (1989) *Bananas, Beaches and Bases: Making Feminist Sense of International Politics* (University of California Press, Berkeley)

Escobar, A. and Alvarez, S. (1992) *The Making of Social Movements in Latin America: Identity, Strategy and Democracy* (Westview, Boulder, CO)

European Industrial Relations Observatory (EIRO), *Annual Review* (Luxembourg, EIRO)

Everard, J. (2000) *Virtual States* (Routledge, London)

Falk, R. (1999) *Predatory Globalization: A Critique* (Polity Press and Blackwell, Cambridge and Malden, MA)

Farrands, C., Worth, O. and Abbott, J. (2001) 'Critical theory in global political economy: Critique? Knowledge? Emancipation?', Paper presented to the 42nd International Studies Association Annual Convention, Chicago

Featherstone, M. (ed.) (1990) *Global Culture: Nationalism, Globalisation and Modernity* (Sage, London).

Federal Reserve Board (2000) 'Recent changes in US family finances: results from the 1998 survey of consumer finances', Federal Reserve Bulletin, January, pp. 1–29

Flood, A. (1996) 'Understanding the Zapatistas' http://flag.blackened.net/revolt/ws96/ws56_Zapatistas.html

Flood, A. (1999) 'The Zapatistas, anarchists and direct democracy', *Anarcho-Syndicalist Review*, 27, winter. Also available at http://flag.blackened.net/revolt/andrew/zap_asr.html

Foucault, M. (1991a) 'Discipline and punish', in P. Rabinow (ed.), *A Foucault Reader* (Penguin, London)

Foucault, M. (1991b) 'Space, power and knowledge', in P. Rabinow (ed.), *A Foucault Reader* (Penguin, London)

Foucault, M. (1991c) 'What is enlightenment', in P. Rabinow (ed.), *A Foucault Reader* (Penguin, London)

Foucault, M. (1997a) 'What is critique?', in M. Foucault, *The Politics of Truth* (Semiotexte, New York), ed. S. Lotringer and L. Hochroth, trans L. Hochroth

Foucault. M. (1997b) 'The ethics of the concern of the self as a practice of freedom', quoted in P. Rabinow, *Ethics, Subjectivity and Truth* (The Free Press, New York)

Frank, A. G. (1967) *Capitalism and Underdevelopment in Latin America Historical Studies of Chile and Brazil* (Monthly Review Press, New York)

Frank, Andre Gunder and Gills, B. (eds.) (1993) *The World System* (Routledge, London)

Frederick, C. A. N. (1999) 'Feminist rhetoric in cyberspace: the *Ethos* of feminist usenet newsgroups', *The Information Society*, vol. 15, no. 3, pp. 187–97

Frieden, J. A. and Lake, D. A. (2000) *International Political Economy*, 4th edn (Bedford/St Martin's, New York)

Friedman, M. (1982) *Capitalism and Freedom* (Chicago University Press, Chicago)

Friedman, T. (2000) *The Lexus and the Olive Tree* (HarperCollins, London).

Fuentes, C. (1993) 'Mexico's financial crisis is political, and the remedy is democracy' in L. Diamond (ed.) *Political Culture and Democracy in Developing Countries* (Lynne Rienner, Boulder). Also at http://www.cs.unb.ca/~alopez-o/politics/fuentes.html

Fuentes, C. (2000) 'Mexico's financial crisis is political, and the remedy is democracy', *Documents on Mexican Politics* http://www.cs.unb.ca/~alopez/politics/fuentes.html

Fukuyama, F. (1991) 'Liberal democracy as a global phenomenon', *Political Studies*, vol. 11, no. 2

G. (1990) 'The political possibilities of postmodernism', *Economy and Society*, vol. 19, no. 1

Gasiorowski M. J. and Polachek, S. W. (1982) 'Conflict and interdependence: east–west trade and linkages in the era of detente', *Journal of Conflict Resolution*, 26

Gaston, N. and Nelson, D. (forthcoming) 'Trade and wages in OECD countries: linking theory and evidence', in Joseph Francois (ed.), *Globalisation and Employment Patterns: Policy, Theory and Evidence* (Oxford University Press, New York)

Gates, B. (1995) *The Road Ahead* (Viking, New York)

George, J. (1994) *Discourses of Global Politics. A Critical (Re)introduction* (Lynne Rienner, Boulder, CO)

Germain, R. D. (1996) 'The worlds of finance: A braudelian perspective on IPE', *European Journal of International Relations* vol. 2, no. 2, pp. 201–30

Germain, R. D. (2000) *Globalization and Its Critics: Perspectives from Political Economy* (Palgrave Macmillan, New York and London)

Germain, R. D. and Kenny, M. (1998) 'Engaging Gramsci: international relations theory and the new Gramscians', *Review of International Studies*, vol. 24, no. 1, January, pp. 3–22

Gerschenkron, A. (1962) *Economic Backwardness in Historical Perspective* (Harvard University Press, Cambridge MA)

Geuss, I. (1982) *The Idea of a Critical Theory* (Cambridge University Press, Cambridge)

Ghosh, D. K. and Ortiz, E. (eds) (1997) *The Global Structure of Financial Markets: An Overview* (Routledge, London)

Giddens, A. (1998) *The Third Way: The Renewal of Social Democracy* (Polity Press, Cambridge)

Gill, S. (1990) *American Hegemony and the Trilateral Commission* (Cambridge University Press, Cambridge)

Gill, S. (ed.) (1993) *Gramsci, Historical Materialism and International Relations* (Cambridge University Press, Cambridge)

Gill, S. (1994) 'Structural change and global political economy: globalizing elites and the emerging world order', in Y. Sakamoto (ed.), *Global Transformation: Challenges to the State System* (United Nations University Press, Tokyo), pp. 169–99

Gill, S. (1995) 'Globalization, market civilization, and disciplinary neoliberalism', *Millennium: Journal of International Studies*, vol. 24, no. 3, pp. 399–423

Gill, S. and Law, D. (1988) *The Global Political Economy* (Harvester Wheatsheaf, Brighton)

Gill, S. and Mittelman, J. (eds) (1997) *Innovation and Transformation in International Studies* (Cambridge University Press, Cambridge)

Gills (ed.), *Globalisation and the Politics of Resistance*, Basingstoke: Palgrave Macmillan, 2000

Gilpin, R. (1987) *The Political Economy of International Reactions* (Princeton: University Press Princeton)

Gills, B., Rocamora, J. and Wilson, R. (eds) (1993) *Low Intensity Democracy. Power in the New World Order* (Pluto Press, London)

Gladwin, M. 'Theory and practice of contemporary social movements,' *Politics*. vol. 14, no. 2, pp. 59–65

Goodlee, F. (1994) 'The World Health Organisation: WHO in crisis', *British Medical Journal*, vol. 309, pp. 1424–8

Gorman, T. (2001) 'Gillian Rose and the project of a Critical Marxism', *Radical Philosophy*, 105, January, pp. 25–36

Gramsci, A. (1957) *The Modern Prince and Other Writings*, trans. Louis Marks (International Publishers, New York)

Gramsci, A. (1971) *Selections from the Prison Notebooks*, ed. and trans. Q. Hoare and G. Nowell Smith (Lawrence & Wishart, London)

Gramsci, A. (1994) *Pre-Prison Writings*, ed. R. Bellamy (Cambridge University Press, Cambridge)

Grant, J. (2000) 'Toehold is now firmer', *Financial Times*, 3 November

Gray, J. (1996) 'No turning back, *The Banker*, vol. 146, no. 850, December, pp. 20–1

Green, S. (2000) 'The pen, the sword and the networked computer', *The World Today*, March, pp. 13–15

Haacke, J. (1996) 'Theory and praxis in international relations: Habermas, self reflection, rational argumentation', *Millennium: Journal of International Studies*, vol. 25, no. 2, pp. 255–91

Habermas, J. (1979) *Communication and the Evolution of Society* (Heinemann Educational, London)

Habermas, J. (1987) *Knowledge and Human Interests* (Polity, Cambridge)

Hebermas, J. (1999) 'The liberal society: constitutionalism vs. democracy', unpublished lecture at Georgetown University, Washington, DC

Hall, P. A. (1986) *Governing the Economy* (Polity Press, Cambridge)

Hall, S. (1988) *The Hard Road to Renewal* (Verso, London)

Hall, S. (1998) 'The great moving nowhere show', *Marxism Today*, November

Handy, C. (1995) *The Future of Work* (Contemporary Papers, London)

Harding, R. (1999) '*Standort Deutschland* in the globalising economy: an end to the economic miracle?', *German Politics*, vol. 8, no. 1, April, pp. 66–88

Harding, S. (1992) 'After the neutrality ideal: science, politics and "strong objectivity"', *Social Research*, vol. 59, no. 3, pp. 567–87

Harm, C. (1992) 'The financing of small firms in Germany', Working Paper 899, spring, World Bank

Harmes, A. (1998) 'Institutional investors and the reproduction of neoliberalism', *Review of International Political Economy*, vol. 5, no. 1, pp. 92–121

Harnischfeger, U. (2000) 'Life still tough for private sector', *Financial Times*, 23 October, p. 4

Harrod, J. (1997) 'Social forces and joining the two IRs', in S. Gill and J. Mittelman (eds), *Innovation and Transformation in International Studies* (Cambridge University Press, Cambridge)

Harrod, J. and O'Brien, R. (eds) (forthcoming) *International Trade Unions: Theory and Strategy in the Global Economy*

Harvey, D. (1982) *The Limits to Capital* (Blackwell, Oxford)

Hay, C. and Marsh, D. (1999) 'Introduction: towards a new (international) political economy?', New Political Economy, vol. 4, no. 1, pp. 5–22

Haynes, J. (1997) *Democracy and Civil Society in the Third World: Politics and New Political Movements* (Polity Press, London)

Heckman, James and Leamer, Edward (1983–2001) *Handbook of Econometrics: Volumes 1-4* (Elsevier Science, Amsterdam)

Held, D., McGrew, A., Goldblatt, D. and Perraton, J. (1999) *Global Transformations: Politics, Economics and Culture* (Polity Press, Cambridge)

Helleiner, E. (1993) 'When finance was the Servant: international capital movements in the Bretton Woods era', in P. G. Cerny (ed.), *Finance and World Politics: Markets, Regimes, and States in the Post-hegemonic Era* (Edward Elgar, Aldershot)

Helleiner, E. (1994) *States and the Re-emergence of Global Finance* (Cornell University Press, Ithaca, NY)

Helleiner, E. (1996) 'IPE and the Greens', *New Political Economy*, 1

Hendry, D. and Morgan, M. (eds) (1995) *The Foundations of Econometric Analysis* (Cambridge University Press, Cambridge)

Herrhausen, A. (1989) 'Es Riecht nach Komplott and Konspiration', *Die Welt*, 27 October

Hilbert, S. (1997) 'For whom the nation? Internationalisation, Zapatismo and the struggle over Mexican modernity', *Antipode*, vol. 29, no. 2, pp. 115–48

Hilderbrand, Werner, and Sonnenschein, Hugo (1986–2001) *Handbook of Mathematical Economics Volume* (Elsevier Science, Amsterdam)

Hilferding, R. [1910] (1981) *Finance Capital: a Study of the latest Phase in Capitalist Development* (Routledge & Kegan Paul, London)

Hindess, B. (1998) 'Politics and liberation', in J Moss (ed.), *Later Foucault* (Sage, London)

Hirsch, F. (1976) *Social Limits to Growth* (Harvard University Press, Cambridge, MA)

Hirst, P. (1998) 'Power article', *Review of International Studies*, December

Hirst, P. and Thompson, G. (1996) *Globalization in Question* (Polity Press, Cambridge)

Hoffman, M. (1988) 'Conversations on critical theory', *Millennium: Journal of International Studies*, vol. 17, no. 1

Hoogvelt, A. (1997) Globalisation and the Postcolonial World: The New Political Economy of Development (Palgrave Macmillan, Basingstoke)

Huntingdon, S. (1997) 'After 20 years: the future of the third Wave' *Journal of Democracy*, no. 8, January/March, pp. 3–13

Hutchings, K. (2001) 'The nature of critique in critical international relations theory', in Wyn Jones (ed.), *Critical Theory and World Politics* (Lynne Rienner, Boulder, CO), pp. 79–90

Hyman, R. (1999) 'Imagined solidarities: can trade unions resist globalization?', in Leisink (ed.), *Globalization and Labour Relations* (Elgar, Cheltenham)

IILS (1999) *Labour and Society Programme*, International Institute for Labour Studies, Geneva

ILO (1995) *Deregulation, Not a Cure All*, World Employment Report, ILO, Geneva

ILO (2000) *Labour Practices in the Footwear, Leather, Textiles and Clothing Industries*, ILO, Geneva

IMF (2000) *Globalisation and Catching-Up: From Recession to Growth in Transition Economies*, International Monetary Fund Working Paper (WP/00/100)

Inayatullah, N. and Blaney, D. L. (1999) 'Towards an ethnological IPE: Karl Polanyi's double critique of capitalism', *Millennium: Journal of International Studies*, vol. 28, no. 2, pp. 311ff

Ingham, G. (1984) *Capitalism Divided? The City and Industry in British Social Development* (Palgrave Macmillan, London)

Ingham, G. (1996) 'Money is a social relation', *Review of Social Economy*, vol. 54, no. 4, pp. 507–29

Institut der Deutschen Wirtschaft (1999) 'Trade union membership and density in the 1990s' (IDW, Köln)

Jahn, B. (1998) 'One step forward, two steps back: critical theory as the latest edition of liberal idealism', *Millennium: Journal of International Studies*, vol. 27, no. 3, pp. 613–41

Jaideep, V. G. (2000a) 'Net activism without borders', *Online Journalism Review*, 13 January, at http://ojr.usc.edu/

Jaideep, V. G. (2000b) *E-Interview*, 9 March

Johnson, P. (1993) 'Feminism and the enlightenment', *Radical Philosophy*, vol. 63, no. 1, pp. 3–11

Johnston, D. S. (1991) 'Constructing the periphery in modern global politics', in C. N. Murphy and R. Tooze (eds), *The New International Political Economy* (Palgrave Macmillan, Basingstoke)

Jones, R. J. B. (1995) *Globalisation and Interdependence in the International Political Economy* (Pinter, London)

Jones, R. J. B. (2000) 'Globalization in perspective', in R. D. Germain (ed.), *Globalization and its Critics: Perspectives from Political Economy* (Palgrave Macmillan, London and New York), pp. 245–66

Kalish, D. E. (1999) 'Global companies form group to curb government regulation of Internet', *Naples Daily News*, 16 January

Kanavos, P., Mrazek, M., and Mossialos, E. (1999) 'Globalisation of pharmaceutical business: a comparative approach', Background paper for The Global Health: A Local Issue Seminar, the Nuffield Trust and Templeton College, Oxford University

Kapstein, E. B. (1994) *Governing the Global Economy: International Finance & the State* (Harvard University Press, Cambridge MA)

Katzenstein, P. J., Keohane, R. O. and Krasner, S. D. (1999) '*International Organization* and the Study of World Politics', *International Organization*, 52

Keohane, R. O. (1984) *After Hegemony: Cooperation and Discord in the World Political Economy* (Princeton University Press, Princeton, NJ)

Keohane, R. O. (1989) 'A personal intellectual history', in J. Kruzel and J. N. Rosenau (eds), *Journeys through World Politics: Autobiographical Reflections of Thirty-four Academic Travelers* (Lexington Books, Lexington, MA)

Keohane, R. O. (2001) 'Governance in a partially globalized world: Presidential Address, American Political Science Association, 2000', *American Political Science Review*, vol. 95, no. 1, pp. 1–13

Keohane, R. O. and Nye, J (1977) *Power and Interdependence: world politics in transition* (Little, Brown, Boston, MA)

King, G., Keohane, R. O. and Verba, S. (1994) *Designing Social Inquiry* (Princeton University Press, Princeton)

Klein, N. (2000) *No Logo* (Flamingo, London)

Klesner, J. (1998) 'An electoral route to democracy: Mexico's transition in comparative perspective', *Comparative Politics*, vol. 30, no. 4, pp. 477–97

Krameae, C. (1999) 'The language and nature of the Internet: the meaning of global', *New Media and Society*, vol. 1, no. 1, pp. 47–53

Krasner, S. D. (ed.) (1983) *International Regimes* (Cornell University Press, Ithaca, NY)

Krishnan, K. (1995) 'The first revolt against globalisation', *Monthly Review*, vol. 48, no. 1, pp. 1–22

Krugman, P. and Obstfeld, M. (2000) *International Economics: Theory and Policy* (Addison-Wesley, Reading, MA)

Lambert, R. (1999) 'International relations and industrial relations: exploring an interface', Paper presented at ISA Annual Convention, Washington, DC, 20 February

Lascano, L. (2000) '10 theses concerning the PRI defeat' http://flag.blackened.net/revolt/ezln/2000/fzln_10theses_july.html

Lash, S. and Urry, J. (1987) *The End of Organized Capitalism* (Polity Press, Cambridge)

Lawrence, S. (1999) 'Widening web', *Far Eastern Economic Review*, 18 November, pp. 54–5

Lawson, C. (1998) 'Mexico's new politics: the elections of 1997', *Journal of Democracy*, no. 8, January/March, pp. 3–28

Lawton, T. C., Rosenau, J. N. and Verdun, A. C. (eds) (2000) *Strange Power: Shaping the Parameters of International Relations and International Political Economy* (Ashgate, Aldershot)

Lee, K. (1995) 'A neo-Gramscian approach to international organisation: an expanded analysis of current reforms to UN development activities', in J. Macmillan and A. Linklater, *Boundaries in Question: New Directions in International Relations* (Pinter, London)

Lee, K. (1999a) 'Globalisation and health policy: a review of the literature and proposed research and policy agenda', *Discussion Paper No 1*, London School of Hygiene and Tropical Medicine

Lee, K. (1999b) 'The Global Dimensions of Health', *Background Paper* for The Global Health: A Local Issue Seminar, the Nuffield Trust and Templeton College, Oxford University

Lefebvre, H. (1991) *The Production of Space* (Blackwell, Oxford)

Lewis, W. Arthur (1978) *The Evolution of the International Economic Order* (Princeton University Press, Princeton, NJ)

Leys, C. (1996) 'The crisis in development theory', *New Political Economy*, vol. 1, no. 1

Leyshon, A. and Thrift, N. (1995) 'Geographies of financial exclusion: financial abandonment in Britain and the United States', Transactions of the Institute of British Geographers, no. 20, pp. 312–41

Leyshon, A. and Thrift, N. (1997) *Money/Space: Geographies of Monetary Transformation* (Routledge, London)

Leyshon, A., Thrift, N. and Pratt, J. (1998) 'Reading financial services: texts, consumers and financial literacy, *Environment and Planning D: Society and Space*, vol. 16, no. 1, pp. 29–55

Linklater, A. (1990) *Beyond Realism and Marxism: Critical Theory and International Relations* (Palgrave Macmillan, Basingstoke)

Linklater, A. (1996) 'The achievement of critical theory', in S. Smith, K. Booth and M. Zalewski (eds), *International Theory: Positivism and Beyond* (Cambridge University Press, Cambridge)

Linklater, A. (1998) *The Transformation of Political Community* (Polity Press, Cambridge)

Lipshutz, R. (1992) 'Reconstructing world politics: the emergence of a global civil society', *Millennium: Journal of International Studies*, vol. 21, no. 3, pp. 389–420

Lipshutz, R. (1996) *Global Civil Society and Global Environmental Governance: The Politics of Nature from Place to Planet* (State University of New York Press, New York)

Loewendahl, H. B. (1999) 'Siemens' "Anglo-Saxon" strategy: is globalising business enough?', *German Politics*, vol. 8, no. 1, April, pp. 89–105

Long, R. (1999) 'Challenge to state hegemony: competing nationalisms and the staging of the conflict in Chiapas', *Journal of Latin American Cultural Studies*, vol. 8, no. 1, pp. 1–15

Lutz, S. (1999a) 'Vom koordinierten zum marktorientierten kapitalismus? Der deutsche Finanzsektor im Umbrach,' *polis Nr. 44*, Institut fur Politikwissenschaft: der Fern Universitat, Hagan

Lutz, S. (1999b) 'From managed to market capitalism? German finance in transition', *German Politics*, vol. 9, no.2, August, pp. 149–70

Lynch, M. (2000) 'Against reflexivity as an academic virtue and source of privileged knowledge', *Theory, Culture and Society*, vol. 17, no. 3, June, pp. 26–55

Macewan, A. (1994) 'Globalisation and Stagnation', *Socialist Register*, pp. 130–44

Maclean, J. (1984) 'Interdependence: an ideological intervention in international relations', in R. J. Barry-Jones and P. Willetts, *Interdependence on Trial* (Pinter, London)

Maclean, J. (1988) 'Marxism and international relations: a strange case of mutual neglect', *Millennium: Journal of International Studies*, vol. 36, no. 10, pp. 295–32.

Maclean, J. (1991) 'Marxist epistemology, explanations of "Change" and the study of international relations', in B. Buzan and R. J. Barry Jones, *Change and the Study of International Relations: The Evaded Dimension* (Pinter, London)

Mallon, F. (1994) 'Promise and dilemmas of subaltern studies: perspectives from Latin American history', *American Historical Review*, vol. 99, no. 5, pp. 1491–1516

Mann, Michael, (1986) *The sources of social power. Volume I: A history of power from the beginning to AD 1760'* (Cambridge University Press, Cambridge)

Marchand, M. and Runyan, A. S. (eds) (2000) *Gender and Global Restructuring* (Routledge, London)

Marcos, Subcommandante (1994) 'First interview with', located at http://flag. blackened.net/revolt/mexico/ezln/marcos_interview_jan94.htm.

Marcos, Subcommandante (1999a) 'Who is working to promote the consulta', http://flag.blackened.net/revolt/mexico/ezln/1999/marcos_who_con_feb.html

Marcos, Subcommandante (1999b) 'People in the most unexpected places are cooperating', 17 March, located at http://flag.blackened.net/revolt/mexico/ ezln/1999/marcos_people_mar99.html

Marcos, Subcommandante (1999c) 'Communique of March 10th', located at http://burn.ucsd.edu/archives/chiapas-l/1999.03/msg00222.html

Marcos, Subcommandante (1999d) 'The Consulta, the victories and the questions of the moment', located at http://flag.blackened.net/revolt/mexico/ezln/1999/ marcos_post_consult_ap99.html

Marcos, Subcommandante. (1999e) 'Underground culture to a culture of resistance', located at http://flag.blackened.net/revolt/mexico/ezln/1999/marcos _under_culture_oct.html

Marcos, Subcommandte (2000) 'Hope for a new dawn in Chiapas: a letter from Subcommandante Marcos of the Zapatistas to Vicente Fox the new president of Mexico', 2 December 2000, located at http://www.thirdworldtraveler.com/ Mexico/Marcos_NewDawnChiapas.html

Marcuse, H. (1964) *One Dimensional Man: Studies in the Ideology of Advanced Industrial Society* (Beacon Press, Boston)

Marcuse, H. (1969) *Eros and Civilisation: a Philosophical Enquiry into Freud* (Allen Lane, London)

Marden, P. and Clark, G. L. (1994) 'The pension fund economy: the evolving regulatory framework in Australia', in S. Corbridge, R. Martin, and N. Thrift, (eds), *Money, Power and Space* (Blackwell, Oxford and Cambridge, MA), pp. 189–217

Marks, J. (2000) 'Foucault, Franks and Gauls', *Theory, Culture, Society*, vol. 17 no. 5, pp. 127–48.

Marsh, D. (1995) 'Positive effects of a culture clash', *Financial Times*, 15 May

Marx, K. (1973) *Grundrisse: Foundations of the Critique of Political Economy*, trans. Martin Nicolaus (Penguin, Harmondsworth)

Mayor, T. (2000a) 'Shrewd moves shore up broker's position in Europe', *Financial Times*, 23 October, p. IV

Mayor, T. (2000b) 'Powerful lender faces a tough Challenge', *Financial Times*, 23 October, p. VI

McGowan, P. (ed.) (1993) *Reassessing Foucault* (Routledge, London)

McLellan, D. (1977) *Karl Marx: Selected Writings* (Oxford University Press, Oxford)

McMichael, P. (1997) 'Rethinking globalization: the agrarian question revisited', *Review of International Political Economy*, vol. 4, no. 4, pp. 630–62

McMichael, P. (2000) 'Globalization: trend or project?', in R. Palan (ed.), *Global Political Economy: Contemporary Theories* (Routledge, London), pp. 100–14

McNamara, R. (1981) *The McNamara years at the World Bank: Major Policy Addresses of R. S. McNamara 1968–1981* (World Bank, Washington, DC)

McNeil, W. H. (1976) *Plagues and People* (Dulasuy, L London)

Meiksins-Woods, E. (1995) 'What is the post-modern agenda?', *Monthly Review*, vol. 47, no. 3, pp. 1–13

Meiksins-Woods, E. (1996a) 'A reply to Sivanandan', *Monthly Review*, vol. 48, no. 9, pp. 21–31

Meiksins-Woods, E. (1996b) 'Modernity, postmodernity and capitalism', *Monthly Review*, vol. 48, no. 3, pp. 21–40

Meiksins-Woods, E., and Bellamy-Foster, J. (1996) 'Marxism and postmodernism', *Monthly Review*, vol. 48, no. 2, pp. 42–52

Miles, J. (2000) 'Can governments control the Internet?', *BBC News Online Network*, 29 January, at http://news.bbc.co.uk

Milkman, R. (1998) 'The new American workplace: high road or low road?', in Thompson and Warhurst (eds), *Workplaces of the Future* (Palgrave Macmillan, Basingstoke), pp. 25–39

Mills, C. Wright (1959) *The Sociological Imagination* (Oxford University, New York).

Minns, R. (1996) 'The social ownership of capital', *New Left Review*, 219, pp. 42–61

Minns, R. (1996a) 'The political economy of pensions', *New Political Economy*, vol. 1, no. 3, pp. 375–91

Mittelman, J. (1996) *Globalisation: Critical Reflections* (Lynne Rienner, Boulder, CO)

Moguel, J. (1999) 'Key elements of the Zapatista Consultation', *National Commission for Democracy in Mexico (NCDM)*, 20 March

Moody, K. (1997) *Workers in a Lean World* (Verso, London)

Morris, S. (1999) 'Corruption and the Mexican political system: continuity and Change', *Third World Quarterly*, 20, October–December, pp. 623–45

Murphy, C. N. (1998) 'Understanding IR: understanding Gramsci', *Review of International Studies*, vol. 24, no. 3, pp. 417–25

Murphy, C. N., and Tooze, R. (eds) (1991) *The New International Political Economy* (Lynne Rienner, Boulder, CO)

Murphy, C. N. and Tooze, R. (1996) 'The epistemology of poverty and the poverty of epistemology in IPE: mystery, blindness and invisibility', *Millennium: Journal of International Studies*, vol. 25, no. 3, pp. 681–709

Murphy, Craig (1988) *America's quest for supremacy and the Third World: A Gramscian analysis*, London: Pinter; Murphy, Craig and Tooze, Roger (1991) The New International Political Economy (Boulder, Lynne Rienner, CO)

Murray, A. (2000) 'German economic model threatened', *The Times*, 12 January, p. 33

Muschell, J. (1996) 'Privatization: a balancing act', *World Health Forum*, WHO, vol. 17, no. 1, Geneva

Nash, J. (1997) 'Fiesta of the world: the Zapatistas and radical democracy in Mexico', *American Anthropologist*, 99, March/April

NCDM (1998) 'Zapatista communique. Above and Below. Masks and Silences', 18th July

NCDM (1998) 'EZLN communique from CCRI-GC', 15th December

Negroponte, N. (1996) *Being Digital* (Coronet; London)

Neufeld, M. (1995) *The Restructuring of International Relations* (Cambridge University Press, Cambridge)

Nugent, D. (1995) 'Northern intellectuals and the EZLN', *Monthly Review*, vol. 47, no. 3, also at http://flag.blackened.net/revolt/mexico/comment/north_intellect_ezln.html

Nuttall, C. (1998) 'Dissent on the Internet', *BBC News Online Network*, December 4, also at http://news.bbc.co.uk

O'Brien, R., Goetz, A. M., Scholte, J.-A. and Williams, M. (2000) *Contesting Global Governance: Multilateral Economic Institutions and Global Social Movements* (Cambridge University Press, Cambridge)

O'Connor, J. (1973) *The Fiscal Crisis of the State* (St Martin's, New York)

OECD (1994) 'Pension fund investment form ageing to emerging markets', OECD Development Centre, Policy Brief No. 9

OECD (1996) 'The OECD jobs strategy: pushing ahead with the strategy', OECD, Paris

OECD (1997) 'Implementing the OECD jobs strategy: lessons from member countries' experience', OECD, Paris

OECD (2000), 'Cross-border trade in financial Services: economics and regulation, Financial Market Trends', no. 75, March, pp. 23–60

Ohmae, K. (1990) *The Borderless World: Power and Strategy in the Interlinked Economy* (HarperCollins, London)

Overbeek, H. (1990) *Global Capitalism and National Decline: The Thatcher Decade in Perspective* (Unwin Hyman, London)

Palan, R. and Abbott, J. (1999) *State Strategies in the Global Political Economy* (Pinter, London)

Pasha, M. (1996) 'Globalisation and poverty in South Asia', *Millennium: Journal of International Studies*, vol. 25, no. 3, pp. 635–57

Patton, P. (1997) 'Taylor and Foucault on power and freedom', *Political Studies*, 37, pp. 260–76

Pauly, L. (1997) *Who Elected the Bankers? Surveillance and Control in the World Economy* (Cornell University Press, Ithaca, NY)

Peel, M. (2001) 'Opening the books', *Financial Times*, 29 March, p. 22

Pels, D. (2000) 'Reflexivity: one step up', *Theory, Culture and Society*, vol. 71, no. 3, June, pp. 1–25

People's Health Assembly (2000) 'Health in the era of globalisation', www.pha2000.org

Perrit Jr, D. H. (1993) 'The Internet as a threat to sovereignty? Thoughts on the Internet's role in the national and global governance', *Indiana Journal of Global Legal Studies*, vol. 5, no. 2, pp. 423–43

Phillips, R. E. (2000) *The Political Economy of the Artificial: Towards an Alternative Paradigm of Business Organisation*, PhD dissertation (unpublished), University of Sussex

Picciotto, S. and Haines, J. (1999) 'Regulating global financial markets', *Journal of Law and Society*, vol. 26, no. 3, pp. 351–68

Polanyi, K. (1944) *The Great Transformation* (Beacon Press, Boston)

Pollert, A. (1999) *Transformation at Work: The New Market Economies of Central Eastern Europe* (Sage, London)

Pretzlik, C. (2001) 'US banks take Europe by storm', *Financial Times*, 9 February, pp. 8–9

Rabinow, P. (ed.) (1991) *A Foucault Reader* (Penguin, London)

Rabinow, P. (1997) *Ethics, Subjectivity and Truth* (The Free Press, New York)

Radice, H. (2000a) 'Responses to globalisation: a critique of progressive nationalism', *New Political Economy*, 5, pp. 5–19

Radice, H. (2000b) 'Globalization and national capitalisms: theorizing convergence and differentiation', *Review of International Political Economy*, vol. 7, no. 2, summer, pp. 719–42

Reich, R. (1991) *The Work of Nations: Preparing Ourselves for Twentieth Century Capitalism* (Simon and Schuster, New York)

Rengger, N. (1988) 'Going critical: a response to Hoffman', *Millennium: Journal of International Studies*, 17, pp. 81–9

Rengger, N. (1993) *Modernity, Postmodernity and Political Theory. Beyond Enlightenment and Critique* (Blackwell, Oxford)

Rescher, N. (1993) *Pluralism – Against the Demand for Consensus* (Oxford University Press, Oxford)

RIPE Editors (1994) Forum for Heterodox International Political Economy, *Review of International Political Economy*, 1, pp. 1–12

Rodan, G. (1988) 'The internet and political control in Singapore', *Political Science Quarterly*, vol. 113, no. 1, pp. 63–89

Rodgers, J. (1999) 'NGOs, new communications technologies and concepts of political community,' *Cambridge Review of International Affairs*, vol. 12, no. 2

Rodriguez, C. (1999) 'All you ever wanted to know about the Consulta but were afraid to ask', *NCDM*, 22 February

Rosenau, P. (1990) *Postmodernism and the Social Sciences* (Princeton University Press, Princeton, NJ)

Rosenau, P. (1992) 'Modern and post-modern science: some contrasts', *Review*, vol. 15, no. 1, pp. 49–91

Rosenau, J. and Durfee, M. (1996) 'Introduction to poverty in global politics', *Millennium Journal of International Studies*, Special Issue.

Rosenau, J. (1997) 'The person, the household, the community, and the globe: notes for a theory of multilateralism in a turbulent world', in R. Cox (ed.), *The New Realism* (Palgrave Macmillan, London and New York)

Rosenberg, J. (1994) 'The international imagination: IR theory and classic social analysis', *Millennium: Journal of International Studies*, vol. 23, no. 1, pp. 85–108.

Rosset, P. and Cunningham, S. (1994) 'Understanding Chiapas: land and rebellion', *Food First Action Alert, Spring* http://flag.blackened.net/revolt/mexico/reports/back94.html

Rostow, W. W. (1960) *The Stages of Economic Growth: A Non-Communist Manifesto* (Du-tch 1971) (Cambridge University Press, Cambridge)

Rubery, J. (1995) 'UK production in comparative perspective', Paper presented to International Conference on 'Production Regimes in an Integrating Europe', UMIST

Ruigrok, W. and van Tulder, R. (1995) *The Logic of International Restructuring*, (Routledge, London)

Rupert, M. (1995) *Producing Hegemony: the Politics of Mass Production and American Global Power* (Cambridge University Press, Cambridge)

Rupert, M., (1997) 'Contesting hegemony: Americanism and far-right ideologies of globalization', in Kurt Burch *et al.* (eds), *International Political Economy Yearbook*, vol. 10 (Lynne Rienner, Boulder, CO) pp. 113–38

Rupert, M. (1998) 'Engaging Gramsci: a response to Germain and Kenny', *Review of International Studies*, vol. 24, no. 3

Rupert, M. (2000) *Ideologies of Globalization: Contending visions of a New World Order* (Routledge, London)

Said, E. W. (1978) *Orientalism*, (Routledge, London)

Salazar, P., Devereaux, P. S., Herna'ndez, A. L. Aguilera, E. and Rodri'guez, G. (1994) 'Interview with Subcommandante Marcos', at http://flag.blackened.net/revolt/mexico/ezln/anmarin.html.

Sally, R. (1996) 'Ordoliberalism and the social market: classical political economy from Germany', *New Political Economy*, vol. 1, no. 2, July, pp. 233–58

Sanderson, A. (2000) 'Tradition versus competition', *The Banker*, 150, October, pp. 53–4

Sartre J.-P. (1948) *Existentialism and Humanism* (Methuen, London: Lukacs, G. (1971) *History and Class Consciousness*, translated (from the German) by Rodney Livingstone (Merlin Press, London)

Sassen, S. (1998) 'On the Internet and sovereignty', *Indiana Journal of Global Legal Studies*, vol. 5, no. 2, pp. 545–59

Sayer, A. (2000), *Criticism and Social Theory* (Sage, London)

Schneider-Lenne, E. R. (1994) 'The role of the German capital markets and the universal banks, supervisory boards and interlocking directorships', in N. Dimsdale and M. Prevezer (eds), *Capital Markets and Corporate Governance* (Oxford University Press, Oxford)

Scholte, J. A. (1996) 'Beyond the buzzword: towards a critical theory of globalization', in E. Kofman and G. Youngs (eds), *Globalization: Theory and Practice* (Pinter, London), pp. 43–57

Scholte, J. A. (2000) *Globalization: A Critical Introduction* (Palgrave Macmillan, Basingstoke)

Schonfeld, A. (1965) *Modern Capitalism* (Oxford University Press, London)

Schumpeter, J. A. (1951) *Imperialism and Social Classes* (Kelley, New York)

Schumpeter, J. A. (1976) *Capitalism, Socialism and Democracy* (Allen & Unwin, London)

Schumpeter, J. A. (1982) *Business Cycles: A Theoretical, Historical and Statistical Analysis of the Capitalist Process* (Porcupine Press, Philadelphia)

Scott, A. (1990) *Ideology and New Social Movements* (Unwin Hyman, London)

Scott, J. C. (1990) *Domination and the Arts of Resistance: Hidden Transcripts* (Yale University Press, New Haven)

Screpanti, E. (1999) 'Capitalist forms and the essence Capitalism', *Review of International Political Economy*, vol. 6, no. 1, spring, pp. 1–26

Sen, A. (1981) *Poverty and famines: An Essay on Entitlement and Deprivation* (Clarendon Press, Oxford)

Sen, A. (1995) *The Political Economy of Hunger: Selected Essays* (Oxford University Press, Oxford)

Sen, A. (1999) *Development as Freedom* (Oxford University Press, Oxford)

Siddiqi, J. (1995) *World Health and World Politics: The World Health Organization and the UN system* (Hurst & Company, London)

Sinclair, T. J. (1999) 'Synchronic global governance and the international political economy of the commonplace', in M. Hewson and T. J. Sinclair (eds) *Approaches to Global Governance Theory* (State University of New York Press, New York) pp. 157–71

Sklair, L. (1991) *Sociology of the Global System* (Harvester Wheatsheaf, London)

Sklair, L. (1998) 'Social movements and global capitalism', in F. Jameson and M. Miyoshi (eds. , *The Culture of Globalisation* (Duke University Press, Durham and London)

Smart, B. (1992) *Postmodernity* (Routledge, London)

Smith, S. and Booth, K. (eds) (1995) *International Relations Theory Today* (Polity Press, Cambridge)

Somavia, J. (1999) 'Trade unions in the 21st century', Keynote speech, (ILO, Geneva)

Spegele, R. (1997) 'Is robust globalism a mistake', *Review of International Studies*, vol. 23, no. 2, pp. 211–41

Spero, J. E. (1977) *The Politics of International Economic Relations* (St Martin's, New York)

Sproull, L. and Kiesler, S. (eds) (1991) *Connections: New Ways of Working in the Networked Organization* (MIT Press, Boston)

Stephen, L. (1996) 'Democracy for whom? Women's grassroots political activism in 1990s Mexico City and Chiapas', in G. Otero (ed.) *Neoliberalism Revisited: The Economic Restructuring of Mexican Politics* (Westview Press, Boulae)

Stopford, J. M. and Strange, S. (1991) *Rival States, Rival Firms: Competition for World Market Shares* (Cambridge University Press, New York)

Story, J. (1997) 'Globalisation, the EU and German financial reform: the political economy of "Finanzplatz Deutschland" ', in G. R. D. Underhill (ed.), *The New World Order in International Finance* (Palgrave Macmillan, London)

Strange, S. (1970) 'International economics and international relations: a case of mutual neglect', *International Affairs*, 46, 2 April, pp. 304–15

Strange, S. (1983), 'Structures, values and risk in the study of the international political economy', in R. J. B Jones (ed.), *Perspectives on Political Economy* (Francis Pinter, Lata).

Strange, S. (ed.) (1984) *Paths to International Political Economy* (Allen & Unwin, London)

Strange, S. (1986) Casino Capitalism (Blackwell, Oxford)

Strange, S. (1991) 'An eclectic approach', in C. N. Murphy and R. Tooze (eds), *The New International Political Economy* (Palgrave Macmillan, Basingstoke)

Strange, S. (1994) *States and Markets* (Pinter, London)

Strange, S. (1995) 'Political economy and international relations', in K. Booth and S. Smith, International Relations Today

Strange, S. (1998) 'The new world of debt', *New Left Review*, 230, pp. 91–114

Streek, W. (1997) 'German capitalism: existence and survival', in C. Crouch, W.

Stubbs, R. and G. D. Underhill (2000) *Political Economy and the Changing Global Order*, 2nd edn (Oxford University Press, Dons Mills, Ontario)

Targett, S. (2000) 'The sleeping giant awakes', *Financial Times*, 23 October, p. viii

Taylor, P. (1996) 'The modern multiplicity of states', in E. Kofman and G. Youngs (eds), *Globalization: Theory and Practice* (Pinter, London), pp. 99–108

Thompson, E. P. (1963) *The Making of the English Working Class* (Penguin, Harmondsworth)

Tickner, J. A. (1991) 'On the fringes of the world economy: a feminist perspective', in C. N. Murphy and R. Tooze (eds), *The New International Political Economy* (Palgrave Macmillan, Basingstoke)

Ticktin, H. (1983) 'The transitional epoch, finance capital and Britain', *Critique*, no. 16, pp. 23–42

Tilly, C., (1990) *Coercion, Capital and European States* (Oxford University Press, Oxford)

Toffler, A. (1991) *Powershift: Knowledge, Wealth, and Violence at the Edge of the 21st Century* (Bantam, New York).

Towers, B. (1997) *The Representation Gap: Change and Reform in the British and Amercian Workplace* (Oxford University Press, Oxford)

Tully, J. ed. (1994) *Philosophy in an Age of Pluralism* (Cambridge University, Cambridge)

Turkle, S. (1996) *Life on the Screen* (Weidenfeld & Nicolson, London)

Unattributed (1999a) 'The turtle salutes', *Voice of the Turtle* at http://www.voiceoftheturtle.org/salutes/pga.htm

Unattributed (1999b) 'Web is shrinking', *BBC News Online Network*, (25 August, at http://news.bbc.co.uk

Unattributed (2000) 'English loses ground', *The Standard* 7 February, http://www.thestandard.com/research/metrics/display/0,2799,10125,00.html)

Underhill, G. (1991) 'Markets beyond politics? The state and the internationalization of financial markets', *European Journal of Political Research*, vol. 19, no. 2, pp. 197–225

van der Pijl, K. (1984) *The Making of an Atlantic Ruling Class* (Verso, London)

van der Pijl, K. (1993) 'Soviet socialism and passive revolution', in Gill (ed.), *Gramsci, historical materialism and international relations* (Cambridge University Press, Cambridge)

van der Wurff, R. (1993) 'Neo-liberalism in Germany', in H. Overbeek (ed.), *Restructuring Hegemony in the Global Political Economy* (Routledge, London)

Veblen, T. (1899) *The Theory of the Leisure Class* (Macmillan, New York)

Vilrokx, J. (1999) 'Towards the denaturing of class relations? The political economy of the firm in global capitalism', in P. Leisink (ed.), *Globalization and Labour Relations* (Elgar, Cheltenham) pp. 57–77

Vipond, P. A. (1993) 'The european financial area in the 1990s: Europe and the transnationalization of finance', in P. G. Cerny (ed.), *Finance and World Politics: Markets, Regimes and States in the Post-Hegemonic Era* (Elgar, Aldershot)

Visker, R. (1992) 'Habermas on Heidegger and Foucault', *Radical Philosophy* 61 pp. 15–23.

Vogel, S. K. (1996) *Freer Markets, More Rules: Regulatory Reform in Advanced Industrial Countries* (Cornell University Press, Ithaca, NY)

Waever, O. (1999) 'The sociology of a not so international discipline: American and European developments in international relations', *International Organization*, 52

Walker, R. B. J. (1991) 'State sovereignty and the articulation of political space/time', *Millennium: Journal of International Studies*, vol. 23, no. 20 pp. 445–61

Walker, R. B. J. (1993) *Inside/Outside International Relations as Political Theory* (Cambridge University Press, Cambridge)

Walker, R. B. J. (1994) 'Social movements/world politics', *Millennium Journal of International Studies*, vol. 23, no. 3, pp. 669–700

Walker, R. B. J. (1988) *One World, Many worlds: Struggles for a just world peace* (Zed Books, London)

Walker, R. B. J. (1999) 'The hierachalisation of political community', *Review of International Studies*, vol. 25, no. 1, pp. 151–7

Warf, B. and Grimes, J. (1997) 'Counter-hegemonic discourses and the Internet', *The Geographical Review*, vol. 87, no. 2, pp. 259–72

Waters, M. (1995) *Globalization* (Routledge, London)

Weiss, L. (1998) *The Myth of the Powerless State: Governing the Economy in a Global Era* (Polity Press, Cambridge)

Wendt, A. (2001) 'What is international relations for? Notes toward a postcritical view, in R. Wyn Jones (ed.), *Critical Theory and World Politics* (Lynne Rienner, Boulder, CO)

Whale, P. B. (1968) *Joint Stock Banking in Germany: A Study of the German Creditbanks Before and After the War* (Frank Cass, London)

WHO (1946) WHO Constitution, *www.who.int*

WHO (1950) *Annual Convention Report, www.who.int*

WHO (1977) *Mandate on health for all, www.who.int*

WHO (1993) *IWC, Health Development in Countries in Greatest Need*, Geneva

WHO (1995a) 'The rise of international cooperation in health', *World Health Forum*, 16 (4) Geneva

WHO (1995b) 'The World Health Report 1995: Bridging the gaps', *World Health Forum*, 16 (4) Geneva

WHO (2001) 'History of WHO and international cooperation in public health', www.who.int

Wickham, G. (1990) 'The political possibilities of postmodernism', *Economy and Society*, vol. 19, no. 1

Wilkinson, R. and Hughes, S. (2000) 'Labour standards and global governance: examining the dimensions of institutional engagement', *Global Governance*, 6, pp. 259–77

Winkler, H. A. (1974) *Organisierter Kapitalismus* (Vandenhoeck & Ruprecht, Gottingen)

Wittgenstein, L. (1975) *On Certainty* (Blackwell, Oxford)

Woodruff, D. (1999) *Money Unmade: Barter and the Fate of Russian Capitalism* (Cornell University Press, Ithaca, NY, and London)

World Bank (1993) *Investing in Health: World Development Indicators*, World Development Report (Oxford University Press, Oxford)

World Bank (1994) *Averting the Old Age Crisis: Policies to Protect the Old and Promote Growth* (Oxford University Press, Oxford)

World Bank (2000), *Annual Report 2000: Annual Review and Summary Financial Information* (World Bank Publications, (Washington, DC)

Worth, O. (2000) 'Counterhegemony to neoliberalism: progressive or nationalistic?', Paper presented to BISA Conference, Bradford

Worth, O. (2001) 'Consolidating neoliberal hegemony: a critical analysis of the third way', unpublished.

Wriston, W. (1992) *The Twilight of Sovereignty* (Charles Scribner's Sons, New York)

Wyn Jones, R. (ed.) (2001) *Critical Theory and World Politics* (Lynne Rienner, Boulder, CO)

Zedillo, Prince de Leon, President of the Federal Republic of Mexico (1998) 'Initiatives for Constitutional Reform Regarding Indigenous Rights and Culture', http://zedillo.presidencia.gob.mx/pages/chiapas/docs/ini15mar98.html

Zysman, J. (1983) *Governments, Markets and Growth: Finance and the Politics of Industrial Change* (Cornell University Press, Ithaca, NY)

Zysman, J. (1996) 'The myth of a global economy: enduring national foundations and emerging regional realities', *New Political Economy*, 1, pp. 157–84

Index